'This rewarding book provides a fundamental contributio psychotherapy. Dilys Daws' compassionate understandin climate which is the necessary foundation for successful it can itself feel therapeutic. It is indeed a masterpiece in
– Juliet Hopkins, Hoi

CW00687756

'I am delighted that a new generation of practitioners will benefit from this updated edition of Dilys Daws' thoroughly professional and practical book of wisdom. It is like a calm, reliable friend who is always there to help those supporting families with sleep problems. I have used *Through the Night* successfully over many years to inform and guide my health visitor practice and can highly recommend it.'
– Maggie Harris, Specialist Health Visitor for Infant Mental Health (Retired), Former Hon Sec of AIMH UK

'This book by Dilys Daws is an essential resource for any clinician working with distressed infants and their families. The author has woven an amazing tapestry from clinical wisdom, psychoanalytic understandings and infancy research to create a thoughtful and practical guide to working with infants with sleep difficulties. Drawing on the knowledge of relationship-based neurophysiology of infancy, psychoanalysis, attachment theory and infancy research we are given a powerfully rich picture of the baby as a person within her intimate relationships. Through this book we see how brief psychoanalytic therapy can be used to help sleep disrupted infants and parents seen in the family medical practice through to the psychotherapist's clinic. Through exploring the meaning of the infant's behaviour, we learn how to support parents to ensure that the baby falling asleep feels safe and loved from the very beginning of life.'
– Associate Prof Campbell Paul, Consultant Infant Psychiatrist, The Royal Children's Hospital Melbourne and the University of Melbourne, President-Elect, World Association for Infant Mental Health

'This book still remains so completely relevant, essential and interesting to anyone working with babies and their families. The combination of clear explanations behind sleep problems and case studies, written with such compassion and understanding, makes it very accessible to exhausted parents with their sleepless infants, and professionals trying to support them. I just wish I had known about this book sooner both as a parent and as a GP.'
– Dr Jane Sackville-West, GP and Trainer at the James Wigg Practice

Praise for *Through the Night: Helping Parents With Sleepless Infants*:

'*Through the Night* is the most interesting, readable and memorable book on human infant development I have ever read. Almost effortlessly, the reader learns about some of the most important theories of human development and infant psychiatry. Daws manages to teach both lay person and professional alike, equally well, by introducing us to a particular problem: how and why infants sleep, or fail to sleep, as their parents wish them to. Parent-infant sleep struggles are discussed beautifully within a context that deals simultaneously with the psychological landscapes of the parents and the larger cultural context within which they intersect. Students, parents, psychologists and psychiatrists will be captivated and enthralled.'
– James McKenna, PhD, Professor of Anthropology, Pomona College and Department of Psychiatry, University of California, Irvine School of Medicine

'In *Through the Night* Dilys Daws demonstrates her firm grasp of the two interacting sides of sleeplessness in children: the one that reflects the biological basis of children's sleep, and the other that reflects the psychological factors which impact upon sleepless children and their parents. Daws clearly recognizes that to help families with sleepless children it is necessary to take both of these into consideration. And – which others often fail to do – she helps parents first recognize the specific nature of their child's problem before deciding upon a treatment programme to deal with it. She does all this with warmth, reason, understanding and compassion. This is a welcome addition to a limited literature dealing with a major problem.'
— Richard Ferber, MD, Center for Pediatric Sleep Disorders, Children's Hospital, Boston, Mass., and author of *Solve Your Child's Sleep Problems: A Practical and Comprehensive Guide for Parents*

'The writing on the therapy provides the highlights of the book. Lively case vignettes are followed by some beautiful writing on therapeutic process . . . as a powerful and sensitive way of working with parents in the context of young families, her clinical descriptions will be absorbing and instructive reading for many professionals.'
— *British Journal of Psychiatry*

'. . . a beautifully recounted and carefully conceptualized account of sleeping difficulties in small children . . . It is clear that Dilys Daws' sensitive and empathetic handling of the parents' problem creates a space of security within which new ways of thinking, not only about each parent's relationship to the perturbed infant, but also about their relationship with one another and with the significant figures of their personal past, can for the first time come into existence. As the author puts it, she "listens and takes seriously the 'cries' of the family as a whole".'
— Joyce McDougall, *International Review of Psycho-Analysis*

'As a family doctor I need to be able to offer realistic and helpful advice to distressed parents. This book has it all. Written with real authority, *Through the Night* is an essential guide to understanding the basis of sleep problems. Dilys Daws' depth and range of experience make her uniquely qualified to help all parents. At last her wisdom can be shared, bringing calm to shattered nerves. Everyone can benefit from the simple, often dramatic, exposure to sleep problems so brilliantly revealed in this penetrating and absorbing résumé of many years' commitment to parents and infants. Unequalled, unrivalled and unsurpassed, this book stands alone as a masterpiece in its field.'
— Dr Roy Macgregor, GP, presenter of ITB's The Full Treatment and family doctor appearing regularly on Sky TB and ITN

Parent-Infant Psychotherapy for Sleep Problems

Sleep problems are among the most common, urgent and undermining troubles parents meet. This book describes Dilys Daws' pioneering method of therapy for sleep problems, honed over 40 years of work with families: brief psychoanalytic therapy with parents and infants together.

Offering tried and tested ways of helping parents work things out better with their babies when such problems arise, this new edition of Dilys Daws' classic work, updated with expert help from Sarah Sutton, frees professionals from the burden of feeling they need to rush to give advice to families, showing instead how to begin the challenging journey of discovering new emotions that every baby brings. It sheds light on the sleep problem in the context of a whole range of aspects of the early world: the regulation of babies' physiological states; dreams and nightmares; the development of separateness; separation and attachment problems; and connections with feeding and weaning.

This much-needed, compassionate and well-informed guide to helping parents and babies with sleep problems draws on twenty-first century development research and rich clinical wisdom to offer ways of understanding sleep problems in each individual family context, with all its particular pressures and possibilities. It will be treasured by new parents struggling with sleeplessness and is enormously valuable for anyone working with parents and their babies.

Dilys Daws was a consultant child psychotherapist at the Tavistock Clinic, chair of the Association of Child Psychotherapists, founding chair of the Association for Infant Mental Health-UK, and continues as a visiting consultant at the Baby Clinic of the James Wigg Practice, Kentish Town. She is joint author with Alexandra de Rementeria of the BMA prize-winning book *Finding Your Way with Your Baby: The Emotional Life of Parents and Infants* (2015).

Sarah Sutton is the author of *Being Taken In: The Framing Relationship* (2014) and *Psychoanalysis, Neuroscience and the Stories of Our Lives: The Relational Roots of Mental Health* (2019), which reframe mental health symptoms as adaptations to a particular intergenerational context. She is the founder of Understanding Children and co-founder of the Learning Studio, writing, teaching and working on the interface between development research and psychoanalytic ideas.

Parent-Infant Psychotherapy for Sleep Problems

Through the Night

Dilys Daws
with Sarah Sutton

Routledge
Taylor & Francis Group

LONDON AND NEW YORK

First published 2020
by Routledge
2 Park Square, Milton Park, Abingdon, Oxon OX14 4RN

and by Routledge
52 Vanderbilt Avenue, New York, NY 10017

Routledge is an imprint of the Taylor & Francis Group, an informa business

© 2020 Dilys Daws with Sarah Sutton

The right of Dilys Daws with Sarah Sutton to be identified as
authors of this work has been asserted by them in accordance with
sections 77 and 78 of the Copyright, Designs and Patents Act 1988.

All rights reserved. No part of this book may be reprinted
or reproduced or utilised in any form or by any electronic,
mechanical, or other means, now known or hereafter invented,
including photocopying and recording, or in any information
storage or retrieval system, without permission in writing from
the publishers.

Trademark notice: Product or corporate names may be trademarks
or registered trademarks, and are used only for identification and
explanation without intent to infringe.

This book has been adapted and updated from *Through the Night:
Helping Parents with Sleepless Infants* by Dilys Daws, published by
Free Association Books, 1989.

British Library Cataloguing-in-Publication Data
A catalogue record for this book is available from the British Library

Library of Congress Cataloging-in-Publication Data
A catalog record for this book has been requested

ISBN: 978-0-367-18779-8 (hbk)
ISBN: 978-0-367-18782-8 (pbk)
ISBN: 978-0-429-19821-2 (ebk)

Typeset in Times New Roman
by Apex CoVantage, LLC

To Sam & William
and to Eric.

Contents

Preface

The earlier version of this book, *Through the Night*, was published 30 years ago. Much of what I wrote in my Preface to the first reprint is still relevant now. I said,

> I have had many letters from parents and professionals telling me of the emotional impact it has had on them . . . most have also told me some small bit of personal history that it has led them to recall. I am gratified that the book has helped to create an atmosphere in which people feel freer to think of emotional relationships in connection with their babies, and that so many readers have felt that the book was relevant for them. I believe it has enabled quite a few professionals to think about their own experiences first, either as parents or as children, and allowed them to 'slow down' in their response to patients and clients. It has perhaps given them the confidence not to offer immediate solutions to problems, but to help these parents tell the 'story' of their baby, and help them to discover what the links between the experiences in their own lives and problems with their baby might be.

Since then I have had many more letters and conversations, and in these 30 years much has happened. My children and stepchildren have grown up and are now the leading generation. I have six grandchildren, all teenagers, and an 'honorary' one in her twenties, and I am learning about the world afresh through them.

My discovery of how much impact *Through the Night* had on parents and professionals led me to develop and spread ideas about infant mental health, and I have spent much of the past three decades enjoyably doing that. As well as helping develop an Under 5s service, and workshop and also an MA programme in infant mental health with Juliet Hopkins at the Tavistock Clinic and Paul Barrows in Bristol, I have spent time writing, teaching and presenting at conferences in the UK and abroad.

In 1995, I went to Australia with my husband Eric Rayner, where we both spoke at a regional conference of the Australian Association for Infant Mental Health (AIMH). I was impressed with how the various professional disciplines working with infants and their families inter-related with each other. On the long plane journey home, I thought, 'We in the UK could do that'. I wrote to several prominent workers in different disciplines who all responded with interest. We set up AIMH-UK in 1996, as an affiliate of the World AIMH, and several of these original people, including Penelope Leach, Lynne Murray, Joan Raphael-Leff, Juliet Hopkins and Sebastian Kraemer are still involved. We encouraged each other in setting up trainings and clinical services, running conferences and workshops, lobbying politically, and generally spreading ideas about the value of early intervention. The current president of AIMH-UK, Professor Jane Barlow, has greatly increased its influence with online training for front-line workers, Infant Mental Health Online (IMHOL). Jane and I helped organize a World Congress in Edinburgh in 2014. Jane Barlow and Per Svanberg's book, *Keeping the Baby in Mind* (Routledge, 2009), describes the range of infant mental health theory and practice in the UK, and Penelope Leach's *Transforming Infant Wellbeing* (Routledge, 2018) is aimed at politicians. My friends at the World Association of Infant Mental Health (WAIMH), especially Astrid Berg, Antoine Guedeney, Campbell Paul, Frances Thomson-Salo and Stephen Seligman, and I have similar aims, and we inspire each other with writing, teaching, and spreading the influence of infant mental health round the world. All these initiatives have been aimed at getting people thinking about the importance of babies' development and creating the much-needed growth of infant mental health resources.

With Alexandra de Rementeria, I fulfilled my ambition to write a much simpler, more accessible book for parents: *Finding Your Way with Your Baby: The Emotional Life of Parents and Babies* (Routledge, 2015).* Like this book, it does not tell anyone what to do!

This new version of *Through the Night*, enhanced by the superb input of my colleague Sarah Sutton, is written in the hope of helping parents work things out better with their babies, and perhaps helping free professionals from the burden of feeling they need to rush to give advice to the families who consult them. Rather, as parents or professionals, we need to find the courage to begin the sometimes painful, frightening and potentially liberating journey of discovering the new emotions that every baby brings.

Note

* Winner of BMA Medical Books Award 2016 1st prize Popular Medicine

Acknowledgements

Writing this new book, I have had the good fortune to have Sarah Sutton, an imaginative writer who specializes in connections between neuroscience and psychotherapy, collaborating with me in updating the original *Through the Night*. It is great to find a new friend in your 80s!

The book comes from over 40 years' work as a child psychotherapist with babies and families. It started in two places in London, at the Child Guidance Training Centre, which then merged with the Tavistock Clinic, and at the Baby Clinic of the James Wigg Practice in Kentish Town Health Centre. I am grateful to colleagues in both places, first to the Tavistock, for years of supporting me, and for taking this on as an 'outreach' part of the Tavistock contribution to the community, and doing similar work in other practices and children's centres. Graduates from the Tavistock have set up similar services round the country. I now have a child psychotherapy trainee, each for a year, which is specialist training for them and a rewarding partnership for me. As an administrator, Dawn de Freitas holds it all together.

My appreciation of the James Wigg practice continues with the feeling that it is a very creative part of my life. I remember with gratitude Alexis Brook who introduced me to the practice, and Caryle Steen, GP and Helen Utidjian, Health Visitor, who welcomed me in. I still feel welcome there, and one GP recently said of me and my trainee, 'I don't know what they do, but it's magic' – the best compliment I have ever had! It is both comforting and stimulating to share with the GPs and health visitors the problems, personal and social, of young families. The work, for us all, can be painful and exhausting, but also deeply satisfying.

In writing the original *Through the Night*, Mary-Sue Moore helped me widen the scope of the book when she enthusiastically introduced me to the world of sleep physiology and psychosomatic ideas. In this new version, Robin Balbernie has been a good source of information and support. I have valued over the years the cooperation of Lisa Miller and the sadly missed Louise Emanuel, among other colleagues in Under 5s work at the Tavistock, and John Launer's role in connecting GPs and psychotherapists.

Again special thanks to my friend Juliet Hopkins who early on helped me think through the principles of this work and encouraged me to write on it and to keep on trying. Janine Sternberg is always there when I need advice.

Robert Young and Ann Scott at Free Association Books made it possible to be published in its first version, and Joanne Forshaw and Alec Selwyn at Routledge have given it new life now. Catherine Alexander's help in getting it to the final stage has been much appreciated.

Thanks to all the families, patients and friends, who shared their stories with me, and to Eric who supported me and was there through the day and through the night! My children, stepchildren, their partners and my grandchildren make the world a more exciting place and keep me feeling competitive.

Thanks to Oxford University Press for permission to quote from Anne Stevenson's 'Poem to My Daughter' from *Minute by Glass Minute*, 1982.

The book is enhanced by the humorous and optimistic cover, designed by Ros Asquith, who followed our theme of giving fathers the same importance as mothers, although of course families come in all shapes and sizes.

Chapter 1

What is a sleep problem?

'Does your baby sleep through the night?' parents ask each other. This book is about infants' sleep, with thoughts about babies who do, as well as those who do not. I will be mainly concerned with the relationship between parents and child within which sleep develops well or badly. This naturally involves exploring the emotions between them which influence the baby's capacity to sleep. The parents' lives, family histories and relationships are the framework within which they bring up their families. I look at how these connect with their baby's development, for which sleep is vital. I will not categorize kinds of sleep problems or systematically give solutions, but I will look at the context and some of the causes of sleep problems.

This book is above all clinically based. It describes my own method of therapy for sleep problems, developed over ten years or so: brief psychoanalytic therapy with parents and infants together. I use many examples from this clinical work, both in order to demonstrate the method itself and as illustrations of my and others' theoretical ideas. Many writers have found statistical connections between infants' sleep problems and other aspects of development or relationships, and I describe some of them here. My purpose is not to add to these statistical findings but to illuminate their connections with particular, individual experiences, so that the nature of the findings can be better understood.

'Through the night of doubt and sorrow', as the hymn says; a highly coloured phrase, but perhaps not too exaggerated a way to describe the long nights that sleepless crying babies and their parents endure. Sleep problems may punctuate uncertainties between parents and baby at any stage of the baby's development and bring out doubts in parents about their parenting abilities. They are among the most undermining troubles a parent has to deal with.

Sorrow is, indeed, also one of my themes; in particular how parents' losses and traumas, for instance the death of the mother's own mother or a birth experienced as disastrous, go on resonating inside the parent and colour such an apparently simple operation as putting a baby to bed. Separations in a parent's life, felt to have been unbearable, may make the small separation of putting a baby down in its cot also seem unbearable.

This book is not so much about how to make sleepless babies behave differently – in fact it is argued throughout that the problem is rarely in the baby alone – it is about how to think differently and more widely about the problem. The sleep disturbance can then be a jumping-off point for real creative thinking by a family about how they all – parents, baby, and other children – interact with each other.

I hope to show that the interchange between parents and baby about going to bed and getting to sleep is, like feeding, one of the crucial transactions between them. First, the way in which this is handled may influence the length and quality of the baby's sleep. Second, it may provide one of the most powerful and influential memories of someone's childhood. Third, the emotional tone and the way in which negotiation happens between parents and child may influence later transactions, even into adolescence. Furthermore, sorting out aspects of what is going on between parents and baby *during the day* may be just as necessary in helping with the sleep problems as going head-on for the events of the night.

In the course of the book, I consider various thoughts that parents have had about their babies' sleep and suggest that parents' dreams about their babies are one form of this thinking. Here, as an illustration, is a dream of my own; I think it shows how dreams can highlight vital aspects of the connections between parents and their children.

On the night before my younger son's first A-level exam I dreamt that he was a little boy again. We were staying in a strange place and I gave him a warm bath, pleasantly confident that he would fall asleep easily afterwards.

In this brief dream are several of the themes of my book. It examines the relationship between parents and baby within which a baby is able to sleep easily or not. It opens up the idea of how much the baby's sleep is a result of his parents' care and how much it is a 'letting go' by the parent so that the baby can attain his own physiological rhythms. How does a parent appropriately follow the changing needs of babies and children at different ages? When a baby falls asleep, do she and her mother experience this as a continuity between them or as a separation? We know now how much experience in the first weeks and months affects what happens later (Perry et al., 1995).

My dream about my teenage son was obviously in part a wish to 'mother' him inappropriately for his age. But mainly perhaps it was a memory of the way he and I had negotiated in the past how I could help him towards what only he could do for himself. No one can fall asleep for someone else, and parents cannot take their children's exams for them! Parents are guardians of their children's sleep, in the words of the psychoanalyst Joyce McDougall (1974, p. 446), who echoes Freud's idea that dreams are the guardians of sleep (1916–17, p. 129). Paradoxically they can often do this best while asleep themselves. The parent who sleeps and dreams about her child leaves the child free to have his own dreams.

This is also a book about strong emotions. I hope to convey the desperation with which parents have told me about their baby's sleeplessness, and the life and death feelings sometimes associated with this. In 40 years of work with such families in a child health clinic and previously at the Tavistock Clinic in London

I have, I think, been able to help many of them improve their situation. I will describe my method in the next chapter; in this one I want to give a context to the problems. This context is in my mind when each new family tells me their problem, their attempted solutions and the expectations about childrearing that have informed their behaviour.

You may be at times taken aback by the connections I make, with little apparent evidence, between parents' own experiences and their children's difficulties. I ask you to bear with me as we look at this throughout the book. The parents I have worked with have often, I think, been relieved and supported by finding these links. It can be liberating for parents to look honestly at the intertwining between themselves and their child, not for blame or self-blame, but as a new chance to take the initiative in a more benign interchange with their child. Something falls into place and problems start to dissolve.

Looking at sleeping problems makes us aware of the complexity of the emotions involved in being a parent. We see just how subtle the process is by which mothers and babies move from such early closeness to seeing themselves as two separate beings. Sleeping problems illustrate difficulties at every stage. Receptivity to the needs of a baby, sensitivity to their fears and spontaneous offering of comfort need to be tempered with a gradual setting of limits. Understanding of a baby's fears enables a parent to contain those fears; the baby gradually learns to manage them himself. A parent does not need to take on the baby's fears as though they are her own.

Having given the context for the book, I will turn now to outline its contents.

A summary of the contents

Part I examines ideas about how to work with families of infants with sleep problems. In Chapter 2, I describe the clinical method that is the foundation of this book. The work I do with families is psychoanalytically based, although it is usually very brief. By this I mean my approach is to take in and reflect upon what parents tell me, so that an understanding and integrative process begins in my mind. A similar reflective understanding can then take over in theirs. I look together with parents at their baby, acknowledging the baby's uniqueness and so helping them to stand outside fixed ways of thinking and reacting. Although some of the success of this work derives from the experience of seeing many families with sleeping problems, it cannot be done in a routine way – the impact of each family's stress and bewilderment must be received afresh each time.

The connections I make between relationships in the family and parents' own early experience also hinge on thoughts about immediate practical solutions. However, I actively suggest these solutions much less often than do some of my colleagues working with sleep problems, although I always have in mind the many devices and practices that help a child to sleep better. I am much informed here by what other parents have told me works for them. Solutions are as much the province of parents as of myself; my task is to help them restore their ability to think effectively so that *they* can provide an answer for *their* child. In trying to evaluate the usefulness for families of this kind of brief work, I compare and contrast it with behaviour modification.

I hope to convey some of my own astonishment and delight at the effectiveness in many cases of this work and also my reactions to the intensity of it. Families come bursting with emotion, not only about their baby's sleeplessness but also about their ordinary hopes and fears for their children. At the risk of sounding sentimental, it is a privilege to be involved with such feelings. Baby clinics, as the health visitors, nurses and doctors who work in them know, are a concentrated experience of life and death feelings about pregnancy, birth and caring for vulnerable little babies. It is exhilarating but also exhausting to be confronted by these everyday dramas.

In brief focused work about a problem like sleeplessness, families come distressed and confused and often feeling fragmented. However, in most cases these are not seriously disturbed families; they are most of the time capable of looking after their own and each other's emotions. What they need is not to have the problem 'solved' or removed, but for an integrating process to start to happen. This putting-together seems often to need an outside person to start it off. Perhaps one of the satisfactions of the work is that the therapist also benefits vicariously from this process of integration. There is a deep pleasure in being involved with the intense feelings of an ordinary baby's development.

Chapter 3 gives a case study of a family I saw with Dr Julia Nelki, the 'Armitages', who have allowed me to give a detailed picture of work with them (I have anonymized all my clinical examples). In this I highlight some of the issues raised in the previous chapter.

This book is principally about people, although it also examines theories; perhaps it is mainly about people's struggle to work out their ideas. In Part I, I describe my own efforts with families to sort something out from a confusion of thoughts and emotions, for the families who come to see me are themselves striving to make sense of their experiences and ideas.

In Part II, I look at research into normal developmental processes in infants, both emotional and physiological, to provide some essential background knowledge for thinking about sleep problems. This is part of an attempt to integrate two very different disciplines – psychoanalysis and physiology. With contributions from Dr Sarah Sutton, who writes on the interface of psychoanalysis and neuroscience, I introduce relevant psychoanalytic ideas and their links with infant development, familiar to me through training as a child psychotherapist. I look too at what can be learnt from the physiological data on the function of sleep for both adults and young children and on the development of the baby's sleep and other states.

It has been fascinating for me to discover neurobiological language for describing developmental processes in infants. I have tried here to continue the work of writers (for example, Stern, 1985) who have already combined neurobiology with psychodynamic ways of describing the infant's emotional development. In this vein, Chapters 4 and 5 describe the functions of normal sleep and the way in which the establishment of the baby's sleep rhythms and other bodily functions is influenced by the parents' handling of their baby, including all the bedtime routines.

Chapter 6 describes the usefulness of dreams and nightmares, both in the physiological organizing function of rapid eye movement (REM) sleep and in the creative imaginings of the mind in remembered dreams. Both of these are different ways of describing how the mind deals with and metabolizes the experience of the day. I show how dreams can illustrate both a person's individual thoughts and anxieties and the connection between the minds of parents and child. Dreams are the dramatizations of the mind. The sleepless families I see have lost much of their time for dreaming. I think that the dramatic playing with ideas about crucial emotions in my meetings with them helps start some of them dreaming again.

Chapters 7 and 8 examine the central hypothesis that separation issues underlie many sleep problems. Here we look at the normal emotional development of a young infant in the context of his relation to his parents. We see how the infant builds up a loving and trusting relationship and from this is able to develop a sense of his own identity. Sleep disorders may be to do with something going wrong in this process and, surprisingly perhaps, it may be the parent who has the difficulty with separation. For vulnerable parents who have themselves experienced rebuffs, putting a baby to bed may seem as though they are rejecting the baby, and a baby who closes his eyes and goes to sleep may seem to be similarly excluding the parent. But it is most important to realize that periods of being sleepless are part of normal maturation. We will look at how new stages of awareness of themselves or of the parents' relationship quite naturally produce anxieties that keep babies awake or give them frightening dreams, or indeed they may simply be a sign of a passionate involvement with all the achievements and pleasures of the day.

Part III takes specific topics and looks at their connection with sleep problems. In Chapter 9, on feeding and weaning, I note that the establishing of both sleep and feeding patterns is an essential part of what goes on between parent and child. Feeding and sleeping also influence each other, and parents may be confused about whether a baby's waking is because of a need to be fed. Problems about feeding, especially in a baby who needs feeding constantly, can often be clearly seen as relationship problems. Problems about weaning may reflect a feeding situation that never quite got sorted out or may represent a mother and baby's reluctance to move on. Sleep problems often accompany these difficulties and, especially when babies have only been able to go to sleep at the breast, mothers may be dismayed at the prospect of losing this when they wean their baby.

Chapters 10 and 11, on parents' own childhood experiences, the father's role, the parents' relationship, single parents and the demands of work outside the home, show how personal experience both in the past and in the present colours how parents interact with their child. Many of the parents I have seen have had difficult relationships with their own parents or have been to some degree deprived. Several of the mothers who came to me had their own mothers die before the baby was born. They have not had confirmation of themselves as a mother from their own mother. This brief work can only touch on such experiences, but making the connection between their own experiences and their interaction with their child does seem to enable parents to differentiate themselves better from their children. Just as there is a drive towards development and integration in young children, so there seems to be a similar integrative thrust towards the development of parental capacity for most people even while carrying personal difficulties inside them.

The final three chapters discuss the way various states of health in parent or baby affect the infant's sleep. Chapter 12, on sleep as a psychosomatic problem, shows how unexpressed conflicts can lead to confused handling of a baby or can turn into psychosomatic symptoms, including sleeplessness. I show how some mothers provoke such a process in their babies. I also show how a shortage of sleep can then exacerbate certain physical conditions.

Chapter 13 describes how mothers and babies normally communicate with each other, and how a depressed mother may be less able to respond to her baby and may miss some of the interactions with him that help set up patterns of sleep. In Chapter 14, I show how various disabilities or illnesses in the baby may themselves directly lead to sleep disorders or may inhibit or confuse parents' handling of the baby, with a subsequent effect on establishment of sleep patterns.

My argument throughout is that the setting up of a baby's sleep/wake rhythms is influenced by the interaction between parent and baby. This interaction is itself influenced by the baby's own temperament and personality and by the stage of development it has reached.

It is also essential to note that having a baby sleep for very long periods is not the main aim of parenthood. Newborn babies need long hours of sleep in which to grow and perhaps to recover from the experience of birth, but soon they are awake for longer hours, and parents and babies use this time not only for feeding but also for cuddles, looks, smiles and 'talking'. It is known that babies in institutions sleep for long periods, probably because no one is eager for them to wake up for this enjoyable play and loving interaction. Babies at home who sleep for inordinately long periods may also sometimes be in a situation where they do not feel that their company is sought; alternatively, they may be temperamentally slower-paced or withdrawn.

Conversely, babies who have slept well in the first months and later have difficulties in sleeping may be babies who are flourishing – their sleeplessness may be the outcome of their development. Towards the end of the first year many babies are fascinated by their discoveries of all that the world has to offer and are loath to shut this off and go to sleep. Babies who start to realize that their parents have a sexual relationship that excludes them may feel very cross about being put alone in their cots. Even the anxieties of the second year, which give many babies nightmares or develop into fears of tigers behind the curtains, are also signs of maturing minds and creative imaginings. In this book I am therefore thinking of sleep problems as those that persist after parents have made allowance for such natural causes of sleeplessness.

Defining sleep problems and statistical research findings

Sleep problems can tear a family apart, but it is only in recent decades that sleep disturbance has been recognized as a major problem, affecting about 30 percent of babies and children under four (Hiscock & Davey, 2018). What is it that has brought about the increase? Do more babies these days have a problem? Are parents less tolerant of broken nights? Or is it simply that more are reported to health visitors and doctors?

The definition of what constitutes a sleep problem, of course, is variable. A baby waking in the night does not necessarily have a sleep problem. Newborn infants wake as a matter of course to be fed during the night, and parents usually respond instinctively to this need. If the baby only wakes once or twice during the night and falls asleep after a feed, it is likely to be a satisfying experience for both parent and baby.

At later ages babies may wake from some physical cause or to seek comfort from parents. Change or stress in the family, or even the impact of their own developmental progress, may cause babies to wake in the night. Parents on the whole take this in their stride. A problem could be considered to exist when the baby's reason for waking is not understood; when the parent feels the waking up is not reasonable; or when an apparent reason has passed but the baby continues to wake as a fixed habit. All these can be thought of in terms of how parents and infant are getting on with each other in their managing of the baby's physiological state.

Richman (1981a) used quite a specific definition in a questionnaire about one- to two-year-olds in Waltham Forest, London. In this a child was considered to have a severe waking problem if the problem had existed for more than three months and the child was waking five or more nights a week. In addition, the child had to be doing one or more of the following: waking three or more times a night; waking for more than 20 minutes during the night; or going into the parents' bed. I would like to note that there is disagreement among researchers and indeed among parents as to whether going into the parents' bed is a problem. Co-sleeping is an increasingly common practice across cultures, encompassing a number of sleeping arrangements, which we will look at in Chapter 8.

Such definitions of sleep problems, though, give us specific criteria for establishing what is being described, so that useful comparable research figures can emerge. One definition of the problem (Zuckerman et al., 1987) was when an infant took an hour or more to get back to sleep after waking at night or woke three or more times a night, or when a problem caused severe disruption to the mother's sleep. This definition in fact allows for an evaluation of the mother-infant relationship in which the problem occurs. This third category of disruption to the mother was included so that lesser problems, such as waking twice a night, would not be missed. In considering the problem in the context of how it is seen by the mother, these researchers say that regular waking once a night, while considered a problem in older children, may reflect an ongoing comfortable adaptation for mother and child at eight months and should not be used to define a sleep problem at this age.

Lozoff et al. (1985) also have a definition with an evaluative component. Their criterion is that a problem existed if 'night waking involving parents or bedtime struggles occurred three or more nights a week for a month preceding the interview, accompanied by conflict or distress'. Here we see that the frequency of waking alone does not constitute the problem and that conflict or distress must be a part of the constellation.

It is also interesting that parents may not even be aware of how often their baby wakes, if she does not wake them. Mothers regularly report less night waking than is evident from video recording:

> A sleep problem in infancy is usually so defined only when it disturbs the sleep of the parents. Some infants may awaken and call in the middle of the night, but its parents do not describe this as a sleep problem. Other infants may awaken for short periods during the night and not signal their parents. These infants have been assumed asleep by studies relying on maternal reports. Finally some infants may awaken before or after the conventionally defined hours (12pm to 5am) and not be defined as night wakers by investigators.
>
> (Anders et al., 1983, p. 163)

Paret (1983) also shows fascinating evidence from video recording babies' sleep habits. She studied 34 mother-infant couples, when the infants were about nine months, and from these distinguished 11 night wakers from 23 night sleepers. The two groups were separated out by the mothers' own reports and validated by 12 hours of video reporting. The mothers' own reports, taken over five days, were reliable enough to separate the two groups of babies.

In distinguishing the wakers from the sleepers, Paret says that none of the 23 sleepers woke more than twice, whereas 8 of the 11 night wakers woke between three and six times and not one woke only once. Interestingly, Paret shows that the total amount of sleep over a 24-hour day was the same for both groups, though the distribution of it differed significantly. Wakers averaged many more naps during the day, making up for their missing night's sleep not by taking longer daytime naps but by a greater number of naps. Thus, even in daytime their sleep cycles were shorter than those of the other group.

The discovery that these particular 'waking' babies slept as much as 'sleeping' ones is indeed surprising and of course contradicts the belief of most parents of children with sleep problems. However, parents' impressions may be intuitively correct in that these frequent, short periods of sleep are of less use to an infant than a longer, continuous period would be. These nine-month-old babies were of an age where, as we will see in Chapter 5, the periods of REM sleep have moved to the latter end of sleep cycles. With too short a time asleep, an infant will have a sufficient amount neither of the indispensable REM sleep nor of deep sleep for restorative and consolidating processes to take place.

As well as this intuition that their infants' sleep is not physiologically efficient, parents' belief that their babies are not getting enough sleep may also derive from a feeling that there is something inherently emotionally unsatisfactory in such short periods of sleep. In addition, they are viewing the situation from the position of the feelings stirred up by their own disturbed sleep.

Settling – does your baby sleep through the night?

In an early pioneering paper on sleep problems, Moore and Ucko (1957) touched on most of the issues that later research has expanded on. They described the settling process as a form of learning at the level of biological adaptation, which requires no consciously directed training by the parents. Generally it takes its course and if disturbed by illness or change, will be resumed when the disturbance is past. If, however, the settling process is delayed beyond the fourth or fifth month, the automatic gravitation to the diurnal cycle will be lost and adjustment may then be very difficult to attain, perhaps because the baby's system has reached a point of stabilization on a different rhythm. Around 70 percent of babies will have settled and stopped waking between midnight and 5am by three months, 80 percent by six months and 90 percent by the end of the first year. Although this research suggests that the settling process is a biological adaptation which cannot be influenced by consciously directed training from parents, we do see, from families who report their children's sleep problems, that parents have a very large part to play in either supporting and reinforcing this biological adaptation or interfering with it.

Video recordings of 40 full-term normal infants without sleep problems in their own homes (Anders et al., 1983) have shown what actually happens during the night in a family and how babies do settle. At two weeks of age *all* babies were removed from the cot during the night and 95 percent were removed between midnight and 2am. At nine months, only 10 percent were taken from the cot, but at a year this had risen again to 25 percent. In fact at this age, 55 percent of babies were seen to have awakened, so that 30 percent had woken without disturbing their mother.

Other interesting findings in this study of mothers and babies in their own homes was that 23 percent of two-week-old babies were put into their cots at some point whilst awake and 77 percent were put in awake at one year. At both ages it was more likely for babies to be put in their cot awake after awakenings that happened later in the night. The sleep latency time, that is, the time it took the baby to get to sleep, was similar over the age span and varied from nine to fifteen and a half minutes.

From these figures we can also see that settling to sleep at an early age does not guarantee future undisturbed nights. The same study shows from a small sample that babies who settle before five months of age have a 50 percent likelihood of developing night waking. Babies who settle later have less likelihood of developing night waking, at least before the end of the first year.

Putting these and Moore and Ucko's (1957) findings together suggests that five months is an important physiological landmark. It might appear that they disagree about the benefits of settling by this age. However, later night waking is not necessarily part of a failure in the physiological consolidation of sleep. Babies who start night waking later on are in the throes of a developmental stage where emotional anxieties and conflicts can be strong enough to waken them. This waking represents a newly based disturbance from within an established sleep rhythm.

The prevalence and continuation of sleep problems

I will turn now to look at what studies have shown about the number of children with sleep problems at various ages and how long the problem continues.

Overall, studies using a fairly fluid definition (see 'Defining Sleep Problems' in a previous section) have found that about a third of children under four have a sleep problem. The figure of 30 percent seems quite compelling. It seems to apply over the whole period of early childhood; for example, Zuckerman et al. (1987) say that up to 30 percent of children have a sleep problem at some time during their first four years.

About 40 percent of children with a sleep problem at eight months still had a problem at three years. Only a quarter of children without a problem at three months had developed a problem by three years (Zuckerman et al., 1987). Richman (1981a) found that just under a fifth of one- to two-year-olds in her sample woke regularly, around 10 percent with severe sleep disruptions. Tracing back, she found that about half of the wakers in her sample had had difficulties since birth.

From a clinical viewpoint, it is worth noting that about a third of children referred to a hospital for psychosomatic problems were suffering from sleep disorders (Guedeney & Kreisler, 1987). This study suggests differentiating primary and secondary sleep disorders, depending on whether the trouble begins before or after three months of age. After all, the factors starting off a sleep problem may not be the same as those maintaining the problem. Richman (1981b) suggests that some infants may have a predisposition not to fall asleep again after waking because of high arousal determined by physiological factors or anxiety. Perinatal activity and early irritability, as well as family stress, are all important factors in this difficulty of going back to sleep.

Who has the problem?

Five experiences seem to distinguish children with sleep problems from those without: accident or illness in the family, unaccustomed absence of the mother during the day, maternal depressed mood, sleeping in the parents' bed and a maternal attitude of ambivalence towards the child (Lozoff et al., 1985). Some of these factors may be partially the cause of a sleep problem, but others, like sleeping in the parents' bed, as we will see later, may be connected with either the causes or the effects of the problem.

We are looking here at stressful circumstances that trigger sleep problems in children. Sleep disturbances, however, are not necessarily seen as sleep problems by the children's parents. They may be understood as a reasonable part of the child's development. Children call out for their parents after being put to bed and express fears of the dark, but such behaviour is not necessarily thought to be a problem by parents. One of parents' tasks is to help a child grow towards eventual independence and separation from them. Getting to bed and falling asleep mirror this separation process. Parents' own experiences affect how they help their children get to bed, including how bedtime was negotiated in their own families. Indeed, 16 percent of mothers of babies with sleep problems examined in a study (Giorgis et al., 1987) had had such problems themselves. Interestingly, a quarter of the mothers had families with sleep problems, compared with only a tenth of the fathers. One wonders if the mothers' memories were better or whether these figures show the greater influence a mother's experience has than the father's on their baby's sleep.

The continuation of sleep problems and their connection with other behaviour problems

Opinions differ about whether sleep problems foreshadow future psychological and behavioural difficulties. We have seen that about 40 percent of children with a problem at eight months still had it at three years (Zuckerman et al., 1987). There was no connection at eight months with other behaviour problems, but at three years they were more likely to have temper tantrums and other behaviour problems. The one problem in the baby that was found to correlate with sleep disturbance at eight months was difficulty with teething, although it is debatable whether teething can cause sufficient discomfort to awaken the child during lighter sleep stages or whether a low sensory threshold for discomfort might explain both teething and sleep problems at eight months.

Giorgis et al. (1987) argue that sleep problems can be transitory, not indicative of future psychopathology. Lozoff et al. (1985), on the other hand, suggest that bedtime conflicts and night waking seem to be quantifiable and easily ascertainable behaviour patterns that could alert paediatric health professionals to the existence of other more pervasive disturbances in the child and its family. What is clear, though, is that a mother's state of mind and health are crucial to her baby's wellbeing. Maternal depression has been found to be the most important psychological factor associated with sleep problems (Armitage et al., 2009). What increasingly emerges from the research is the connection between infants' sleep problems and the quality of the emotional relationships in the family. I will look more closely at the various elements of this important connection throughout the book. We turn in the next chapter to my discoveries of this emotionality in meetings with families.

Part I

Chapter 2

Brief psychoanalytic therapy for sleep problems

In this chapter, I describe the way I work with families on their babies' sleep problems, in consultations which enable them to discover how some of the ways they relate to each other influence the baby's sleep. The process of the consultation in itself has an integrating effect for the family. I describe my approach and compare the principles of this work with those of behavioural therapy, and I also think about the ways in which different approaches – going to therapy, reading baby books, or getting advice from elsewhere – may be used by families.

Coming for help

My own work with infants who cannot sleep is in child health clinics, known as baby clinics, currently at a general medical practice and previously at the Tavistock Clinic, London. In both places, families bring problems with their babies' or small children's development. When families come with a sleep problem, it is always urgent and they need to be seen quickly. Although they may have been suffering with one or more sleepless children and apparently tolerating the situation for some time, when they do get to the point of seeking a referral, they often feel 'at the end of their tether' and bursting with emotion. They come in distress, in anger, overcome by helplessness. In looking at such problems with them, I have come to realize that the clue to the work lies within this emotionality. The strong feelings are not only the result of sleepless nights. I will try to show how they are also both a cause of the problem and a route into discovering how to alleviate it.

In spite of the urgency of the problem and often the distress of the entire family, I have found that as few as one or two consultations may allow a change in the parents' approach to the baby that breaks the deadlock between them. I usually find that if a change is going to occur, it does so after the first or second meeting; I then often see the family several times more to consolidate these changes. This is a departure from the longer term intensive work of psychoanalytic child psychotherapy, and I will examine the principles underlying it.

It has been remarked that no one is ever the worse for having a sleep problem cured. What is more, sleeplessness, which can spread throughout a whole family, actually stops useful thinking by parents about what is going on in the family.

Helping them think during the day can start a process that enables them to manage the chaos of the night. When a sleep problem has been resolved, parents may deal more effectively with the normal run of the family's and children's developmental problems. However, curing a problem, without also having thought through its possible origins in the context of family relations, means at best that an opportunity for the family to look at their dynamics or their handling of their infant has been lost; at worst, the 'cure' may appear to confirm that the child alone was the problem.

Sleep disturbances often illustrate what is going on in a family, but families often need help to discover for themselves what is being represented by the problem. Also, issues uncovered between parents and children, or between the parents themselves, often lead back to parents' own experiences in their childhood with their parents. Repeatedly the theme of how to deal with and survive separations comes up; we will come back to this important topic later.

I am about to describe the way I work, but I hope that the style of the book is itself evidence of this. It does not describe solutions, and I do not myself immediately 'reassure' parents, declare the normality of their child's behaviour or give them advice, although some of this may happen during the work. In reading accounts of interchanges between families and myself, I hope that other professionals working with families with sleep problems, or parents themselves, will consider the issues we have covered (see also Daws, 2008).

The clinical illustrations are not intended to 'prove' that this method works. They are there to indicate how many different facets of people's lives can interlink with one symptom or disturbance, such as a sleep problem. Furthermore, it need not be daunting to take this on board in brief therapy. My central idea, and experience, is that the process of acknowledging and gathering in for the parents all the relevant aspects of a baby's life and its relationship to them, within the brief framework of the consultation, is itself therapeutic.

With this in mind, the method I use combines three elements. First, there are questions about the baby's routine; as I ask for the details of day and night, a vivid picture builds up in my mind of what actually happens in this family and what they think should happen. My mental picture also involves the physical placing of cots and beds and who sleeps with whom and in which room. The questions themselves sometimes begin to clarify a confused situation as the parents both let me know and think about the implications of the questions. Second, there is a free-ranging enquiry into memories of the pregnancy, birth and early weeks; I tell parents that I need to know the baby's life-story to make sense of what is happening now. Third, I ask questions about the parents' relationship with each other and with their own parents, so that we see the family context of this particular baby.

I start by letting parents tell me in their own way what the problem is, so that I do not lose the particular flavour of what they feel is the problem and how it started. It also means I have the chance to experience the key emotion with which parents tell their story. Once I have begun to ask questions, I am perhaps felt to be looking after them and intense emotions often subside. My sense is that whatever emotion comes out strongly in these first few moments is what the baby may feel directed towards him during his sleepless nights, be it anger, anxiety or responsible concern. After the parents have told me the problem, I explain that I would like to ask them questions about the baby and the family in general, so that we can discover what links there may be. I start with questions of detail and then feel free to get into the general area of family relationships. (In later chapters I describe how these connect with the problem.) In every interview I have in mind very specific information to collect. However, no two interviews are the same. The order and the nature of my questions are always different, dependent, I hope, on picking up the special and unique links in each family's story.

Who actually comes to the first interview varies. I always invite both parents to come with their baby. If there is a good relationship, it does not seem to matter particularly for the effectiveness of the work whether the mother comes alone or whether both parents attend. Most parents naturally bring the baby along with them. If not, I always ask to see the baby on the next occasion. It not only adds greatly to the information for me to see how mothers, fathers and babies interact with each other, as well as to listen to what is reported, but as the work progresses it is *about* this interaction. Mothers are the ones who usually bring their children to the child health clinic for routine check-ups. It often seems natural to them to come alone with the baby in the first place and bring their partner along the next time, if I have made enough sense to them in the first encounter!

The parents I see have usually been offered much advice already and often feel they have 'tried everything'. What I give them in the first place is simple – ordinary psychoanalytic free-floating attention. As they tell their story, unconscious threads draw together and connections emerge. Because I do not at once offer solutions, they are less likely to react negatively. They are left able to free associate, that is, let their minds lead freely from one related theme to another. They may perceive me as interested, receptive and capable of holding on to a great deal of information. In this setting, it is striking how parents can economically convey much focused information. It seems as though all ordinary parents have a 'story' to tell about their baby, as dramatic and moving as any work of literature. What is also communicated, and confirmed by my interest, is the uniqueness of each baby and its family.

As this story unfolds, themes emerge about the nature of the family's relationships. For instance, the meaning of not sleeping may change with the age of the child. But underlying it at every stage seems always to be some aspect of the problem of separation and individuation between mother and baby, with feeding and weaning problems closely related.

Separation problems

Simplistically speaking, the problem for a mother in getting a baby to sleep is the basic act of putting the baby down, that is, of separating herself from her baby and the baby from her. McDougall (1974) describes how a baby needs to come to terms with the loss of the available mother and 'create psychic objects which will compensate for his loss'. His capacity to do this will be circumscribed by his parents' unconscious fears and desires. Through over-identification, many parents tend to spare their children 'the inevitable confrontation with reality . . . The anxieties to which this primal separation give rise are usually qualified by terms such as annihilation and disintegration' (p. 438).

This conjures up for us powerful images of psychic processes. The consultations in which parents relate to me the details of their confused nights of wakings and feedings are a live illustration of the disintegration McDougall refers to. The fragmented experience which is conveyed to me starts to come together, as I listen to these details and make a more integrated pattern of them, initially within my own mind.

One extreme example illustrates this. The mother of Barnaby, aged four, and Clare, aged six months, had consulted many doctors and other professionals about many different complaints in herself and her children. She came in great distress about both children's sleeping problems. She talked non-stop about her many attempts to get help for this multitude of complaints and her confusion about what to attend to first. There was no dialogue between us, and ten minutes before the end of the session I stopped her to point out that she was leaving no time for *me* to talk. I then said that I had had two thoughts while she was talking. One was that it was very difficult to bring up children. The second was that she had consulted many professionals and that they had all got it wrong for her.

This mother was very taken by these thoughts. Because I offered no advice, I was in no danger of getting it wrong myself! More seriously, I had recognized that she was so full of conflicting anxieties that she had no space to let in yet another opinion. The next week she brought her husband and both told me, very painfully, of their own difficult childhoods. I remarked that, as well as leaving them unsure of their individual ability as parents, their different childhood experiences had given them conflicting ideas of how to be parents; these were reinforced by contradictory ideas from the many professionals they had consulted.

Thinking about this enabled both to be more effective with their older child. Barnaby's alarming temper tantrums went within the next week and his sleep problems slightly improved. Their attention then turned to the baby, Clare, who was waking frequently during the night and needing to be breastfed by her mother. They repeatedly asked me, 'Should we leave her to cry?'

I described how there seemed to be no idea of any middle way between going to her every time and absolutely abandoning her. They then asked if it would make her feel insecure and damage her if she was left for a while. I said that perhaps we could turn the question around and think about how insecure it would make Clare feel if she thought that they *had* to come in to her every time she called out – that they could not trust her to manage for a while on her own and that they could not trust their love and care for her to carry on for a while from the last feed. The parents could feel, I think, that this reversal of mine was not superficial and 'gimmicky'. They could see I was moved by their accounts of their own childhood insecurity and the damage it had caused. While seriously keeping in mind the dangers of insecurity, I was able to suggest that Clare's position was not the same as theirs; with two loving parents safely at hand, *her* need was to experience herself as *separate* from them. They reported that when she cried they no longer went in, picked her up and fed her. Each time she cried they now would call out to her or go in and talk to her briefly, telling her to go to sleep. They said that her cries no longer sounded frantic; they were indignant or complaining or sad. Having thought about the meaning of Clare's cries, they then perceived the sound of them differently and were then also able to respond to them less frantically.

Barnaby and Clare's parents found the three or four consultations they had with me helpful; both children were happier and slept better. What made the difference? My choice of this family as the first clinical example in the book comes from two elements in the work: first, it was overwhelmingly evident that the parents' own childhood experience underlay their present problem in handling their children; second, they asked a question, 'Should we leave her to cry?', that seemed to call irresistibly for a straight answer. In the response to such a question, we have the ideal chance to examine the differences and the common ground between this way of working and behaviour management colleagues who give more specific advice than I usually do.

Comparisons with behavioural work

Those who have well-structured programmes for parents to follow are of course also interested in and respectful of the relationships and situations of the families who consult them. But they may also be careful to define a cut-off point. For instance, Douglas and Richman suggest:

> In practice we have found that generally it is not useful to delve back into the past or into the parents' or the child's psyche to find out the cause of a sleep problem. It is more profitable to concentrate on the here and now of how parents are responding at night-time and how that might affect the sleep pattern.
>
> (1984, p. 47)

It seems from this that professionals may feel reticent about going too far into a family's privacy and that too much attention to the family's history is intrusive and not particularly relevant. I do not think this is quite right; in fact there is a deep human need to be known and understood. Sleep problems may often arise when families are having difficulty in straightforwardly understanding and responding to each other. Even brief work where families are really listened to may enable them to feel that something crucial about them has been understood. They may then be better able to understand and respond to each other.

From informal comparisons, I gather that my own results in helping babies to sleep better, taken from the family's expressed satisfaction or otherwise, are similar to those of other workers. My impression, based on improvement claimed by families to have happened by the end of treatment, is that in half of all refer-rals there is a noticeable improvement in the baby's sleep. In looking at whether improvements last, and hold over the following year, for example, complications arise. Two opposing factors must be taken into account: first, that many sleep problems 'cure' themselves over time without treatment; second, that new stages of development in babies may lead to difficulties in sleeping. For any method of treatment it is therefore worth considering how much 'success' at the time should be held to imply non-recurrence of the problem.

In comparing differing methods, it is interesting to speculate whether parents who are determined that they will solve the problem *now* can use whatever method is confidently offered or whether one method suits the personalities and needs of some families better. Several times I have seen parents who have previously had some behaviour management counselling and have then complained to me, 'They just told us what to do; they didn't *listen* to what *our* problem was'; but I suspect that as many parents have travelled in the opposite direction, complaining of me, 'She wouldn't give us any proper advice; she kept on asking us questions about ourselves'.

A psychotherapeutic method allows parents to work out for themselves impor-tant elements in their emotional relationship with their child. It seems that this might also help them deal with future problems. Behavioural work has equal, per-haps greater, success in alleviation of the problem, but less gain for the families in understanding for themselves the psychological process involved and in thinking about the origins of the disturbance. There are diagnostic implications here in assessing which families are able and willing to manage thinking about their fam-ily dynamics and which are not.

Here I must declare my debt to behaviour modifiers and the thought that they have put into the many questions that parents bring, such as, 'Should we leave her to cry?' Douglas and Richman (1984), for example, clarify different aspects of sleep problems and management techniques for solving them. Richman (1981a, 1981b) usefully differentiates between the causes of the sleep problem and the parental management which maintains it. Behavioural management addresses itself to this prolonging of a problem that no longer has a dynamic meaning for the child and its family. More recently, Ferber (2013) explores both problem and solution.

What most workers in this field have in common is struggling with the essence of the need a baby is expressing and communicating to his parents in waking and crying. What is less thought about is the way parents' hearing of their baby's cry-ing is influenced by their own early experiences. Thus, 'Should you leave a baby to cry?' may initially mean, 'Should I have been left to cry?' The first consultation may in fact be a testing of how seriously the therapist, of whatever orientation, takes the 'cries' of the whole family for some understanding. The urgency of a baby's cries may stir up memories of similar infantile feelings of desperation in the parents themselves, which then render them incapable of acting as adult, compe-tent parents. They identify with the baby's cries and are powerless to change them.

It is necessary then to look at the mixture of relief and hostility with which we ourselves, or the parents we work with, may greet advice which includes the concrete suggestion of leaving a baby to cry. The apparently simple question, 'Should you leave a baby to cry?', contains parents' agonizing and deeply felt doubts about whether their impulses are in fact cruel and sadistic. When their own desperate feelings have been thought about, they may also, like Clare's parents, hear the baby's cries as being less frantic.

Behaviour management techniques also deal with parents' fears by giving firm, sensible advice which tells them what is acceptable behaviour towards little children and what is not. In this way, it enables some parents to use common sense with their children. However, I think it is worth evaluating the logic behind these techniques. Among behaviour modifiers there is considerable debate about different methods. Those who suggest letting a baby cry without picking him up may also emphasize the huge importance of checking on him and reassuring him of the parents' presence.

Weissbluth (1987b) dismisses this checking as delaying the resolution of the problem and advocates leaving the baby alone until she falls asleep, citing many successful examples. His reasoning is that the baby quickly 'learns' to fall asleep and stay asleep and that the baby's ability to sleep in itself improves the relationship between parents and babies. However, in looking at this method we can see that it does not address the underlying relationship, although the change in the baby's behaviour may be a relief to all. Parents are switching from too much response to their baby to apparently none at all. Such an abrupt change of tactic could seem in itself as irrational as the previous practice. By contrast, in techniques where the parents remain near and responsive, the parents can be said to remain responsible to the baby for the change in their management of him. This takes some of the urgency out of the situation, as the baby's communication may be felt to be heard. The relief this entails may mean the baby goes on crying, or gives up and go to sleep, but has been able to express his feelings to his parents about what is going on. Parents and baby are able to communicate and work something out between them.

Leach, in her book *Your Baby and Child* (2010), very clearly shows the dangers of simply leaving a baby to cry without going back to reassure him, explaining that if parents persist with this policy to a point where their child actually gives up crying, they have won the battle at a very high price. The child has been convinced that they did not care enough about him or understand him well enough to take any notice of what he was trying to communicate to them.

She considers the issue further in *Controlled Crying, What Parents Need to Know* (2015). Her advice is salutary, though it is also worth bearing in mind the ambivalent relationship which already exists between parents and children who have been listened to *too much* (Hopkins, 1996). Morrell and Steele (2003) suggest that when there are infants with a sensitive temperament, depressed mothers and ambivalent attachment, then 'the brief psychodynamic approach described by Daws (1989) [in the original version of this book] may be particularly suited to parent-infant dyads with persistent sleeping problems'.

A parent's comparison of ways to solve the sleep problem

One mother of three little girls described to me her first baby's sleep problem at five months, two months after she had returned to work. Bridget refused to settle for the first stretch of sleep in the evening before her 11 o'clock feed. Her parents were desperate to have their own meal and do what was needed in the house, and her mother decided to use advice from a book which according to her said, 'Let them scream'. On the first night, Bridget screamed for three-quarters of an hour before falling asleep, on the second night for half an hour and on the third night for only quarter of an hour. After two or three more nights of screaming for quarter of an hour, Bridget stopped screaming and settled quickly to sleep. Her mother, who had become exhausted, was relieved.

However, when the third daughter Anita also had a period of not being able to sleep, though at the later age of 12 months, her mother felt she needed very different attention. This little girl in fact used to get to sleep easily, but later woke screaming. Her mother thought she suffered from nightmares and needed the reassurance and comfort of her mother's presence until she was able to fall asleep again in her cot.

It is interesting how differently this mother responded to these two babies' sleep disturbances. On the one hand, she was responding intuitively to different aspects of meaning in the wakefulness of the two babies. On the other, she also felt that her attitude to the younger child was coloured to some extent by what had happened between herself and the older one. Bridget's failure to go to sleep had indeed been cured very quickly, by leaving her to cry. Her mother was very thankful about this at the time. She could not have coped with more disturbed evenings. Nevertheless she was left with an uneasy feeling of something unresolved between herself and Bridget, even though the 'cure' did not seem to have harmed Bridget. She was a secure little girl who coped very well with some later hospitalization, when her mother stayed with her.

The transition for the mother from having a very wakeful baby, perhaps demanding attention because of her absence at work during the day, to having a baby who went to sleep quickly was gratifying, but it was also very abrupt. It is possible that what was missing for this mother in the few days of successful action was the chance to think through the implications for her relationship with Bridget of this enormous change. Perhaps the unfinished nature of this business with Bridget was what partly led to her different treatment of Anita, besides being the appropriate response to Anita at the time.

Reading baby books – the pitfalls

Reading books can be extremely helpful and supportive. St James-Roberts' (2012) book, *The Origins, Prevention and Treatment of Infant Crying and Sleeping Problems* is one such; a comprehensive guide to the many aspects of crying and sleeping that trouble babies and their parents. It summarizes a wide range of research evidence and considers approaches to preventing or managing them. The limitation, though, for any book of guidance is that the parent/reader cannot challenge their own questions as they bring them to the books in the way that a therapist can in an interview. The problem for parents in reading books giving advice about sleep problems is therefore whether the choice of advice to take fits in with and is reinforced by the kind of parenting they are already using or whether they are released to try something different.

For example, in a previous generation, Dr Benjamin Spock's (1946) advice to be sensitive to a child's needs came as a great relief to parents who had felt that earlier professional advice ignored the baby's own rhythms in favour of imposing an easily understood schedule of feeding and sleeping. When I chaired him giving a lecture to the Association of Child Psychotherapists in London in 1979, he was very complimentary about my success with sleep problems! However, Dr Spock's ideas could be interpreted by anti-authoritarian parents as a manifesto that any kind of discipline or limit setting was bad for children. Some of these parents may have been communicating their repudiation of the authoritarian style of their own parents. What they may not have been getting any more right than their parents was a sensitive discovery of what their baby's actual needs were.

More recently, behavioural approaches have been promoted purporting to offer tough love and no-nonsense rules, giving very specific advice to parents about behaviour-modifying schemes for getting children to sleep better, among other things. Programmes and books like this may rescue some parents from indecision and confusion, a feeling of not knowing what to do. The pitfall in such approaches, though, is that parents who are already insensitive to the meaning of their children's crying may use them as permission to go on ignoring the meaning. In our book for parents, *Finding Your Way with Your Baby* (Daws & de Rementeria, 2015), Alexandra de Rementeria and I hope to be open-minded. We say,

> This is the baby book that does not tell you what to do. We hope that it will encourage you to observe your baby, to really attend to the detail of what is happening in the moment and the feelings aroused in you. We are not 'teasing' you by withholding knowledge of what to do when there are problems. You know your own baby better than we can, and might be strengthened to find your own solutions. The book describes the emotions involved in having a baby and watching his development. In becoming a parent you develop too. Perhaps nothing else in your life changes you so much.
>
> (2015, p. 1)

One mother told her health visitor that her one-year-old baby slept about 12 hours at night but could not learn how to go back to sleep on his own if he woke. He woke once or twice a night and his mother used to go in, give him a bottle and stay till he fell asleep again. She had now changed to giving him the bottle and a musical toy, instead of staying with him. She then announced a further change.

She said, 'Today it's going to be a traumatic day', because she would not give him the bottle any more. She would leave him just with the toy. She predicted that the baby would start screaming and she would come up after five minutes to stay with him. The next day she would come after ten minutes of crying. After a couple of weeks he would get used to it and not need his mother or the bottle to help get him back to sleep. His mother then showed the health visitor the advice book she was using, looked through it and said to the baby, 'You need a transitional object', handing the baby several different soft toys. The baby wasn't interested and reached for his mother's book; she fetched him two of his own books instead.

In this account we see how a mother has decided to change the baby's behaviour without, apparently, any curiosity as to *why* the baby was still waking up in the night. At any rate she did not pass on any such speculation to the health visitor. It may well be that, for whatever reason the baby was waking, both mother and baby were better served by an unbroken night's sleep, but even so one element would still be missing – the mother's *understanding* of the baby's waking, even while communicating that she was not prepared to tolerate it.

It was interesting that when this mother had an 'intellectual' idea that the baby needed a transitional object and artificially produced one, it did not work. However, she was sensitive to the baby showing her that the book she was using herself was important to him. She then brought the baby his own books. It may well be that the books did have a real transitional significance for the baby and, as something connected with his mother, were satisfying to him. This is what the essential nature of the transitional object involves; it has to do with an idea and memory of being with the mother that then enables the baby to be apart from the mother. This concept, developed by Winnicott, is described more fully in Chapter 7.

This moment of sensitivity by the mother highlights why she had felt that the day of withholding the bottle completely would be traumatic. The plan to remove the bottle from the baby, and hence remove the need for her to come in the night to supply it, seemed to be based *only* on the belief that the baby could/should manage on his own. She was expressing no satisfaction at what she and the baby had achieved together in the mutual feeding relationship, nor was she expressing regret that she and the baby might be losing something between them. Moreover, there was no suggestion that the bottle itself might already have been partly a transitional object for the baby.

How parents use advice

Psychoanalytic work allows parents to put into words their conflicts about what to do and how to listen to the advice given to them. It may help them understand their fears of hostility and violence towards their children, by putting into words the feelings evoked by their baby crying. Paradoxically, it is sometimes those parents who seem most unable to set any limits who are most afraid that firmness might lead to cruelty. It is always vital to clarify what they are afraid of doing. Uninformed reassurance can be really dangerous. It can seem to troubled parents like a validation of their cruelty (which had not been recognized by the therapist) and might lead to them acting it out either passively, by leaving the baby for long periods, or actively, by physical means such as hitting or shaking.

Advice on bringing up children has always swung from one extreme to another, but no one is obliged to take it. It is therefore illuminating to look at the taking or ignoring of advice as an aspect of projection of the unwanted qualities of the self, such as cruelty. For example, getting a professional to recommend leaving a baby to cry is a way of getting someone else to take responsibility for worries about whether this is a cruel way of dealing with a baby. The parent is then free either to follow the advice without owning it or to repudiate it, attributing such advice to others and perhaps only looking at it in terms of cruelty and not, as in some contexts, useful firmness. In extreme cases, parents can project their own unacknowledged aggression so effectively that the professional's own aggression is stirred up and advice is given that does involve cruel or insensitive behaviour towards the baby.

Fraiberg's thoughts about parents looking at their own traumatic experiences are useful here: 'It is the parent who cannot remember his childhood feelings of pain and anxiety who will need to inflict his pain upon his child' (1980, p. 182). She describes how bringing back into conscious memory the *feelings* connected with experience, not just the experiences themselves, can break the chain of ill-treatment.

Whenever an apparently innocuous question by a parent is posed about whether to be more or less firm with a child, it is essential to think, 'Firmer than what?' In what context is the question being asked? Surprisingly often, some cruelty or neglect in the parents' own background is waiting to be revealed. But the telling of this is only the start. Is it the parents' hope that the therapist will condemn this cruelty, or collude with it and insist on repeating it, or dismiss it as irrelevant to present matters? All this has to be clarified. It need not be a lengthy business. These dilemmas have been carried around since childhood, but the therapist does not need to *solve* the problem for parents. Putting the present problem in its context may be enough to enable parents to go away and start thinking about it for themselves, possibly finding that other ways of dealing with the child have become open to them.

Taking these dilemmas one generation further, we see how children themselves, either as babies or later on in childhood, may have difficulty in knowing whether their parents have behaved cruelly to them. Hopkins (1986) describes how they have neither the experience nor the objectivity to evaluate their parents' behaviour towards them. It is difficult to discriminate between their own impulses towards their parents, their perception of their parents and the real behaviour of the parents. It can take much effort in later life to sort this out.

The clinical setting

When working in a general practice baby clinic, referrals come to me from doctors, nurses and health visitors. They may have known about the problem for some time and been working with it. Many such problems are in any case transitory; my colleagues usually consider a referral to me for some time, so as not to hand on the family prematurely. There may be a moment, with or without this background knowledge of the problem, when the professional realizes that the family is desperate. Even so, when I am told about it, I do not usually feel that I should see the family immediately. I am, however, often able to see parents within a few days, and a gap of this length, knowing that they have an appointment, enables parents to think through the problem and perhaps come with a balance of vulnerability and defence, so that they can work with me as their adult parent selves, as well as convey to me some of their infantile desperation.

I do not ask parents to arrive the first time we meet with a written chart of their baby's sleeping and wakings. This could detract from the impact of the 'emotional evidence'. In behaviour management, making such charts can be a first stage in dealing with the chaos in the family. But I prefer to meet the family first in their state of chaos in order to be able to both feel and think about the implications of this state. However, it is then vital to start making a structure from the information they bring, though one that connects with emotions. As mentioned already, I do go through the details of what happens day and night with the baby and may take notes of such details in front of the family. Families may also wish to write things down between our meetings. These notes are sometimes the only way the family and I can remember, in later weeks, exactly how things were before and by what stages changes have been made. Otherwise it can be hard to retain more than an impressionistic memory of the original situation.

Parents' use of the therapist

I do not usually comment on my use for parents in the sessions; I take for granted that I am doing a kind of parenting to them by my interested listening. Perhaps I am a combined parental figure, providing what could be described in a short-hand way as 'maternal' receptivity and 'paternal' limit setting. At other times it does seem necessary for me to spell out what is happening between us. I am more likely to do this with sceptical and hostile parents, where I may point out how little expectation of help from me they seem to have. Sometimes they will then link this to experiences with their own parents. With Simon's parents, (see Chapter 9), it seemed necessary for anger to be experienced by parents and child towards me (and felt by me towards them) before anger could be comfortably dealt with in the family and the parents freed to be ordinarily angry and firm with Simon.

The length of treatment may be an important issue where parents use my support to take bold steps in separating from their child. They may wish me to remain with them, feeling they can manage new phases in their relationships only if this support remains. In work which is intended to be brief, this can indeed be a problem. One mother decided she no longer needed to take tranquillizers after I offered her some weekly sessions. This was a brave decision, but we needed to discuss whether the weekly times with me might become as addictive as she had feared the medication would be. Just as babies' use of their mothers, and vice versa, can be addictive (see Chapter 12), so there was a danger that this mother might need my continuing presence instead of being able to take away for herself the new ideas we had worked out together.

The nature of the problem can influence the parent's use of the therapist when, for example, there is an acute weaning problem and difficulty in separation. A mother's inability to say 'no' to her baby and her constant fitting in with his demands may be passed on as an expectation of how the therapist should behave towards mother and baby, that is, that she should fit in with them. One such mother was feeding her one-year-old baby constantly, night and day. She felt he could not stand it if his needs were not attended to at once. She herself was unusually specific about what times she could manage to see me and when she could not, although she was not working. I found myself feeling very unreasonable in not making special arrangements for her, until I saw these demands as a communication to me of what was going on between the baby and herself, that is, she was fitting in with his unreasonable demands as well as with his appropriate ones.

It will have become clear that I generally did this particular kind of work on my own, though in recent years I have changed this practice and enjoy the benefits of working with an experienced trainee. Working with a colleague changes the situation for both families and myself and has, as one might expect, both advantages and disadvantages. What is gained is another mind, another set of thoughts about a problem, someone who may see through one's blind spots. The co-worker can be a support to the therapist or help the family feel better looked after by a couple that is in some ways analogous to a parental couple. There are also losses. It can be harder for two people to pick up the unconscious links that are emerging from material. Simply by being different, a second person may pick up different, just as valid, themes, but in doing so may cut through the unfolding of something else. The delicate business of putting everything together in the therapist's mind is perhaps impaired by having two minds at work. One solution to these dilemmas is for the co-worker to be present mainly as an observer in the first meeting, joining in enough to prevent the awkwardness of being a totally silent presence, saying enough for the family to have a sense of who this person in the room is, but not cutting across the train of thought of the active therapist. This usually leads naturally on to the co-worker becoming active in later sessions. Such a method has great advantages for therapists training to do this kind of work.

Signals within the family

Returning to individual work, one essential factor is to pick up parents' feelings that I am being critical of them. This may come up in a reverse way, that is, *they* are critical of *my* way of looking at their problems. These feelings influence me when I wonder how much to tell parents of what I observe going on between them and their child in the room at the time. It can sometimes be useful to show parents ways in which they have got stuck in interpreting their children's signals, or it can be persecuting. It is sometimes hard to know beforehand how it will sound when put into words.

One mother came to me, complaining that her two-year-old daughter would not sleep and whined all day. She could not stand it any longer, she told me in an irritated moan. I took my courage in both hands and commented on her way of talking, adding that she and the child were looking at each other with equally disagreeable expressions. At the end of the hour I asked this mother, rather doubtfully, if she would like another appointment; she said she would and I anticipated another hour of moaning. But both came next week, bright and smiling, and the mother said how much better she felt. It seemed as though my remarks were experienced as a willingness to take on her disagreeableness. She started to tell me about her low opinion of herself and her capabilities. Over the next few weeks she was able to get a part-time job and to start losing weight. As her self-esteem rose, she became more confident in her mothering; she and her daughter had happier times together and could sort out bedtime problems more freely.

Less successful was my attempt to show another mother whose child woke frequently in the night how I felt she misunderstood his signals. This 14-month-old little boy, John, fell as he explored my room. His mother swooped on him and picked him up with loud shrieks, before John himself had made any sound. John considered for a moment and responded by shrieking too. It seemed to me that John had neither been given time to work out his own reaction to his fall nor been comforted quietly. I thought it likely that something similar happened in the night, with John's mother reacting immediately to any sound or stirring from him, before really knowing if the sounds were a communication to her to come to him.

I commented to this mother on the sequence I had observed and realized I had offended her; the rest of the session did not go well. I told the health visitor of my tactlessness and she reported John's mother as saying that I had told her off. The health visitor advised her (and presumably me!) to give it another try. Next week during our meeting John fell again. His mother said nothing. John looked around in surprise, waited and came to me for a response. His mother looked 'daggers' at me. I realized this was one family I was not going to be in tune with.

Equally daunting was Kevin's mother. She was a single mother with a two-year-old, Kevin; he had a one-year-old brother and she was again pregnant. Kevin woke frequently during the night. As they came into the room, Kevin jumped on a chair. His mother told him not to. I said I did not mind and his mother explained that if he jumped on the sofa at home, he could fall out of the window. I agreed that this was a serious matter and offered to fetch Kevin some more toys. His mother said, 'That's all right, he can jump on the furniture.' Kevin jumped and his mother said, 'Don't jump on the furniture.'

Surprisingly perhaps, this mother was quite happy for me to tell her how confusing I, and presumably Kevin, found this sequence. I connected it with what might be happening at night. With this 'double-bind' in force, Kevin would be very unsure of whether he was supposed to stay in his bed. Kevin came with his mother and little brother for several weeks; we played and talked together; his mother joined in and followed the children's play and both children became able to concentrate better. Unhappily this brief work was not enough; it did not last outside the room. Life at home was still chaotic, and Kevin's mother did not feel able to accept the offer of a place in a young family centre for long-term support-ive work with her and the children.

What these last three families had in common was a misunderstanding or con-fusion about how to use signals among themselves and what to do with negative feelings about them. With the first family, my interest in them was enough to allow them to make pleasanter allowances for each other; in the second, the mother's misunderstanding of her son was compounded by her feeling that I also misunder-stood *her*. In the third case, there was a feeling that I sympathetically understood the confusion, though this was unfortunately not enough to change anything.

The common element in my work with all three families was the attempt to enable the mother to observe the baby and her own responses to him. This can be supportive, when a mother is helped to see the meaning of her baby's cries and is gratified by discovering her own response to them. Some mothers even lack basic reassurance that their babies need and appreciate them. However, for some mothers it seems that the very acknowledgement of the baby's needs reinforces the problem. Mothers who have already felt alarmed by the life and death quality of an infant's basic needs, or by the strength of his emotional expression of them, will be additionally persecuted by having this pointed out. In such cases the brief work described here may not be appropriate.

Secure adults are able to perceive their baby's signals; insecure ones may need to ignore them (Main et al., 1985). Being unwillingly made to perceive a baby's signals may thus interfere with the parents' defensive attempts not to look at issues of dependence, so very painful in their own backgrounds. An important consequence of looking at the meaning of behaviour between parents and baby during the meetings with me is that the parents also have the chance to start sort-ing out what goes on between themselves and their baby during the ordinary dif-ficulties of the day. This can then carry over into a better understanding of each other during the nights, which can otherwise feel quite out of control.

Other workers confirm the value of some of the elements of the consultations I have been describing. One study of the relationship between sleep problems and other disturbances in family life reported, 'We had the impression that the interview itself was therapeutic for some mothers, as they reflected on their child's behaviour and family circumstances' (Lozoff et al., 1985, p. 482). Work with par-ents and child together brings out connections in their emotional states of being. These connections are also noted by Lebovici (1980), who takes account of what happens when the baby starts to cry during the session, and suggests that perhaps some of the mother's own infantile feelings are expressed through her baby's cries. Often babies, apparently too young to understand the actual words, cry as parents talk about traumatic events in their own lives. I have noticed, for instance, that babies cry as parents talk about difficulties in their relationship. Following from this, we might think that at times a baby's crying in the night is connected with such feelings in the mother or, at any rate, that the mother's inability to comfort the crying baby comes from unresolved grief of her own.

Babies may cry when their mothers would like to escape from the discussion. It often happens that babies cry and their mothers stand up to go at moments of looking at painful matters. Sometimes I think this is to spare *me* the impact of the painful subject. When I describe some of these possibilities and suggest that we continue, many mothers are relieved and are able to console the baby enough for us to hear ourselves speak. Such an incident may also be an insight into a mother's use of her relationship with her baby as an escape from working out painful issues either in her relationship or in her own history.

Emotional attunement and the failure of it is, indeed, one of the themes of this book. In fact the hard work of this method of therapy comes from the need for the therapist to be in touch appropriately with each set of individuals. In order to change something, it is first necessary to know what it is. A family comes in a certain state of mind about their child and his sleep problem. It is necessary for the worker to know and be in touch with this state of mind without feeling that her own is the same as theirs.

The atmosphere of the consultations

The worker who offers this receptivity is assailed by a jumble of information, emotion and memories. At first I thought of this bombardment as just an unfortunate way of behaving by people who are short of sleep. In Chapter 4 we will see how sleep, particularly REM sleep, has a restorative function with respect to focused attention and the capacity to discriminate, and from this we would expect parents deprived by their babies of sleep to be short of such attributes. In time, however, I came to recognize such 'bombardment' consultations as being often the ones that promised most resolution. It requires the use of another set of ideas to understand how this comes about.

Looking ahead to Chapter 6 on dreams and their function in assimilating memories of the day into settled long-term memory, I see one of the main uses of the consultation as being akin to dream-work. Parents nearly always come in a distressed state, with a confused mass of information. What happens in the dream-work by the process of assimilation also happens in my consultations with parents: the scattered information they bring to me is brought together during the consultation. The essential ingredient, I believe, is that the information has to be integrated in my mind before the process can happen in the parents' minds. I cannot just politely listen while they do the putting together.

Main et al. (1985) have shown how the way in which parents talk about their relationships with their own parents predicts how they get on with their babies. Parents who are insecurely attached tend to be incoherent in talking about their childhood experiences. I think the confused and jumbled way parents bring their experiences to the consultation reflects this incoherence.

As well as including a mass of information, the sessions are usually very lively. Babies cry, toddlers have to be taken to the lavatory, turn lights on and off, threaten to put their fingers in electric sockets. There is ample opportunity for families to show as well as describe how they deal with difficult situations. But what usually comes across is the parents' sense of freedom to use the occasion to look at this present problem of a baby who cannot sleep across barriers of painful memories of all kinds. Many mothers cry as they describe the birth of their baby and as they remember moments of pain, humiliation, relief and joy. Sometimes I am shocked to find answering tears in my own eyes as I listen, but at the same time there is a moment of knowing that real emotion has been recollected and connected with the present. I have then been entrusted with knowing about the depth of feeling between parents and baby, however well or badly things might have gone.

If there is no flash of feeling, I am doubtful that anything will happen in the interview. One mother came, having recently taken her daughter into hospital, complaining that she could not cope with the baby's sleeplessness. The hospital had kept the baby a couple of days and sent her home again. This mother came to see me, looking worried and tense. She had no story to pour out and answered my questions dutifully, describing pregnancy and birth blankly. When I asked her about holding the baby for the first time, I again got a non-committal reply. When I said, 'Can you remember the first time she looked at you?', the mother's face lit up in a smile. Suddenly she *was* remembering. This baby, who had become a worrying, persecuting problem, connected for a moment with the baby who had first looked at her mother at a few minutes old.

As with all infant-parent work, one of the main aims is to help parents see their babies more clearly, to look at them without misconceptions arising from misreading signals or re-creating old relationships.

Parents need to talk about themselves, their relationship, their childhood, their jobs, even why they feel their problems are the fault of their relations or their neighbours. When they feel I am really in touch, I may be told a dream, as a way of acknowledging that what goes on in their own minds, conscious and unconscious, connects with their baby's mind. One father dreamt that his not-yet-talking son said to him, 'Why don't you show me how to get to sleep?' We will see in Chapter 6 how much thought this one-liner opened up.

The baby's physical setting at home

As well as looking at the complexities of the family relationships, the actual physical details of the problem, plus the parents' attempt to solve it, are considered in detail. Indeed one of the pleasures of the work is the problem-solving within a framework of physical objects and limitations – beds, cots, rooms, bath times – and the range of behaviours and activities that any set of parents feel is possible for them – lights on or off, doors open or closed, the availability of teddies, books, musical toys.

The way in which physical objects are described reflects the quality of the emotional relationships between parents and baby. If these are going reasonably well, parents treasure even their baby's clothes and blankets. Feelings about them spring from their feelings about the body they cover. Parents, of course, know minutely, and see meaning in, the baby's expressions and gestures and they 'know' what is in their baby's mind. Following from this, the baby's toys are imbued for the parent with the meaning they have for the baby. I in turn picture all this vividly. Parenthood thus involves enjoying and being utterly involved with small objects and routinely performed actions. Similarly, it is necessary for me to have a mental involvement with the tiny details of what I am told about all this. Because I hear so many different versions, I am also aware of what is missing, of parents who are unable to create a routine or furnish their baby's environment with objects. I am then alerted to look at where this lack comes from, although I do not rush in to supply what is missing with my suggestions.

Methods of getting a baby to sleep

Barnaby and Clare's parents were fairly typical of parents who consult me when they told me how many different methods for handling their children they had used. They had tried so many ways, received so much advice and none of it had worked. Moore and Ucko's (1957) study shows how variable handling seems to lead to a significantly higher proportion of chronically waking babies. They suggest a link between this and parental anxiety. The circular nature of this will be evident; cause and effect can get thoroughly blurred. Parents cannot always remember where they have started from to see whether something new makes a difference. One strength of behavioural technique is the way it can be helpful in sorting out the logic of making any change, in a way that parents can understand.

Another strength comes from looking at how one kind of behaviour by the baby links with another. For example, Paret (1983), in the study of waking and sleeping babies I mentioned earlier, shows that wakers could fall asleep only while being moved, held or rocked. In one sample, ten of the eleven babies in the waking groups could not be put down in their cribs until they were already asleep, whereas only one of the nineteen good sleepers was rocked or moved to sleep (p. 174). Here we have some objective data showing that behaviour intended to help a baby sleep, that is, holding him until he falls asleep, does not also help him to stay asleep.

What difference does knowing this make to therapeutic work? I do in fact tell parents of this kind of connection and the conclusions it leads to. In particular Ferber (2013) describes how a baby who falls asleep having been put into his cot awake then has the means to get himself to sleep again when he wakes up later. This is soundly based, logical information and is useful, both for its own sake and also in the context of looking at the assumptions behind methods parents have used that have proved unsuccessful, and their doubts and fears about trying other methods. As we will see in later chapters, these assumptions might involve the mother's ability to permit the baby to reduce his dependence on her and have other forms of gratification instead.

An important aspect of family consultations is of course the presence of the baby or small child themselves. This provides the invaluable opportunity to see how the members actually relate to each other. Not to be underestimated is the direct effect on the child of listening to the conversation. In fraught mother-baby relationships even quite a small baby can appear to respond to the therapist's attempts to 'hold' the mother and baby couple. It is easily apparent that older children are listening and making use of the issues discussed.

One three-year-old, who according to his parents had never been able to settle easily to sleep, said on the evening after the family's first visit to me, 'The lady said I have to go sleep', and asked to be put to bed. It is touching that this little boy needed this simple 'instruction' so much that he had abstracted it from the conversation; I had not in fact directly addressed him in this way. What it allowed, in the following meetings, was a look at the dynamics of why the parents themselves had been unable to supply this much-needed, simple idea to their son and had had to seek my help.

The parents of another three-year-old boy, Noah, told me he had never slept well and had screamed for hours from the day he was brought home from hospital. His mother cried as she told me the details of his difficult birth and the fears she had had, first, that he would die and, second, that he was brain-damaged. (We will see in Chapter 7 the frequent connections between birth difficulties and sleep problems.) Three times during the account Noah asked to go to the toilet and three times his father anxiously took him. On the second and third occasions I commented on the fact that painful things were being talked about when Noah asked to go out. I was not meaning that he ought to stay in the room, but that his parents could start considering whether it would be helpful to Noah to hear his mother's fears about him openly stated. Meanwhile we had the evidence that his father's first instinctive way of helping Noah in anxious situations was to allow him a change of scene, not try to hold him in one place. The immediacy of this, happening in the room, adds greatly to the picture of what happens at home at night when Noah cannot settle down to sleep. We see also in this family a vignette of one constellation of relationships. A vital aspect of the parental role is how much each is able to limit the other's misplaced concern about the child. This father, if anything, intensified the mother's concern, so there was no respite for Noah from his parents' anxieties.

One key factor in a sleep problem is the age of the baby when the family comes to seek help; the problem is very different with a three-month-old baby than it is with a three-year-old child. The issues of adjusting to the life and death demands of a very new baby are different from the negotiations with an older child. As we saw earlier, Richman (1981b) has pointed out that the origin of a problem and the forces that have maintained it as an ongoing conflict need to be disconnected. In the clinical examples illustrating each of the following chapters, I hope this will be made clear.

Also of interest is the personality of the parents and their assumptions of what babies should be like. Raphael-Leff (1983, 1986) has made an interesting distinction between types of mothers she calls 'facilitators' and 'regulators'. In her view, regulators have more fixed ideas about how babies should fit in with their own lives and in fact have babies with fewer sleep problems; facilitators have more of an idea of fitting in with their babies and these babies have more sleep disturbances.

In this chapter, I have suggested that a baby's sleep ability is coloured by the parents' own experience, as well as their perception of the whole question of sleeping, and I have proposed that experiences such as difficult births have a connection with sleep problems.

With most families the presumed precipitating causes of the problem happened some time ago. What is often striking is that these families have already had a chance to talk over such events. Some seem to have forgotten that they have done so. What this suggests to me is that families who have had babies in intensive care or other traumatic experiences may need the chance to talk them through again at different moments in their baby's development. The continuance of a severe sleep or other emotional problem does not mean that talking through a difficult birth early on has not been helpful, but that it needs to be talked about again at different moments of the baby's continued survival and also needs to be talked about in the context of the parents' own childhood experience before it can be thoroughly dealt with.

One factor in perpetuating a family's apparent need for outside help may be that one vital element has not yet been taken up by any of the professionals prepared to listen. One such element may be anger with professionals for what has gone wrong at the birth or some other time. Furthermore, this anger may be displaced outside because of the parents' unbearable feeling of responsibility. A parent told me with scorn of all the advice doctors and health visitors had given her for her three-month-old son Patrick's acute colic. I said she did not seem to expect anything better from me. It took two or three meetings before I was able to show how she trapped unwary doctors into giving opinions she could 'prove' did not work. This made sense, as she saw how it connected with her feelings towards me. There may also be anger with parents' own parents for not being more supportive during a traumatic time. In the logic of the unconscious, if the parents feel responsible for the difficulties with their own baby, then *their* parents must be equally responsible for what has gone wrong for them. Such connections are not often put into words but continue as a reproach. Parents go on perpetuating a communication that someone has got it wrong, which wears out professionals. Finding the origin of this is an enormous relief to all concerned.

Working through it, in terms of feelings towards the therapist now, also allows change to happen. Most families I see do not really need more advice. They need to look at the process by which they have found it difficult to use the advice which is freely available. Either they have felt a conflict within themselves about what to do, or they have felt confused, not knowing which way to turn. In Chapter 10, we will look at the different types of childhood experience which might determine these responses.

Where simple 'advice' from me does appear to be needed, we may be seeing unparented parents needing a grandmothering view to make up for a real lack. At other times I suspect that when I am pressed to give advice, parents in conflict are trying to get me to support one parent's view against the other's, without having the conflict openly recognized.

Finally, a warning: sleep problems are usually a sign of concerned parents who are perhaps just rather confused in what they want for their child; sometimes, however, they can be danger signs of disturbed or very ill parents who are unable to be appropriately in tune with their baby's need to be looked after – they must then be taken very seriously.

Chapter 3

A case study

The Armitage family

This is an account of a family who were seen four times for their baby's sleep problem. In this time, there was an improvement in the baby's sleep. The parents also used the opportunity to talk about their own family experiences. They spontaneously made connections between their own experiences and their baby's situation, though it was actually quite difficult for them to acknowledge, in my opinion at any rate, that this process was what enabled the improvement in the baby's sleep to get going. The first three times we met weekly. There was a gap of a month, while the family and then I were on holiday, before the fourth meeting.

Maria Armitage had telephoned asking for help with her nine-month-old baby Gareth. She, her husband Stephen and Gareth came to meet Dr Julia Nelki and myself. Dr N, with the family's permission, took notes during our meetings. It is important to recognize that although Dr N was present initially as an observer and to record the session, the family found her presence very positive. Probably they also responded to my own experience of her as supportive, although I usually work on my own. As the sessions continued, Dr N took an equal part in the conversations.

This is a chance to see how themes emerge and develop in meetings with a family. I will give the gist of our conversations, as recorded by Dr N; these include the remarks made at the time by her or me to the parents. In italics are my additional thoughts, some from the time of the sessions or soon after; principally they provide an overview, connecting the material with my ideas of how the consultations worked and with theoretical ideas about some of the issues that arose.

First meeting

When we first met, Maria was changing Gareth's nappy in the waiting room. There was some confusion while Dr N and I introduced ourselves and waited for the nappy change to finish. Stephen carried Gareth, a big, alert, chubby and healthy-looking baby, down the corridor. Gareth looked and smiled at Dr N on the walk down to my room.

As we sat down Maria said, looking at Gareth, 'He's the naughty one'. The parents sat down next to each other on the sofa, Stephen still holding Gareth. Maria is an attractive, dark, striking, Greek woman, her husband pale-skinned and precise in manner. Throughout the first interview Gareth sat close to his father and interacted more with him, except when fed from both breast and bottle by his mother.

Maria began talking in a rushed and confused way about their difficulties with getting Gareth to sleep. At first it was hard to understand whether she was talking about a problem of putting him to sleep in the evening or of him waking late in the night. We gradually made clear that at this point they were talking about Gareth waking constantly, after he had got to sleep. He was at present sleeping in their room in his cot, as he needed constant reassurance. He woke every few hours and could be soothed sometimes by breastfeeding and at other times just by being cuddled.

The rushed and confused way that mother described the nature of the problem is common in describing sleep problems. I think it is important not to interrupt this confusion too soon. Firstly, it is necessary to feel the impact of it before trying to sort it out. Starting to sort things out too soon could be experienced by the parents as an unwillingness to know the full extent of how dreadful the nights really are for them. Secondly, by listening to the emotions with which parents convey their description of the night, there is a chance to see what the baby experiences his parents as being like, when they deal with him in the night. The incoherence, anger or total loss of knowing what to do that is conveyed to the therapist as parents recall dreadful nights is likely to be a re-enactment of what they feel then.

Once this confusion and the quality of the emotions has been really registered by the therapist, it is time to ask questions so as to clarify the situation. These highlight the fact that there is a confusion to be sorted out and that they themselves are starting to make some structure out of the chaos. I have mentioned that I prefer families not to have made a chart of the baby's sleep patterns before our first meeting. It takes away some of the raw edge of experience. It is not that I want to delay the family's chance to start sorting things out for themselves, but it comes from a cautionary idea that this structuring on paper might involve losing an opportunity to work out some of the meaning of the sleep disturbance. Some families, however, decide to keep a record after we have started work and this can be a very useful way of keeping straight what changes there have been. As I said earlier, it can otherwise be difficult to retain more than an impressionistic idea of what things were like before; it all gets blurred in memory.

Stephen came in here, saying there was nothing at all wrong with Gareth, he was a healthy, happy boy, but he could not go to sleep normally. He moans and fights sleep even if he is very tired, unless he is in motion, as when Stephen walks around with him or puts him in the car and drives him around.

Here we see the initial fright of parents who come to a child guidance clinic and fear that we will label their child as 'abnormal' or 'disturbed'. We hastened to say that one of our main functions was to help parents look at an ordinary problem in their children's development. We also see here Gareth's conflict about getting to sleep and the way that being in movement does soothe him enough to get him to sleep. So far we have learnt that breastfeeding, cuddling and motion can all get him to sleep.

Maria says that Gareth eats very well. In the preparations towards bedtime he has solids at about 5pm and the bottle at 8pm. 'Sometimes it's like it's not enough', says Maria. She then says that she and her husband disagreed over whether to leave him to cry or not, that Stephen did not like leaving him.

I had asked the parents to tell me first about the nature of Gareth's sleep problems and then about the routine of both day and night. Here we see that while mother attempts to give me an ordered account of Gareth's feeds during the day, leading up to the effect of this on his sleep, she diverts to the statement that she and her husband disagree about leaving the baby to cry. This is obviously a key issue, a major source of tension, and one we come back to during this session and later.

Whether to leave a baby to cry is a major issue which we have looked at earlier. This is such a fraught subject, with so many possible interpretations of what 'leaving a baby to cry' means, before starting to think of whether it is an advisable thing to do, that it is no wonder parents often hold two opposing views from among the conflicting and confusing range of possibilities. For parents at odds with each other already this may be just another battleground, but for many parents this disagreement about their baby's sleep problem is stirred up by the peculiar confusions of the problem and can be an additional source of distress to them.

Gareth sat happily between his father's legs, playing with toys and keys and smiling and looking at Dr N. Maria, a bit separate at this point from Gareth and his father, was thinking through the problem; she pulled a funny face at Gareth when he looked at her. She returned to the issue of leaving him to cry and, pointing to her husband, said, 'He can't leave him'. I asked them to tell me something of their lives, saying that we needed to understand the context of Gareth's sleep problems and that I was interested in finding out how they had all got to the present point. It was necessary at first to ask many questions, though gradually they talked more freely. They had met in England, while Maria was on a visit. She said that although there were many children in her extended family, having her own had been very difficult and it was as if she knew nothing. She could not *talk* to her baby at first. She said twice that she had her baby 'by herself' and 'alone', although in fact her husband had been present.

This is the first hint that mother has suffered by having her baby in a country away from her own family. Her own family experience – of being around small children – had, for the moment anyway, disappeared at this distance from them. Her inability to 'talk' to her baby is perhaps a sign of postnatal depression. It is also worth noting that her own language of intimacy from her childhood is not her husband's language or the language of the country she now lives in.

The pregnancy and labour had been easy, with no problems at all. 'I saw him before you did', said Stephen, though Maria held him first when he was put to the breast.

Gareth was now standing, held by his father. Stephen said Gareth does not crawl but likes to be held in this standing position. He also uses the baby-walker at home.

I thought, but did not speak, about the possible confusing effects of 'baby-walkers'. By allowing babies to move quickly across the room before they can really walk, are they having a physical experience before being psychologically ready for it? Does it take away from imagining *being able to cross the room, if movement can magically be made to happen?*

'He is not very happy sitting down', said Stephen, adding, 'I'm speaking for him'. Apparently prompted by this, Maria said that Gareth was more like his father and that Stephen chose his name. Stephen said, 'I wanted a name that couldn't be shortened, not like mine'. (Gareth, and the parents' names, of course, are not their real names.)

This alerted us to thinking that father did not want Gareth to have some of the experiences he himself had had. Talking about the choice of name for a baby can often be a way for parents to bring in ideas about their relationship to their own families or their aspirations or fantasies about their baby before its birth.

Maria now said that the beginning had been very difficult. 'Every time I was changing him he was screaming, I didn't know what to do. I couldn't relax. My husband said I was like a machine. After my parents had been to visit, I realized Gareth had been aware of everything.' I said that it sounded as if Maria had been helped by her parents' coming, at which point Maria began crying. Stephen did not appear to notice this. He was now very involved in the interview, sitting forward in his seat and talking freely. He said that he and Maria had disagreed about how to get Gareth to sleep. Stephen stands up to rock him. Maria is too tired to stand with Gareth, but feels that if Stephen does, then Gareth wants her to as well. Stephen said he had stopped doing it to give Maria a chance. He said they had disagreed in the past but 'Not now. I've no recriminations against her'.

We can see here the honesty with which the parents are struggling to let us know of the arguments between them about how to help their child.

Stephen spontaneously said that he recalled being left to cry himself as a baby and being desperately unhappy at those times. His parents had to work hard because money was short and were away a lot, leaving him in a large house in the care of his grandmother, who was too old to climb the stairs to see to him. His earliest memories were of *being left* and *crying.* He added later that the wind blowing through an aerial on top of the house made a whistling noise that terrified him, though nobody realized it for a long time.

He said he could not bear Gareth crying, even for ten minutes, and that they did try being firm for three to four days, but that these were the hardest times for him in Gareth's life. Gareth, still sitting in front of his father, gave one cry and Stephen immediately gave him lots of toys.

Father is illustrating one of the themes of this book, that parents' own experiences colour their interpretation of what their child is going through. With his memories of being left alone and unprotected, he does not want his son to have to go through anything like that.

The parents told us of their visit to Greece and Gareth's illness on their return two months ago. He had a chest infection and was admitted to hospital for a week and Maria slept with him there and he slept well. He is now better and it was never clear what the diagnosis was.

Here we see that the hospital provided a respite for both Gareth and his mother from whatever unresolved issue in their relationship, or other cause, was keeping Gareth from sleeping.

Maria said she was 'full of confusions' and also sounded desperate at 'being 24 hours with him', which, however, Stephen feels is extremely important for Gareth. Gareth started to moan and cry. Stephen picked him up and he struggled in his father's arms. I commented that in this state he did not look at either of his parents. His father gave him a toy, which he accepted and played with. Stephen described Gareth as irritable, cantankerous and tetchy when going to sleep. Sounding rather irritable himself, he seemed to be still reliving his own experiences, saying that he was put to bed early and just left.

We see how Gareth's father is using our suggestions to help him connect the present problem with past experience.

I asked how Gareth gets to sleep. Maria said she would give him a bottle and hold him in her arms and he would fall asleep, before being put in the cot.

With so much essential thought about the past it was necessary for me to ask questions to anchor this to the details about the present.

Stephen said Gareth does not go to sleep gracefully, but fights. He remembered how upset his wife had been in the early days after Gareth's birth. Maria took this cue and said that her mother had not come until Gareth was one month old. This was because of an earthquake in their hometown. Maria told us that the earthquake happened two weeks before Gareth was due. It brought on her labour and for several days she did not know whether her parents, or the rest of her family, were alive or dead. She heard a few days later that they were safe, but it was a few weeks before her mother was able to come to this country. Maria was very distressed not to have her mother there earlier. She said her pregnancy had only gone well because she knew her mother was coming.

Maria's mother stayed three months, then they went back home to Greece together and Gareth slept well there until Stephen arrived, though this coincided with the hotter weather.

I said it sounded as if the earthquake in Greece had been one for them too, that Maria had been shaken up and worried about her family and had not got her confidence back until her mother came over. She had perhaps felt more secure and settled in her home country, as well as relieved to see all her family were safe, and that was perhaps why Gareth could sleep better there. Stephen intervened and said that Maria 'was dying to get home'. Gareth was beginning to cry and was handed to mother for breastfeeding. She was confident and relaxed with him. He settled immediately and soon fell asleep. As he fed, Stephen told me in reply to my questions that Gareth does not have teeth yet and is beginning to make recognizable sounds, such as 'Pa, Pa'.

We could speculate as to why Gareth cried at this particular moment – perhaps for his own internal reasons – perhaps he was picking up the painful emotions of the adults' conversation. We note how confident mother is in dealing with him. Gareth has no teeth yet, so conflicts about biting have not yet arisen. When I asked about Gareth's words, his father picks out for notice his saying the sounds 'Pa, Pa'. We were also able to see how Gareth is comforted by his mother's breast-feeding. Although he also has a bottle, he apparently has not yet got other self-soothing things to do.

I asked the parents what changes ideally they would like to happen. Maria said she would like Gareth to sleep through the night, but did not mind where, though preferably in his own room.

Stephen asked if we thought Gareth was hyperactive; he then observed that every child was different and there could not be pat solutions. He said several times that if we convinced him it was good to let a baby cry, he would of course accept it. The implication was that he wouldn't. I agreed with him that each family had to find their own solutions and said that it was important to recognize the difference between Stephen's experience as a child and Gareth's experience now, with both parents around a lot, loving and available; and that to be left to cry in that situation could be different. It was also important to clarify just what we meant by 'leaving to cry'. We talked about the difference in giving a baby room to protest and the sort of abandonment Stephen had undergone himself. I also said that if children get used to falling asleep in their cots, they are not as worried when they wake up there as when they have fallen asleep in someone's arms.

Stephen said that Gareth was very sensitive and if they so much as moved in their bed, he would move or wake. I said that for Gareth his parents being present in the same room was perhaps comforting but also arousing. Perhaps he needed his own room now. Both parents seemed to agree with this.

As we ended, I suggested that the parents, father in particular, think about the following:

1   What was so painful for him in his childhood that it was colouring the situation now?
2   How can Gareth be more independent?

I felt it premature to discuss any change in behaviour at this point. They were both keen to come again the following week.

Both parents came to this first meeting upset and agitated. They left in a much calmer mood. What happened in between? Looking over the events of this meeting, I find myself surprised that Gareth's father, who had a very businesslike manner, quickly accepted our decision not to provide 'advice' as to what to change in his behaviour towards his son. Both parents seized on the opportunity to talk about the personal issues that affected their relationship with Gareth – his father needed to talk about his partly unhappy childhood; his mother about being cut off from her happy one and the shock of the earthquake involving her family. Both got lost in these accounts. They also came to the session at odds with each other about what to do with Gareth. Telling us about this also seemed to help them to be more in agreement.

Father's need to put himself first with Gareth was a crucial aspect of what we observed in this meeting. His emphasis on having seen Gareth first at his birth or Gareth's first words being 'Pa, Pa' were examples of this. It did not occur to me until later that father's feeling as a child at the times that he was left alone that he was not important to his parents made it vital for him to be important to his baby now, even if this meant sometimes competing with his wife. Stephen, who had hoped for 'advice', was perhaps relieved not to get it. In fact he told us what advice he expected to hear from us, i.e. 'leave the baby to cry', and that this would be unacceptable.

Later I also noticed that the overriding catastrophic event of the earthquake, which sent mother into labour, was not told us until well after the middle of the first meeting. Although her parents survived, at the time she was giving birth to Gareth and for four days afterwards she did not know whether they were alive or dead. Mother told us of this devastating experience in a hesitant, detached way, so that it was left to Dr N and myself to exclaim at the awfulness of it. We could guess that this was partly the flatness of postnatal depression, perhaps brought on by the trauma, and also that not having allowed herself to know consciously how dreadful this experience was had left her more vulnerable to its consequences. Being out of touch with some of the feelings of what she had herself gone through made her prone to be out of touch at times with her son and his communications.

Second meeting

We met the family a week later, and they seemed much calmer. They said Gareth was settling better. Although they were quite hesitant and reluctant to admit it, it emerged that Gareth had slept well three or four times in the last week. Stephen in particular seemed unable to acknowledge either any changes that had been made or any benefit that might have come from talking last week, or, indeed, that things really were any better. He said he was worried about how Gareth goes to sleep, that he fights it and is fretful and moans, though he now seems content with himself in the mornings.

I said that perhaps what we talked about last week had seemed rather nebulous; they couldn't see what connection talking about their own problems had with Gareth not sleeping, though it had felt to be making sense at the time. Perhaps after our meeting they had felt rather embarrassed that they had said so much about themselves to strangers. They agreed and seemed to relax.

Maria went on to talk more about when Gareth moans, that, just as we had seen last week, it is 'as if he is looking for something that isn't there' and they feel angry with themselves because they don't know what he wants. Since last week, when I had pointed it out, they had noticed how he doesn't look at his parents when he is in that mood.

Both parents talked about not having their own mothers around to help them. Maria's mother is in Greece and Stephen's died some time ago.

It did not feel right to use these remarks as an invitation to say that perhaps Dr N and I were perceived as parents who could help them. If anything, we were being felt like the absence of their own mothers. They were perhaps depicting feeling like Gareth when he moans, not knowing how to capture his parents' attention and look to them for help.

I asked what the parents felt about weaning Gareth. Maria said the health visitor had advised her not to breastfeed, particularly at night, but she wanted to carry on for a long time still. I realized that the parents thought I was advising them to stop breastfeeding now and said this was not what I had meant.

We talked about what had happened during the week to make the difference to Gareth. Maria said she had covered him with a blanket; perhaps that had done it. She had also left him in the crèche a couple of times while she went to keep-fit classes. She said Gareth had enjoyed playing with the other children there. I said that perhaps our talk last week had enabled Maria to think about being able to be separate from Gareth for a short time. Because she felt all right about leaving him, he could also enjoy it. Because he also found that she came back to him when she left him during the day, he might have realized that when he was put down to sleep at night his parents would still come back to him. Perhaps Gareth had worried that he could not manage without his parents and was beginning to learn that he could. They said, however, that he can still only play with toys in his parents' presence and speculated whether his delay in crawling is because that also means more independence than he is ready for.

I asked if there was one thing they now thought they could change. After a silence Maria said, 'Leave him to cry'. We emphasized that if they did leave Gareth, it was important to tell him where they were going and to come back within a few minutes. Maria confessed she had left Gareth in the crèche without saying goodbye. We talked about the importance of saying goodbye and about the difference between leaving Gareth for a few minutes and Stephen's own childhood experience of being left for a long time.

Maria said she always used to pick Gareth up when he cried; her mother had advised it because you would know that if he stopped crying when you picked him up he was not crying because he was in pain. It was clear that Maria was now trying to sort out the consequences of this well-meant advice.

In this meeting it seemed that, having poured out their own stories last time, the parents were at first rather ashamed of having done so and therefore rather ill at ease. Perhaps they were afraid of being sucked into more revelations about themselves, beyond their usefulness for this piece of work. When I commented on this, they were relieved and able to work more purposefully this time on thinking about making changes for Gareth.

It is also very common to find that parents report a change in an offhand way, as though it has no relevance. It may be that they are worried that the therapist will count the change prematurely as success and stop seeing them too soon; or alternatively that even if they have not openly admitted it to themselves, they do actually see at another level that the connections they are making about relationships and about their feelings on separations are as important as the actual cure of the baby's sleep problem. This is not luring people into interminable therapy, but resolving important issues stirred up in the work, so that these issues can be comfortably left. It was also apparent in this meeting that the parents were more in agreement on how to think about and act for Gareth.

Third meeting

Both parents seemed more relaxed this time. Last night they had had the best night ever with Gareth. The rest of the week had included a couple of bad nights but mostly things were better. Gareth was still enjoying the crèche and Maria said she had been able to say goodbye to him. Stephen had also started to say goodbye when he went off to work in the mornings. It seemed also that Maria was realizing the importance of preparation time. She had established much more of a bedtime routine for Gareth. The transition from waking to sleeping was becoming easier to think about, since the parents had stopped feeling so hopeless about it.

Gareth can still only go to sleep before he is put in his cot, usually in his mother's arms, but Stephen said that once last week he had fallen asleep while lying on his tummy on their bed. It seemed as if Gareth was starting to take responsibility for his going to sleep. We suggested that they try to find a moment to say goodnight to him before he falls asleep, to help him take account of being in this transition stage.

We talked about why Gareth doesn't look at his parents when he is tired. 'It's as if he's not looking to us for help', Maria said. She added that when he gets in a state and she firmly says to him, 'Gareth, stop it', he does respond at once. However, she worried about saying it. I said that talking sharply was a way of bringing him to focus on his parents and enabled them to help him better.

I asked the parents to think ahead to when Gareth might be in his own room. The parents had thought they would need a two-way intercom, but then realized that they would be able to hear him from the next room without one.

Gareth was quite happy in this session and played a lot with his father. At one point he played with a toy telephone, which allowed us to think about how to keep in contact from a distance. Stephen said that Gareth now enjoys playing on a slide, allowing his father to let him go and trusting that he would be caught again. We talked about how this was a sign that he is beginning to separate and become more independent.

The parents again said on this occasion that they could not see how coming here had caused the changes in Gareth. This time I did take it up in terms of their relationship with Dr N and myself and said there was a problem that if they felt there was a benefit in coming here, it would make it hard to separate from us after this brief piece of work.

It was noticeable that the parents had left after the second meeting torn about whether to leave Gareth to cry. They had achieved the better nights without having had to do anything that seemed drastic to them. In fact saying goodbye to herald separations during the day was what probably had the biggest impact on the symbolic separation of going to sleep at night-time. They had in no sense 'left him to cry'.

Fourth meeting

Dr N is away on holiday. We had told the parents when we were arranging this meeting, but they are surprised at her absence. They report that Gareth is now in his own room. They have to stay with him for half an hour while he falls asleep in his cot. He wakes up once in the night and falls asleep again quietly. He wakes up again at 6.30am, has a feed and goes back to sleep after it.

As the parents tell me this, Gareth crawls around the room, pulling himself up on the table. Stephen says everything very mournfully; no hint from his voice that we are talking about considerable progress.

I guess that he is very put out by Dr N's absence. It was perhaps important that we had been there as a couple and was perhaps a mistake to resume work without Dr N. But the accident that the family, I and she, were all on holiday one after the other seemed to make too long a gap in what had started off as very urgent work.

It seems clear that the parents intend this to be the last meeting. Maria says how delighted she is at their progress and thanks me. I say that they have worked hard. Stephen says they don't begrudge Gareth the time.

This was a successful brief piece of work. In four meetings this little boy changed from being wakeful throughout the night to having a long night's sleep with only one brief awakening. He was also by the end sleeping in his own room. It was necessary, however, for Dr N and I to hang on to our own optimism throughout this piece of work. These parents had to convey to us much confusion, indecision and hopelessness. By listening to their communications, we knew also what separation meant to them and why they found it so difficult. It can be tempting in such a case to think of keeping oneself at a distance and simply give out advice. Apart of course from this not being our way of working, both parents made it clear they could not have borne that. I really think that the only effective way to help these parents was to bear with receiving and understanding their feelings, so that we could then try to help them understand better how such feelings connect with behaviour.

I think it is significant that the ending of this brief work was painful for both parents, but especially for Gareth's father. It seemed to me that he particularly felt Dr N's absence as a rejection, having suffered rejections repeatedly as a little boy. His apparently narrow summing-up of the work, 'We don't begrudge him the time', has much more meaning than at first seems apparent. His own parents did begrudge the time spent in thinking about his needs, and his receptivity to his little boy was a striking sign of his ability to be different from them. His initially distant way of talking covered considerable emotional feeling. These parents had both been affected by traumatic situations or events. This work was about their struggles to make sense of it all on behalf of their little boy.

This work was successful; the parents and Dr N and I were pleased with the results, but looking at it after a period of time I am aware that we failed to communicate directly to Gareth more than exchanging smiles and friendly comments. We did use our observations of him to help the parents notice more about his reactions to them. These days we would bring him into the interactions much more, especially inspired by Thomson-Salo's (2018) recent book, *Engaging Infants*, where she writes about the active contribution that even young infants make to the therapeutic encounter and their therapeutic alliance.

Part II

Chapter 4

The physiology of sleep states

For the next two chapters we are going to change gear, as it were, from a clinical casework orientation to a more theoretical viewpoint, looking at the research data on sleep, both in adults and infants, and on infant development. As a child psychotherapist trained in psychoanalytic ideas, my natural mode of work is that of clinical cases, as illustrated in the first three chapters, not the appraisal of scientific research. But during my time working on sleep problems I have come to be fascinated by, and see the vital importance of, sleep and dream physiology. So I hope to convey some of the excitement I have felt in discovering links with what I already know from observing infants clinically. Researchers over the past three decades have begun to bridge the gap between physiology, neuroscience and clinical practice by putting biological data into a psychological framework. Others have looked at connections between neurobiology, infant mental health and psychotherapy (Music, 2019; Sutton, 2014, 2019).

Though this chapter is rooted in physiology, we will see how the development of sleep and other states is inextricably bound up with the parents' handling of the baby. We will see the effect of this handling both on the baby's psychophysiological state, that is to say, its feelings, and on the relationship between parents and baby. I will start by outlining the nature of adult sleep.

Adults' sleep patterns

It used to be thought that falling asleep was a simple process and that sleep was a kind of negation of waking. However, recent research has shown how complex sleep states are; there may be even more mental activity going on during sleep than during waking states. On falling asleep, our rhythmical brain waves, measured in electroencephalograms (EEGs), go through certain characteristic changes, which can be divided into five distinct patterns (Lowy, 1970). Stages 1–3 involve gradually less wakeability and variable EEG activity; Stage 4 is the deepest stage of sleep, from which there are virtually no reports of mental activity. Vital signs like pulse rate, respiration and blood pressure are very regular. The fifth stage is characterised by rapid eye movement (REM), during which people report dreams if woken, in contrast with the other stages.

For adults, a night's sleep includes more REM sleep in the last third of the night and more Stage 4 in the first third. Each has its own particular function. To get the benefit of all these functions, a person needs to remain asleep long enough for each cycle to continue through to Stage 4 in the early part of the night and for the whole night's sleep to be long enough for the later REM periods to take place.

The functions of sleep

We know that the function of sleep in general is restorative and that the various stages provide different aspects of this. For example, Stage 4 sleep is the one in which physical growth and the maintenance of the immune system are promoted. Subtle connections with other bodily systems have also been established, as we will see in Chapter 12 on psychosomatic problems. Walker (2017) describes it as 'a veritable treasure trove of mental and physical benefits for your brain and body respectively'.

Sleep research also points to links between emotional adaptation and self-confidence and the ability to focus on what is important. REM sleep, in particular, seems to 'have a restorative function with respect to systems of focused attention' (Hartmann, 1973, p. 147), protecting the ability to focus on one thing at a time, to discriminate and pick out what is important. Research has shown people were unable to ignore distracting information after sleep deprivation, resulting in similar processing of neutral and negative distractors and disabling accurate emotional discrimination (Ben-Simon et al., 2015).

The ability to maintain an optimistic mood, energy and self-confidence and to adapt emotionally to the physical and social environment are also affected by REM sleep. Sleep, especially REM sleep, is all the more needed after days of stress, worry or intense new learning and seems to have a role in consolidating learning or memory, particularly for those who, like new parents, have had to restructure under stress their way of doing things (Hartmann, 1973).

In Chapter 6, we will look in a bit more detail at the usefulness of the dream dramas that take place during REM sleep. It seems that they help to consolidate learning and, more particularly, are a way of integrating emotional experiences through both conscious and unconscious levels of imagining.

Parents' sleep

We have been looking at the general functions of sleep in adults, and will now turn to look at the implications for parents. The consolidations happening in sleep are especially important for parents of newborn babies who are going through tremendous emotional changes.

The experience of going through pregnancy and childbirth, having a new baby and following the many astounding changes and leaps of development made in the first months and years has an emotional impact that is stressful, however enjoyable it may be too. Parents have the exhilarating but terrifying task of being responsible for a new life. Their experience of themselves and their relation to society changes radically; this inevitably involves a great deal of emotional readjustment.

New parents are arguably the people most in need of a good night's sleep! From the research mentioned earlier, we begin to see how, when disturbances in babies' sleep lead to loss of sleep by parents, their own ability to deal with the problem is in itself impaired. Focused attention and optimism, which are both affected by REM sleep, are the very qualities needed to help solve such problems.

We can start to see, too, how the actual process of waking can be difficult, either from the deep preoccupations of the dreaming period or from the deeply unconscious physiological state of Stage 4. Parents woken by their babies at either of these stages are likely to have difficulty dealing with the baby. In a REM period, they may be reluctant to emerge from their dream state, caught up in the process of working out their own stresses and anxieties. In a disintegrated state themselves, their child's anxieties cannot be put into perspective. Parents who are deeply asleep in Stage 4 may awake shaky and confused, not easily in control of their bodily movements and not able to work out what their baby needs.

In spite of these inevitable difficulties, waking in the night in the early weeks to feed or attend to a baby does not in itself constitute a sleep problem for either parent or baby. 'Regular waking once a night, which is considered a sleep problem in older children, may reflect an ongoing comfortable adaptation for mother and child at eight months' (Zuckerman et al., 1987, p. 665).

As we will see, attunement to the baby's rhythms is more important for most mothers in the early weeks than following their own biological sleep/wake rhythm. Mary-Sue Moore (1989) shows that mothers of new babies do not in fact sleep deeply; they do not often proceed into Stage 4 sleep, because they wish to be able to hear their baby cry. McKenna et al. (1990) demonstrate that mothers' waking is not only because they have already heard the baby's cries; they have already produced alpha waves during deep sleep which pull them up into light sleep again. This may not be so much to do with 'good' or 'unselfish' mothering as with finding the freedom for mutually satisfying exchanges of biological cues and signals between mother and baby. Inability to respond to her baby's rhythms may be as deeply disappointing and disturbing to the mother as to the baby. This is a glimpse of the intrinsic connection between biological and emotional processes and the way that the imperatives of parent-infant attachment can override the parents' personal physiological cycles. Patterns and rhythms are established between them. What happens is that when baby and mother are relatively close at night, the baby's neurologically based responses to the mother's breathing, movements and touch tend to reduce infant crying while positively regulating the baby's systems like breathing, body temperature, stress levels, immune status and oxygenation (McKenna et al., 2007).

Infants' sleep patterns

How does infant sleep differ from adult sleep? The most obvious difference is that babies sleep for much longer than adults do. These long hours are essential for physical growth and development, and it is increasingly clear that they are needed for consolidation of emotional and cognitive development, too (Tham et al., 2017). As well as sleeping longer, though, infants' sleep patterns are rather different from those of an adult. Let us now look at these and how they develop.

At birth, newborns sleep through most of the day and night, in short bouts. By six weeks, day and night patterns begin to emerge, and by about 10–12 weeks, the early stages of a daily rhythm develops, with a longer stretch of sleep through the night. The change in total sleep decreases by 16 weeks, with daytime sleep now appearing as well-defined naps punctuating a longer wakeful period. Day sleep gradually decreases and night sleep increases, so that by six months babies tend to be spending half the time asleep and half awake. By this stage, 70 percent of babies are sleeping through the night; by nine months it is 90 percent.

The circadian rhythm is the daily flow of physiological and behavioural functions including sleeping/waking. It is generally tied to the day-night cycle, although it can be measurably different when light/dark and other time cues are removed. Some basic physiological functions, like temperature and heartbeat, become entrained to this rhythm early on, others later. Kidney function, for example, does not entrain until approximately two years of age.

The changes in the circadian distribution of sleep and wakefulness are accompanied by changes within the sleep cycle itself. Interestingly, newborn infants go directly into REM sleep. Given that babies have evolved to seek developmentally necessary stimulation, not shut it out, and that they spend so much time asleep, stimulation would have to mainly come during sleep states. REM periods are most likely to provide this. Somewhere between three and six months the nature of falling asleep changes and the baby goes not into REM or 'active' sleep but into non-REM or 'quiet' sleep. As the baby matures, perhaps a greater proportion of 'quiet' sleep becomes necessary to balance an increase in stimulating wakeful periods.

However, another process, that of establishing rhythms and sequencing, is equally important. Developmental changes are not simply the maturation of the sleep/wake cycle, but are also part of interactions between a number of independent biological rhythms. For instance, the cyclical alternations of active and quiet sleep in the newborn are manifestations of a basic rest-activity cycle. The origin of this cycle has been shown in the foetus from three months on, but Emde and Robinson (1979) describe its presence in the first hours after birth. The cycle remains throughout our lifetime, lasting 90 minutes in adults as compared with 45 minutes in newborns.

It is useful to think of these less alert periods while awake as times for losing focused attention and being reflective, which have restorative functions similar to REM sleep. We can thus begin to see how the basic rest-activity cycle interacts with the sleep/wake cycle. For infant and adult it is seen in variations of activity both during sleep and in waking states. In infants, quiet and active states within sleep are matched by similar quiet and active waking states, with crying as the most stimulated state of all.

Let us now take a closer look at the REM/non-REM sequence in a baby's sleep. Ferber (2013) describes the baby's behaviour in different states of the sleep cycle, which is readily observable by parents. REM sleep appears in the foetus at about six or seven months' gestation, and non-REM sleep at between seven and eight months' gestation. Parents can easily see the baby in REM sleep twitching and breathing irregularly, with eyes flickering under their eyelids. In contrast, in quiet, non-REM sleep the baby breathes deeply and lies very still, occasionally making fast sucking motions or experiencing a sudden body startle.

After the first three months, the baby falls straight into non-REM sleep and plunges rapidly into Stage 4 within ten minutes. In youngsters this is an extremely deep sleep; waking a child from Stage 4 may be almost impossible. Thus a child who is rocked to sleep in his parent's arms may waken if put down in his cot while still in an early light stage of sleep, but will not do so if put down after reaching the later deep stage. A child woken by parents during Stage 4, perhaps to visit the toilet, will return to sleep instantly and have no recollection of the arousal in the morning. At the end of the deep sleep phase, there may be sudden body and eye movements, and the child may either wake or begin a fresh sleep cycle.

These descriptions are in order to help parents understand the physiological aspects of their baby's sleep cycles. An interesting issue is how individuals deal with the facts of their own sleep cycles, which include arousals, and how these are interpreted by parents on behalf of their babies. Many of us will easily recognize that as adults having a periodic arousal during the night, we can either turn over and go back to sleep or can find that pressing anxieties pull us into wakefulness if the previous REM time has not dealt with these sufficiently to allow sleep to continue. Babies, similarly, may wake in the early weeks to be fed at the times of these arousals through the cycle. Later on, waking may still signal such a need or it may simply be an arousal in the sleep cycle. It is easy to see how differently parents can behave at these times and the potential effect on their baby's sleep. Some, perceiving their baby to be awake, may let them drift back into sleep. Others, interpreting the arousal as a sign of some need, respond by waking the baby more completely. We shall look carefully at these different responses in later chapters.

Every new baby as they develop is reaching and managing new and different psychobiological states. Parents are intimately involved in both following and influencing these states. Stern (1985) has shown how a baby needs an 'other' to engage in mutual regulation, in the service of developing self-regulation. The other is of course usually the parent. Let us now look at this mutual regulation process in a little more detail.

Chapter 5

Babies' physiological states and parenting

The relation between parents and baby plays a vital part in the growth of the baby's physiological states. The handling of the baby by his parents helps him regulate his bodily states and has an effect on his psychological state; in other words, it affects his feelings. This then has an effect on the feelings that build up between parents and baby. Sleep, together with other states, seems inextricably bound up with parents' handling of their baby; let us examine this more closely.

In looking at the development of the baby's physiological states, we can see that right from the first few minutes after birth there is an interplay between the baby's own state and that of his mother. Mother and baby are open and receptive to each other. Gerhardt describes how:

> Physiologically, the human baby is still very much part of the mother's body. He depends on her milk to feed him, to regulate his heart rate and blood pressure, and to provide immune protection. His muscular activity is regulated by her touch, as is his growth hormone level. Her body keeps him warm and she disperses his stress hormones for him by her touch and her feeding.
>
> (2004, p. 22)

These mutual physiological processes are part of the way in which attachment forms between parents and baby. Beebe et al. (2012) show how, for future disorganized infants, not being sensed and known by the mother leads to confusion in sensing and knowing themselves. Research into the earliest postnatal interactions confirms the need for mothers, fathers and babies to be as much together as possible in the early stages after birth. To put this in perspective, it is worth saying that the bonding process can indeed get a good head start in those early moments, but the first hours after birth are *not* the only time bonding can possibly take place. Leaping ahead for a moment to clinical interchanges, mothers have several times told me with anguish that they have not been able to bond because their baby was, for example, taken away to an incubator for the first few hours. In such cases I say to them that what they have missed is *not* the only chance to bond with their baby, but a useful moment to start the long process of doing so.

When a mother and infant have achieved a sustained reciprocal rhythm, how does this affect the baby's sleep? One of the ordinary universal tasks of a mother is to help her baby regulate his sleep rhythms. Kreisler (1974) has remarked that of all the functions of the body, 'sleep is without doubt the most fragile' (p. 96). A mother who has intuitively achieved a reciprocal rhythm with an adaptable baby will probably be puzzled by this comment. To others the fragility will be all too recognizable, with regular patterns seemingly unattainable.

We have seen how in the first weeks the sleep/wake cycle goes on irrespective of the time of day. It takes until 12 to 16 weeks before day and night are clearly distinguished. We can now put the establishing of a day and night rhythm into a wider context. As well as being a physiological maturation, it is also a sign of psychological maturation. For the baby, this achievement is the product of a complex interaction between innate biological factors, environmental stimulation, satisfaction and frustration. It is a vital aspect of his self-development. It comes as part of the relationship between mother and infant and their reciprocal exchanges of feeding, holding and playing. Through her face, tone of voice and touch, the mother's responses to the baby soothe and regulate his level of tension and help him settle into a stable sleep pattern. Here again we see a connection between parent-infant interaction and neurological processes. Sander et al. (1976) emphasize the significance of the first ten days of life for mother and baby in organizing the time and rhythm of the baby's sleep. They deplore the 'nonchalant separation' of mothers and babies in some maternity units, which is to the detriment of this process.

As the day and night rhythm gets established, changes take place within the sleep cycle and the baby has a smaller amount of stimulating REM sleep. As the weeks go by, some of this stimulating function is taken over by social relations, such as those between parents and baby. Thus the social relations of parent and infant affect physical development. Put another way, emotional growth mediates physical growth as much as vice versa.

In terms of the baby's sleep cycles, Wolff (1974) suggests three levels: regular, irregular – or quiet and active as discussed in Chapter 4 – and drowsy. He distinguishes three waking states: alert inactivity, waking activity and crying, the most stimulated state. Our baby moves from one to another of these six states; our next question is, therefore, how and why she does this. I will now turn to look at some of the influences upon these transitions.

Newborn behaviour

We all know that babies are different from each other. Research into the relationship between innate characteristics and the effect of the environment has developed enormously over recent years (for an overview, see Music, 2010). Psychoanalytically based infant observations have accurately captured the way the infant and his parents interact through the early weeks and months (Reid, 1997). Research on mother-infant pairs has also been able to show subtle aspects of this nature-nurture interaction from very early on (Beebe & Lachman, 2002).

One aspect of the interaction concerns the baby's temperament. Brazelton's *Neonatal Behavioural Assessment Scale* (1973) offers a way of assessing temperamental variations in newborn babies and the effect they may have on their caregivers, showing the infant's adaptation to the environment in the service of his motor, emotional and cognitive development. It assesses the infant's response to stimuli of various kinds as a way of exploring his capacity to recover from the demands of labour, delivery and exposure to a new environment. The researcher looks at the interaction between himself and the infant, measuring his own responses and evaluating them as those most likely to be elicited by that infant from his own parents. The infant's eliciting characteristics are then specified, in terms of cuddlability, irritability, consolability and self-soothing ability. Differences emerge between one baby and another in tempo and style at birth and the way these might influence the newborn's parents.

In their study of this scale, Als et al. (1977) pick out two major attributes, 'attractiveness and need for stimulation'. These measure how much initiative the newborn takes, or how much stimulation he needs, as well as how he is able to respond to the researcher's stimuli. One infant may be stressed and unable to tolerate handling, even while being soothed, while another shows periods of sustained responsiveness, while being able to maintain physiological stability and availability for social stimulation. With regard to a slightly different function, the examiner looks at the newborn's use of, and need for, stimulation in order to organize his responses. Many newborns become more organized and stable as they are handled, while others are quite the opposite; they cannot tolerate handling and clearly give cues that they are better off alone. Some can deal with stimulation but do not necessarily need it to become well organized.

These tests were originally designed to detect infants at risk, to screen for difficulties and to see the effect of medication during delivery, but they have a wider interest for us. They alert us to the effect of the new baby's behaviour on parental response and to just how varied the behaviour systems of a baby are to which a parent has to become attuned. You will note that the Brazelton Scale criteria are a combination of the physiological and the social responses of the infant to the researcher's cue. The researcher, in turn, then responds to the infant. In everyday parenting, in picking up and responding to the infant's cues, parents are doing so in ways they may not be directly aware of; they are at an unconscious level. Brazelton's ideas of 'attractiveness' and 'need for stimulation' are perhaps similar to ways that psychoanalysts have thought of parents' unconscious intuitive and empathic knowledge of their baby's state of feelings. Parents have found it illuminating to have these intuitive responses and an indication of the range of their baby's behaviour pointed out to them.

In everyday ways, parents describe their newborn babies' states in such terms as 'friendly', 'responsive', 'suspicious', 'bad-tempered', 'fussy', 'inconsolable', 'easy' or 'difficult to please'. They also speculate on which characteristics the baby was born with, whom she takes after or what in the environment has affected her. These debates are not just theoretical; they are practical discussions going on during active care of the baby. Wolke and St. James Roberts (1987) note that parents' perception of their baby may be personally determined and not fit in with the views of professionals. They show how closely the parents' perception of the baby can influence its behaviour and argue that

> a mother who initially perceives her infant as slightly easier than an observer is believed to be more likely to positively interact and consequently influence infant behaviour than a mother who perceives her infant, in agreement with the observer, as difficult.
>
> (p. 65)

Conversely, Nover et al. (1984) show, as we will see in Chapter 13, how a mother's negative perceptions influence her baby's behaviour adversely. Indeed, from the field of infant mental health, Jones describes how the process of parent-infant psychotherapy can work to reclaim projected aspects of the parent, so that 'the baby becomes freer to be noticed as a separate being with thoughts and feelings of its own' (2006, p. 109).

Parents' influence on a baby's states

Stern (1985) describes how closely the baby's physiological development is tied up with her relationship to the person looking after her, showing how this interplay gives the baby experience of her own body. The baby needs the physical mediation of another person to satisfy her hunger or deal with other physical states, such as getting to sleep. Stern says, 'others regulate the infant's experiences of somatic state . . . in all such regulations a dramatic shift in neurophysiological states is involved' (1985, p. 103). However, his view is that although the baby undergoes a dramatic transformation in her self-state through her interaction with this other person, she retains her feeling of being separate from that other person; she does not feel as though she has merged with that person.

Stern shows how strong feelings and important representations come not just from the acts of being fed or put to sleep, but also from the way in which they are performed. The infant's own states of consciousness and activity are in fact socially negotiated states, affected by the other person who feeds and physically cares for the baby. How does the infant experience within himself the social actions of the other person and feel changed by what this other person does? One example is the way in which a bedtime routine affects what a baby feels about himself; this then has an effect on his somatic state. At its simplest, a baby who is cuddled and played with before being put to bed will have a different feeling about himself than one who has been perfunctorily put there. He will feel different about himself and about the mother or other person who has put him there. These feelings will stay with him and, if he is in a cot or room on his own, the separation will be coloured by the feelings produced during the bedtime routine.

Sleeping with parents

The way in which a parent helps the child regulate his own sleep/wake state includes of course whether the parent actually sleeps at night with the child or instead helps the child to manage to be on his own. Here again physiological and relationship issues connect with each other. McKenna (1986) describes the physiological aspects of parents sleeping with their babies and demonstrates connections between parents' and their babies' somatic processes. He synthesizes anthropological and physiological data on bodily contact with parents, suggesting:

> we have pushed too far the concept of the infant's physiological independence from the parent. For example, one inference that can be drawn from the cross-cultural and evolutionary data is that by having them sleep alone through the night and at very young ages we may be conditioning urban infants to sleep for artificially prolonged stages of the sleep cycle before their systems are best able to do so.
>
> (1986, p. 10)

He describes sleeping apart as a severe deprivation for small infants not neurologically independent enough to be separate from their parents. He explains, for example, the vital effect of the way parents and infants respond to each other's breathing sounds and movements: a vulnerable infant can be 'reminded' to breathe by close contact with the parents' breathing. He emphasizes the value physiologically, and by implication psychologically, of physical contact between parent and baby. (We come back to the emotional implications of this in Chapter 8.) Smith and Steinschneider (1975) give an interesting example of the connection between mothers' and infants' body states, showing that infants born to mothers with low heart rates sleep longer, fall asleep faster and cry less often than infants born to mothers with higher heart rates.

If we think of McKenna's argument as applying particularly to the early weeks of infancy, it accords well with mothers' common feelings of anxiety and of being somehow incomplete when separated at all from their infants. When hospital practice is to remove newborn babies to a nursery to give mothers a 'rest', mothers may be confused by feeling that even after the arduous experience of childbirth they feel less in need of respite than of closeness to the baby.

As we have seen, sleeping with parents has an effect on the baby's physiology, but parents are of course rarely aware of this. Their choice of whether they have their babies sleep with them derives from a whole range of cultural and personal reasons (see Chapter 9). Other childrearing practices also often have a calming physiological effect on babies. These practices include swaddling, rocking, massage and carrying of the baby; they involve holding, touch and movement close to the parent's body. Similar also is the non-nutrient use of sucking, though this is more of a self-soothing mechanism, whether the baby finds its own thumb or whether the means is provided by the parent who gives the baby a dummy.

(Sucking at the nipple or bottle-teat also fulfils such functions, in addition to the getting of milk.) Let us look at some of these practices in more detail.

Swaddling

Swaddling, wrapping the baby in bands or a tightly folded blanket with or without the use of a board or cradle, affects the baby's physiological and emotional states and also the relationship between mother and baby. It can be an effective way of calming a baby who finds it hard to settle. Lipton et al. (1965) found that 'infants who were swaddled slept more, had reduced levels of motor activity in response to stimulation, fewer startles and lower heart-rate variability than non-swaddled infants' (p. 259). The tactile quality of swaddling may be as important as constraining movement.

The cradleboard is used in Navajo child care (Chisholm & Richards, 1978). There is an initial protest at being put on the board, but part of the Navajo tradition of cradleboard use is the accepted wisdom that babies often fret when first put on the cradleboard. Mothers believe the cradleboard itself will stop the child's crying and do not respond within 15 seconds. This delay appears to give the baby space to 'protest' as part of a process of settling into sleep, without the confusion of being picked up again by the parent. The baby withdraws into sleep because of the lack of response by the parent, but this does not seem to be a pathogenic process of reciprocal emotional withdrawal. It is also not the same as 'leaving a baby to cry', as the parent remains close to the baby. It would be interesting to see the way in which mother and baby greet each other when the baby wakes from a long sleep on the cradleboard.

The study raises the question of whether this reduced mutual responsiveness and infant activity level is detrimental developmentally. The suggestion is, however, that the opportunity for interchange may be as important as the interchange itself and note that compared with European infants, Navajo babies spend more time in actual or potential social contact with adults. After looking at the effect of the cradleboard on Navajo infants, the study suggests that if newborn babies with heightened responsiveness are calmed early on by the cradleboard or swaddling, they may avoid sleep problems.

Wrapping a baby tightly in a blanket or shawl can have a similar effect. One baby I observed being put to bed in the first few weeks was tightly wrapped in a shawl, with his arms inside. As he was wrapped up each time, a peaceful look spread over his face; he would shut his eyes and fall asleep instantly. After a few weeks he struggled to have his arms out, though he still liked his body to be closely wrapped. As he got older and his movements increased, the shawl soon worked loose and the calming effect lessened.

Perhaps the dilemma for some parents with babies who have to be held in their arms for long periods in order to fall asleep, and who tend to wake again when finally put down, might be solved by a cradleboard. In such cases the baby is in a sense using the mother as a 'cradleboard' – requiring her to go on holding him, without any acknowledgement of the mother's own need, that is, *not* to be holding him all the time. He is also not taking into himself any experience that could carry over to enable him to feel he could be put down. The neutral ground of the board might release both mother and baby from this impasse.

These thoughts must also be connected with the finding that babies given extra carrying in the early months cry less later on (Hunziker & Barr, 1986). Somewhere in all this is an issue about timing. Mothers who have to go on holding their babies to get them to sleep may have somewhere missed the right timing in helping the baby regulate her *own* somatic states of sleeping and waking.

Rocking

Bowlby (1969) has described rocking as an effective way of terminating rhythmic crying. He notes that the effective speed at which rocking stops a baby crying is 60 cycles a minute or above. Sixty steps a minute is also the rate of a very slow walk. Bowlby makes the connection that when carried on her mother's back or hip, a young baby is rocked at not less than 60 cycles a minute and does not cry unless she is hungry or in pain. He suggests that although this may be a happy chance, it is more likely to be one of the selective pressures operating during the course of human evolution. To demonstrate the bodily effect that rocking has, Bowlby also shows that while being rocked the baby's heart rate usually returns to near resting level.

Sucking

Sucking obviously has primarily a feeding function, but its non-nutrient uses are also very important. Dunn (1977) summarizes some of the issues and shows how it stops a baby crying. Sucking on a dummy, for example,

> relaxes the movement of the guts and of the major muscles, and also reduces the number of eye-movements the baby makes when given something patterned to look at. While the baby is sucking in this way, not only is the stimulation from his mouth regular and rhythmic, but his random thrashing about is greatly reduced.

(p. 28)

Dunn questions whether the sucking reduces the active thrashing of arms and legs and so calms the baby or whether the calming effect of sucking reduces the movement.

Sucking also has great emotional significance as a way for the baby to be in contact with the mother through sucking at the breast. Sucking on, for example, a dummy can therefore also represent a memory of sucking at the breast and thus be both a way of keeping in contact through the mind and at the same time be a way of being separate in body from the mother.

Massage

Massage can be helpful in promoting sleep. Gerhardt (2004) says, 'in mothers' or fathers' arms, where it is safe and warm, muscles can relax and breathing can deepen as tensions are dispersed by gentle stroking or calm rocking'. When relationships are going well, massage may be just another way of experiencing this, but where there are difficulties massage may be a way for parents to reach out to their babies. Underdown (2009) shows that by reducing stress, massage can improve sleep and control colic. Given at the right level of pressure it can significantly influence melatonin levels, which are important in establishing circadian levels (Goldstein-Ferber, 2002). Also, parent and baby may start to pick up each other's cues and feel more warmth. As a result, parents with postnatal depression may also benefit from massaging their baby (Glover et al., 2002).

Conclusion

We have seen that babies need considerable help in the development of their own neurophysiological states. It is obvious that a helpless little baby needs to be fed by someone else. It may not be quite so evident that it is through another person's intervention that a baby has an experience of the workings of his own body and, what is more, that through this his body gradually becomes more organized. We have also seen how the closeness of the parent's body has an effect on the baby's body, as does swaddling or wrapping the baby up tightly, while the parent remains near.

All this help from the parent or caretaker is essential in facilitating the baby's capacity to be separate from other people. Closeness starts a process which helps enable the baby to look after the workings of her own body, so that she can achieve eventual separation. In Chapter 7, we will see the parallel psychological process by which a baby needs intimate emotional contact with a parent or carer, in order to build up a sense of the self and eventually be able to separate from the parent. A baby's somatic functioning requires an interested other person's presence. It is also vital that the other person sees the baby as being separate from themselves, but we will come to this later.

Dreams and nightmares

People have always been interested in their dreams and believed that there was a meaning to them. The telling of dreams to another person has also always been important. Sometimes there is an excited compulsion to relate the dream, the dreamer being preoccupied with it until the telling brings a feeling of relief. At other times there is a caution and reticence in the dreamer, who feels that telling the dream would be too revealing.

In early history, as we see from the Bible or from ancient Greek and Roman literature, the meaning of the dream was thought to lie in foretelling the future. Freud brought an entirely new perspective to this search for meaning. He developed a method of free association, of letting thoughts flow freely so that connections could emerge. In the course of this he found that his patients often dwelt upon their dreams because they seemed to carry great import. He realized that they seemed to be determined in part by present problems, but they also often led straight back to profound experiences at all stages of earlier life, even infancy, and were thus the 'royal road to the unconscious'. Freud looked in detail at his own dreams and those related to him by patients, colleagues and friends. In *The Interpretation of Dreams* (1900), he showed how present-day anxieties and conflicts intruded into sleep, disturbing it. He described how dreams seemed to include an imagined wish-fulfilment that apparently solved these conflicts and allowed sleep to continue. The dramatic action portrayed in a dream contained multiple images, which were disguised and condensed representations of present-day conflicts combined together with past memories.

Psychoanalytic understanding of present difficulties partly in terms of past relationships and experiences evolved from this view of dreams. Even more importantly, it has offered since then a way of relating thoughts, fantasies and dreams to our emotional life and long-term life-events. Our dreams can be a useful way of checking our state of mental wellbeing. At its simplest, nightmares are often understood as a sign of turbulence and stress in the mind. At times of change in life, dreams, in their linking of events from childhood with present-day occurrences, are a way of learning from and using past experience, consciously or unconsciously, or of seeing common themes in a life-history. We know ourselves through our history. Dreams are a bit like works of art. In both,

forgotten experience becomes accessible to be used, without conscious awareness, as part of the creative imagination.

Sleep and dream research confirms Freud's insight that what is remembered in
dreams relates to sleep disturbance and also is the link between present and past.
Dreams seem to perform the very efficient function of internal communication,
from one aspect of a person's mind to another. Since Freud's day, we have learnt
that the function of dreaming is much more than a protection of sleep, solving
conflicts and thus allowing sleep to continue. It also serves to assimilate current
experience into long-term memory, and, as I suggest later, performs a psychologically integrating function, whether or not the dream is remembered or its meaning
consciously understood.

Meltzer (1983), a Kleinian psychoanalyst, takes further Freud's connection
between moments from the day before the dream and their links with infantile
experience. He picks up Freud's point that a particular link to infantile experience was necessary for a daytime event to qualify for dream representation and
suggests that in fact infantile experiences are ongoing and underlie the waking,
conscious experiences of the day.

> We would consider dreaming to be as continuous in the mind as is digestion
> in the body, but concentrated more fully on its task when the other mental
> processes of dealing with the outside world are in abeyance during sleep.
>
> (1983, p. 88)

REM or D sleep

Let us now look at dream-time from another point of view, in the context of the
theory of REM or D sleep, in which we dream, as explained by sleep researchers.

I outlined in Chapter 4 the biological progression of the stages of sleep and the
function of REM sleep in restoring the ability to focus on one item at a time and to
maintain an optimistic mood, energy and self-confidence. More D sleep is needed
when there have been emotional changes or new learning to absorb, especially
when there is stress involved in the impact of whatever is new. D sleep seems to
have a role in consolidating learning and memory and in reconnecting the important changes made during the day.

We see from this the importance to both parents and baby of achieving
enough D sleep. Its restorative functions are particularly relevant both to the
situation of a baby developing and trying to master the implications of its own
learning processes and to parents who are having to make changes in themselves to be in tune with the physical and emotional changes taking place in
their baby. We also can see that, if their sleep process is interrupted, parents
whose systems of focused attention have become impaired will have less ability to solve the sleep problems of their baby. Parents in this situation know only
too well that systems that maintain optimism, energy and self-confidence are
indeed impaired by lack of D sleep!

It is important to notice that the cyclical nature of sleep and the point at which D sleep occurs during the cycles affect the quality of sleep of parents who are woken by their babies, as well as that of the babies themselves. We have seen that newborn babies plunge straight into REM sleep. Older babies and adults go into D sleep later in the cycle. So an older baby who wakes frequently during the night may be waking both himself and his parents at the stage in the cycle before there has been enough D sleep for the vital restorative processes to take place. Noting that D sleep happens principally towards the end of a night's sleep, parents (or anyone else for that matter) woken in the middle of the night are, in fact, at their lowest ebb in a 24-hour cycle before the renewal of the D sleep period.

Palombo's work (1978) on dreams suggests that 'the dream itself . . . and not merely the interpretation of the dream – plays a positive integrating role in normal emotional development' (p. 6). He illuminates what may be a crucial occurrence in dreams, suggesting that dreaming plays a central function in assimilating memories of the day into settled long-term memory. Thus if dreaming is insufficient or interrupted, the consequences are very serious for child and adult alike – they are left with a jumble of unassimilated memories. Here it is worth differentiating between the dream process itself and the memory of the dream. Unremembered dreams perform this important co-ordinating function for the mind, without the dreamer being aware that this has happened. Remembered dreams have an additional function in illuminating in symbolic form present conflicts, choices and changes and connecting these with experiences from the past. The dreamer has a chance to ponder over these images and symbols and the memories they release.

It has occurred to me that what goes on in my consultations with parents is somewhat akin to the co-ordinating aspect of dream-work. As I have said, parents nearly always come in a distressed state, with a confused mass of information. It seems to be compulsively necessary for them (and equally fascinating for me) to tell me the fullest details of the baby's behaviour through the day and night. All this is set in the framework of relationships and emotions. I think that an integrative process comparable to that of dreaming is set in motion by my listening to all of this and, to begin with, putting it in place in my mind. I think that I then help the parents to start to think and then dream it over; this then leaves the baby freer to have her own dreams.

Parents' dreams

Luke and his mother illustrate this well. This mother, with her six-month-old baby (described further in Chapter 9), came to see me, agonizing over the process of weaning. She had to return to work in two months' time, but was still breastfeeding Luke night and day. The coming separation felt arbitrary to her, and this made it difficult for her to sort out whether Luke still needed her and her breast or whether both of them were ready to be more separate from each other.

When she had got to the point of being able to own natural feelings of *not* wanting to be with her baby all the time and was becoming ready to stop breastfeeding,

I asked if she had had any dreams about it all. She laughed and said, 'I don't get to sleep for long enough to dream'. Then she recalled a dream a week previously, just after Luke's christening. In the dream she was wearing a white dress with buttons down the front. One button was open and the baby's godfather had done it up for her. The economy of this dream is quite startling: the allusions to this mother beginning to button herself up from breastfeeding and the associations to sexual feelings and a wedding brought together the themes of our work. She had begun to speculate whether her extreme closeness to Luke had caused her to feel more distant from her husband. She was starting to think about whether a more appropriate space between her and Luke would enable her marriage to come back to life. The white dress perhaps alluded to a new 'wedding' with her husband. The christening, a ceremony of recognizing Luke as an individual, was well timed for this family. I pointed out to Luke's mother that her dream was a kind of commentary, running through her mind, on all these issues.

Bion (1962) has described how the mother's thinking about her baby helps him deal with his confused emotional experiences in a way that enables him to start thinking and dreaming. I would add that the mother's dreaming is part of this process. This mother's dream seemed to have helped her prepare for the partial weaning process later in the week. Luke, in turn, was set free to sleep and dream.

Dreams can be a way of anticipating progress before it has been openly achieved, not as a form of prophecy but as an acknowledgement of mental work. Parents' dreams may herald progress in dealing with the problems between them and their children. One father (already mentioned in Chapter 2) dreamt that his little son Stanley, who could not yet talk, asked him, 'Why don't you show me how to get to sleep?' This released into consciousness memories that helped him connect what was happening now with similar problems from the generation before, between his own father and himself. This dream thus linked the past with the present, reminding Stanley's father of his own childhood difficulties and apparently informing him that *his* father's failure to help him was part of the background of his own failure to help his son now. However, I think Stanley's question in the dream, 'Why don't you show me how to get to sleep?' actually came from a dawning ability by his father to do just that. The dream words show that Stanley's father is beginning to imagine himself as being able to help his son.

In a sense, therefore, parents' dreams are one of the many aspects of caring for their children. The first example of this may be dreams in pregnancy. This is one of the routes of the psychological preparation that is a major task of pregnancy. Dreams in pregnancy enable the mother to absorb the changes taking place in her own body and in her position within her family and her wider community. These dreams can provide a shape to her fantasies. Some may be an extension of her day-dreams about what the baby will be like, its gender, appearance and character; others may express disturbing fantasies about what the being growing inside her is doing to her body; and others may be a representation of anxieties as to whether the foetus is developing normally. In particular, anxiety-dreams about the impending childbirth may be one means towards mastering this anxiety.

The turbulence of the actual experience of the birth may be demonstrated later by highly disturbing dreams, which may both denote a mother at risk and be a way of absorbing the psychic stresses.

Moving on to after the baby has been born, one mother, whose baby had colic and slept badly, dreamt that she took the baby's penis into her mouth. It seemed as though this was partly a reversal of the breastfeeding experience of *her* nipple going into *his* mouth. We see from this simple example how disturbing new bodily experiences like breastfeeding can be; they can arouse worries and confusion about forbidden sexual feelings in the mother towards her baby. Shocked by this dream, although able to confide it to her husband, the mother found the breastfeeding awkward. It was not until she told me the dream and could make the conscious connection between it and breastfeeding that she was able to get more comfortable with these disturbing dreams.

Later this mother dreamt that her baby turned into a small furry animal with big teeth. I commented to her that this seemed to represent fantasies that she was breastfeeding a small biting animal and that this might be affecting her way of feeding him in such a way that it produced pain in him. Perhaps she strained away from this imagined biting, so that the baby took in gulps of air as he sucked, or something else fraught between them may have affected his digestion of the milk. This is one possible sequence of events, which can only be a hypothesis (in Chapter 9 we look at some of the explanations for colic). Given my explanation, the dream illustrated the mother's fear of being bitten, which then indirectly caused the baby's pain. Another possible chain of events is that the baby's pain was what precipitated the dream – perhaps the screaming of the baby was experienced by the mother as a kind of biting into herself, so that she pictured him in her dream as a biting animal.

Parents may thus dream about their children in many ways, ranging from dealing with their own trauma in having babies and differentiating themselves from their babies to a mature ability to dream altruistically on behalf of their children.

Parents' understanding of children's dreams

How can parents help their children with their own dreams? Palombo (1978) suggests that parents are the original interpreters of dreams. This should not be misunderstood as meaning parents should act as 'therapists' or enquire intrusively about dreams.

> The repeatedly reassuring presence of his mother or her substitute after the experience of an awakening dream is a crucial element in any infant's learning to distinguish between his inner and outer worlds . . . The child just beginning to talk brings his awakening dreams to his parents both for reassurance and to take advantage of their ability to translate his strange experience into

words . . . The parent's failure to supply what is needed at this point may have a serious effect on the later accessibility to the child of his early memories and of fantasy material in general.

(Palombo, 1978, p. 164)

Through dreams and nightmares in children we can, in fact, see revealed the stages of emotional and psychic development. These are conveyed in both the dreams that wake the child and those that do not. What are the differences between these dreams? Scott suggests one possibility:

When Freud began to listen to patients' stories of their lives their dreams were naturally part of the story . . . He discovered that dreams showed disguised attempts to fulfil wishes which often dated from infancy . . . These wishes were disguised in such a way that sleep was preserved or protected, unless the emotion connected with the attempted wish-fulfilment was so great, or the dream was repeated with such increasing emotion, that continued sleep becomes impossible.

(1975, p. 253)

With young infants we can only guess at the content of their REM states, using the clues we observe of sucking mouths, crying out and so on. But these clues can be very persuasive. One mother said to me spontaneously of her sleeping two-month-old, 'He's dreaming of sucking'. When a crying baby wakes in distress, not seeming to need food, parents may empathically guess at a 'bad dream'. It becomes much easier when a child who can use words is able to recount a frightening dream at the time of waking or obtain the relief of telling in the morning the memory of one that did not wake him. However, in talking of the seriousness of the need to understand a child's dream, we must include in this the need for empathy with the dreams of the preverbal child and the anxieties that lie behind them.

Joanna's mother showed me how hard it can be in reality to be an interpreter for a child's dream. Joanna, aged one, would cry out during a nightmare, but when her mother went in to her she was rejected, that is, treated as a part of the nightmare. Joanna slept badly, had many of these nightmares and had frequent temper tantrums during the day. Joanna's mother vividly described feeling that her baby saw her as a 'witch' in the night.

It seemed appropriate to go quite explicitly through a simple Kleinian version of child development and talk about the child's difficulty in managing her own aggressive and destructive impulses and her need to project these into her mother. This mother was interested intellectually, but also responded instinctively. The sleeping difficulties had started at six weeks, after a brief period when Joanna's father had to go away. We connected the sleeping difficulties with her mother's own panic at this separation and her resentment with her partner for not being there to support her. After ten months of bad nights, Joanna slept through the night for two weeks. After that there were some broken nights, but the relationship between mother and daughter changed dramatically from mutual fury to a loving, teasing one. By understanding the nature of her baby's fears in the night, Joanna's mother was better able to respond to them. The baby now had the experience of being understood and was comforted by this understanding. She no longer needed to wake repeatedly to seek it.

All this activity through the night is as universal and matter of fact as the parents' ability to tolerate the small child's daytime outburst of 'I hate you', which stems from the same instinctual source as the equally passionate 'I love you'. The significance of the child's confiding her nightmares to her parents is thus that they give her both protection over the strength of the impulses and anxieties that the nightmares represent and that there is an unspoken forgiveness by the parents for themselves being at least in part the focus of these impulses.

One mother told me in some distress that she felt she was the cause of her two-year-old daughter's nightmares. After an angry outburst where she shouted irrationally at her, her daughter dreamt about an angry witch. She felt her daughter was putting this real encounter into symbolic form. It is important to differentiate between actual events which are dealt with psychically through our dreams and the grappling with emotions that also fills children's dreams with witches, monsters and so on. These witches and monsters can be both the child's own impulses and the feared retaliation from parents for these imagined attacks.

The child's conflicts

In this book I have considered the effect of parents' own difficulties on the child's ability to sleep, suggesting that at times the child's disturbance is a direct reflection of the parents'. Secondly, I have shown how a child's own difficulty in sleeping can be eased or not by the parent. Some sleep disturbances may be symptoms serving a parent's psychopathology, and some may arise through conflict within the child himself, which may give rise to sleep problems and be illustrated by dreams and nightmares. We will start by looking briefly at the connections between the physiological development of sleep, including REM or D states, and emotional growth.

Metcalf (1979) suggests that both physiologically and psychologically the psychic precursors and prototypes of dramatic dreaming begin during the period of switch-over in sleep patterns at about three months, when babies move away from falling straight into REM sleep. As the central nervous system matures, so do the physiological possibilities of the nature of dream states become more complex.

This change in sleep physiology coincides with psychological change in the infant. His developing physical attainments are matched with a growing sense of self and psychological differentiation from the mother. Developing at the same time are memory and anticipation. We may speculate that emerging dreams are facilitated by these. It can only be hypothesis as to what the content of an infant's dream is, but like the mother who said of her two-month-old, 'He's dreaming of sucking', we are using something of our own experience when we speculate that an infant's dreams are memories and desires of states he has experienced, re-enactments of present gratification or unfulfilled states.

We will look in more detail at the psychological development of babies in the next chapter, but meanwhile I would like to note that the various anxieties emerging at different stages of development produce their own effects on sleep. As we will see in Chapter 9, the stage of weaning, both actual and psychological, and stranger-anxiety are important examples of a potentially stressful developmental stage. Babies who have slept well previously may now have sleep disturbances under the stress of this period. The dreams of this time probably reflect the internal preoccupations of the baby. Klein (1959) vividly describes the concern of the growing infant for the mother, with the infant now *worrying* about how her impulses have affected the mother and how to deal with her aggressive feelings. This stage is called by Klein the 'depressive position'; it does not mean that the baby is depressed, but implies sensitivity and concern for others. This is also the age of teeth coming through. What is the psychological meaning of the sensations in gums, of the presence of these hard, biting new bits of the baby? Does the baby experience this as pain and suffering within her own body or as a tool with which to enjoy biting into hard rusks, teething rings and so on? Does she feel joyfully ruthless or depressively guilty when she bites her mother, inadvertently or on purpose? And what does she make of all this in her dreams? No wonder parents of babies of six to nine months or so, intuitively aware of so much going on, are not surprised at anxious cries in the night.

Dreaming does not always herald anxiety. It is also a vital part of the attainment of psychic individuality. Tustin (1972) writes of the stage where

> identification with a mother who can bear the pains of bodily separateness begins to take place . . . Thus the capacity for representations and the use of skills develop. Dreams begin to take the place of random discharges and bodily movements. Innate forms begin to be transformed into thoughts and fantasies. The psyche as we know it begins. The child becomes psychologically viable and continent.
>
> (p. 61)

As the baby gets older and is able to talk, he may then tell his parents of the content of his dream. As with adults' dreams, the manifest content may simply be an illustration of the themes underneath. For example, the monsters and wild beasts in many little children's dreams would seem to depict aspects of themselves or of their parents. Perhaps jealousies of parents and also jealousies of new babies may account for some of these dreams.

The book *Where the Wild Things Are* (Sendak, 1963) can have an amazingly therapeutic effect on children in the grip of these feelings. Max, the hero of this book, makes so much mischief that his mother calls him a 'wild thing' after he says to her, 'I'll eat you up', and is sent to bed without his supper. In bed he dreams that he goes to where the Wild Things are, tames the monsters and becomes their king. After a year of this he becomes lonely and goes home to 'where someone loved him best of all'.

What seems to work in this story for a small child is the acknowledgement of the wild feelings inside himself, making friends with them and overcoming them within himself and getting back to a loving relationship with his mother. Having this book read to them may often help children manage their nightmares, as also may patient listening by parents to children recounting the content of these dreams. The parents' task is to listen and help children deal with the forces of their dreams – the actual having of the nightmare may be a useful path to self-awareness for the child about the fierceness of his own emotions.

Dreams and playing

We have looked at dreams and nightmares as ways of expressing and communicating anxieties and conflicts. The dreams may also help to resolve these conflicts. We have also noted that through the images that symbolically represent conflicts, we can make connections, consciously or not, between past and present issues. We have also seen that the dream itself has an integrating function and helps sort out, make sense of and put into memory our continuing daily experiences.

Meltzer (1983) describes the dream process as continuing to run underneath our waking lives. In children, this continuous process can best be seen in their play. Children can often be seen engaged in reflective 'dreaming' play and, in a more active state, in playing out some make-believe. This can easily be thought of as a carry-over from the work of dreaming. Anna Freud observed that children could relate their dreams but not go on to talk about the meaning of the images that arose in them. Both she and Klein evolved (though from very different theoretical standpoints) methods of therapy with children that involved understanding their play as a communication of some of the thoughts and phantasies underlying everyday ones. Just as some children cannot easily relax into sleep and dreaming, so some children are unable to play. Pound (1982) has shown how some children of depressed mothers cannot relax their vigilance enough to turn their attention to play. Attuning to the baby through play can work through the defences of both baby and parents (Paul, 2014a).

Children's nightmares follow the pattern of their emotional development. Babies becoming independent may appear to dream of feelings of abandonment, judging by their 'sorrow on arousal', to use Terr's (1987) poignant phrase. Toddlers struggling with their impulses may create daytime waking symbols of their fears and then produce these same symbols in their dreams. For example, fierce dogs, feared in the street, may represent newly acquired biting impulses. They may appear unchanged in dreams or be changed into even fiercer 'Wild Things'.

Terr (1987), looking at how children's nightmares progress developmentally, remarks on how the acquirement of language enables the child to tell his dreams. She suggests that 'the absence of language to label emotions may actually predispose' the toddler to nightmares. We can see from this that the organizational effect of having words in which to express feelings may start to get them under control. 'Nameless terrors' are less likely to remain so when a child has words to name them; we have seen earlier the therapeutic benefit of a child telling his parent his dreams. The manifest content of the dream changes as the child's cognitive capacities develop. Dreams become more complicated: for instance, small children dream of small figures such as rabbits, while school-age children dream of their peers. We see how growing independence takes children out of the home in their dreams, as it does in waking life.

Nightmares and night terrors

A nightmare is 'a long frightening dream which awakens the sleeper, and is clearly remembered as a very detailed, vivid and intense dream experience' (Hartmann, 1984, p. 19). By contrast, the night terror is not a dream, but a 'disorder of arousal' (Broughton, 1968). It is a different biopsychological phenomenon, generally triggered out of deep (slow-wave) sleep, not REM sleep. It happens early during the sleep period, usually in the first two hours of deepest sleep, and consists of a sudden arousal in terror, most often accompanied by a scream, sweating, body movements and sometimes sleepwalking. Sleepers do not remember night terrors as they might a dream; they either recall nothing at all or are aware of a single frightening physical image or sensation. 'The person . . . who sits upright in bed, or gets out of bed, screaming, with a glazed expression on his face, is a person having a night terror, not a nightmare' (Hartmann, 1984, p. 21). This description will be familiar to many parents. Most commonly reported between the ages of three to eight, parents often describe the child as screaming and then either going back to sleep or sleepwalking. A particular difficulty for parents in dealing with their children's night terrors is the sudden arousal, which also rouses the parents with alarm and no warning. Their ability to deal calmly with the child is inevitably affected by their own psychological and physiological response to this awakening.

A child having a night terror may cry out, talk or moan, but he is not awake. He will not recognize his parents or allow them to comfort him and he will not remember it in the morning (Ferber, 2013). A child waking from a nightmare can report a dream if he is old enough. He will cry or call for his parent, will recognize the parent and want to be held and comforted. He will remember the dream on waking and also in the morning. One of the interesting consequences of the differences in remembering nightmares and night terrors is that after a remembered nightmare a child may be frightened to go to bed or to sleep. After a night terror he does not have this fear, but will relax and be able to return to sleep quickly; with no memory of the night terror, he is not afraid to go to sleep on other nights.

There may be a tendency for night terrors to run in families, and some children may have a genetic susceptibility to them. Night terrors can be considered a minor abnormality in the brain's sleep/wake mechanisms, producing unusual arousals. However, night terrors can also be influenced by environmental or emotional factors. A child susceptible to night terrors may have them whenever there is stress or a difficult period in the family. Since sleep deprivation and extreme tiredness aggravate night terrors, keeping to a regular sleep schedule may in itself be a partial cure. Reassurance both to parents and by parents can be helpful, and short-term psychotherapy can be useful. It may reduce stress by helping parents handle potentially stressful events in new ways and give them an opportunity to examine their own dangerous emotions – anger and rage – in a safe daytime setting. Magagna (1986), in her paper on older children, has described night terrors in latency as being a way of expressing unacknowledged hostility within families. Dangerous matters that cannot be openly talked about may be expressed in this way.

Non-symbolic post-traumatic nightmares

Moore (1989) has highlighted a particular kind of non-symbolic recurring 'nightmares' and a link between these and significantly reduced Stage 4 deep sleep. They are arousals out of Stage 2 sleep and are repetitive memories of a traumatic event. Somebody having this kind of nightmare awakes in a highly aroused state. The link is made between feeling or being vulnerable to external threats and being less likely to go deeply into Stage 4 sleep. Self-preservation keeps us from becoming deeply unconscious. In a circular process that may reinforce the trouble, in this situation people also experience fewer REM dreams or ordinary nightmares that would follow Stage 4 sleep and thus are deprived of the reparative work that a REM dream or nightmare could offer. When people in this situation have also suffered a traumatic event, they often experience nightmares coming out of the lighter Stage 2 sleep. During these Stage 2 nightmares, traumatic memories or situations are played over and over again, with little symbolic alteration. However, there may be some REM nightmares at the same stage which do help the person deal with the perceived dangers. As the traumatic experience is gradually integrated, fewer Stage 2 nightmares occur and REM dreams become less frightening.

Terr (1987) similarly describes children after a traumatic kidnapping having an exactly repeated, recurrent nightmare. As time went on, the children were able to add current material from their lives to the nightmare. The dreams became 'modified repetitions' and became increasingly disguised with symbolism. Moore points out that in a post-traumatic dream the people involved are portrayed as themselves, not as someone symbolically standing in for them. As the dream begins to play a part in the recovery process, the dream itself gradually changes and settles into the context of other experiences. We are straying here into ideas derived from children older than those discussed in this book, but this available material sheds light on processes also pertaining to younger infants.

Moore (1989) also shows that night terrors which come out of Stage 4 deep sleep, rather than Stage 2 or REM sleep, may be understood as a conflict between two ways of surviving. When the anxieties of the night terror appear, there are potentially two ways of defending the threat to the self – either going into deeper unconsciousness or arousal. The disturbed arousal from a night terror where the child does not properly awake is the result of this unsolved conflict. The child wakes screaming and does not recognize the parent; the parent also becomes terrified by the child's state.

Who has nightmares?

Hartmann (1984) makes the observation that nightmare-sufferers see themselves as having been unusually sensitive in childhood.

> The word sensitive occurred frequently; referring sometimes to perceptual sensitivity – to light and sound, for instance; sometimes to interpersonal sensitivity – empathy, awareness of others' feelings; and almost always to being themselves emotionally sensitive – easily hurt by others. They saw this personality characteristic as having been present more or less from birth.
>
> (1984, p. 70)

Why go into details of adult nightmare-sufferers in a book about infants? Children do have more frequent nightmares than do most adults; it is a developmental phase and may be one of the things most people grow out of. However, the question of sensitivity has an important bearing on how parents deal with childhood nightmares. The paradoxical solution is, I think, that facing the content of the nightmare commonsensically with the child may reduce this over-sensitivity – the child may be relieved that the universality of his terror is acknowledged. We all have demons within us – sharing them by recounting our dreams can make them manageable. Nothing could be more robust than the monsters in *Where the Wild Things Are* or than Max in his way of dealing with them. These thoughts tie in with Hartmann's findings that nightmare-sufferers frequently see themselves as having been sensitive children. One factor in this may have been the failure of their parents at the time to deal matter-of-factly with infantile terrors. These children seem to grow up with one 'skin' less of parental protection.

Sometimes the parental protection has been compromised in more serious ways, and night terrors and other sleep problems ensue (Insana et al., 2014). In one such case, a mother described how her baby's father, since diagnosed as schizophrenic, used to wake her up in the night by thumping her for no apparent reason. When the baby, Jerry, was born, the father sat by his cot and woke him repeatedly, saying it was to check that he was still alive. Jerry's mother left his father, went back to him and then, after several occasions when he violently beat her up in front of the baby, she finally left. At three this little boy woke repeatedly in the night, often with night terrors, screaming, being hard to rouse and unable to tell his mother what was frightening him. His mother was terrified that he was taking after his father, that is, becoming schizophrenic. I talked with her about the need to understand with Jerry what the terrors in the night were about – that they were replaying the frightening things he had witnessed before he had words to describe them or ways of understanding them.

We know now just how damaging it is for children to witness domestic violence (for an overview, see Kitzmann et al., 2003) and how formative the impact is upon a child like Jerry's developing mind. Even when a baby is asleep, the same brain areas fire up as if they were awake. Sleeping babies (and babies in general in fact) are far more sensitively open to environmental inputs than people tend to realize. The indirect effects too of Jerry's mother being preoccupied with his father's serious mental health problems will have had an effect on his wellbeing and development and of course his sleep – beyond that of his father's troubling treatment of him, including waking him repeatedly in the night. It seemed to me that the mother's attitude now was vital for Jerry's future mental health. Thus if she could convey to him that she *understood* the nature of his terrors and let him know about actual protection for him now, he may gradually feel secure enough to sleep better. Little children need parents to do an actual sweep under the bed to get rid of any potential lurking monsters; saying they are gone is not enough. For Jerry, it may take some time, but physical safety and his mother's receptive attention to his fears could begin to help him feel safe enough to settle and sleep better. Jerry's mother had felt that his father had slipped away from her into an incomprehensible, mad world of schizophrenic thinking and impulse. She had tried to make sense of it for him, tried to help him, reassure him and look after him, and it had not worked. In fact I was suggesting that what had not worked for Jerry's father might work for Jerry.

We have seen in this chapter how dreams and nightmares are a way of dealing with, understanding and organizing into memory the experiences we encounter throughout life. The symbolic way in which dreams refer to people, places and events means that dreams can be a vivid illustration of thought processes. The story-telling of a dream punctuates an individual's life-history. We have seen how dreams can get hold of themes from the past and can express anticipatory thoughts about the future. Our dream thoughts underlie our conscious thoughts even in waking time. Perhaps with parents and infants, unconsciously so closely in touch with each other, dreams are a vehicle of communication about these intertwined thoughts.

Chapter 7

The development of separateness of the self

We have looked at how a baby develops physiologically, influenced by his parents' handling of him. Now we will turn to the normal emotional development of the baby, which is also influenced by the parents, at first principally the mother, who is so often the main carer to begin with. Various psychoanalytic writers have described this process in different ways; their theoretical languages are sometimes at odds with each other, but all have an interesting original way of adding to our picture of what happens between parents and babies.

This is a chapter about feelings, about how the baby's sense of self develops, how his sense of who he is on his own derives from who he is with his mother, and conversely how this depends also on his mother's picture of him. The process starts as early as pregnancy; one of the mother's first tasks is thinking about her coming baby and herself in relationship to him. How she manages it can even affect the birth and the early weeks of life.

Mothers and babies establish intimacy and are then able to become more separate from each other. This is not an automatic development; rather it is a human drama, containing both pains and achievements. The mother of eight-month-old Dominic said to me, 'When he closes his eyes, I feel left out'. In one sense the problem for a mother in getting a baby to sleep is the basic act of putting the baby down, that is, of separating herself from the baby and the baby from her. It can be as difficult for the mother to do without the baby as it is the other way round. Much of psychoanalytic and child development literature is occupied with showing us the process by which a baby starts from a state of dependence, physical and emotional, on its mother and gradually moves apart.

Winnicott was a paediatrician and psychoanalyst who worked with mothers and babies and wrote for professionals and parents. His book *The Child, the Family and the Outside World* (1964), although written from outdated assumptions about the social context of the family, describes the deeply emotional world of babies and their parents in a fresh and moving way. He emphasizes, 'There is no such thing as a baby', only 'a *baby* and *someone*'. The baby depends on his mother for survival, and the mother is for a while almost totally bound up with the baby. Winnicott called this 'primary maternal preoccupation'. The baby moves through various states to the separation and individuation we associate with maturity, and the mother reciprocally pulls apart from the baby. This process and its vicissitudes have been described within various theoretical frameworks. As we look at some of these ideas, we should hold in mind the question posed in Chapter 1, whether sleep is experienced as a disruption or as a continuation of the being together of mother and baby. We will also see how the ability to sleep, or sleep disturbance, may punctuate the various stages of the baby's development.

How do babies manage to separate from their mothers and how do mothers separate from their babies? One important factor is highlighted in Paret's (1983) study of the connection between sleeping and the ability of babies to separate from their mothers. In a sample of babies at the crawling stage, the 'sleepers' were able to move significantly further away from their mothers than the 'wakers'. It seems that babies who sleep well are more secure and can put some distance between themselves and their mothers.

Pregnancy

It is just as well that pregnancy, from conception to a full-term baby, is a process that takes nine months. Prospective (especially first-time) mothers need at least this time to deal with the enormous changes taking place in their bodies, their minds and their lives. Pregnancy is a preparation time, both physical and emotional. Incidentally, it is no accident that pregnant mothers need a great deal of sleep, particularly in the first three months. One might think that the later stages, with a larger baby to carry inside, would make a mother even more tired. However, if we think of one of the functions of sleep as being to deal with the effects of change, we can see that both physically, with the body accepting the new foetus growing inside it, and emotionally, as the mother thinks over the consequences to herself and adjusts to the existence of a new life, this early stage will require much more sleep.

The theme of separation is present even in pregnancy. Raphael-Leff (1982) describes pregnancy as a process whereby the mother at first feels the baby is a part of herself and then gradually feels it to become separate. In the psychological tasks of pregnancy which serve as a rehearsal for motherhood, she says that there are three major tasks, which may be seen as:

a) achievement of emotional fusion with the foetus in early pregnancy; b) gradual differentiation of foetus and self after the quickening; and c) progressive psychic separation of baby and mother, culminating in the physical separation at birth.

(p. 3)

She points out that women who are not able to make use of their pregnancy to prepare in this way will tend to have corresponding difficulties in their relationship with their child and may also have repercussions on the birth itself and on the early months afterwards. Related to this preparation and the whole task of becoming a mother to her own baby, the mother-to-be is dealing with the feelings and memories stirred up about herself as a baby in relation to her own mother (Emde,

1988). Later on, in Chapter 10, we will see how the particular quality of the relationship a mother has had with her own mother colours her way of dealing with her baby, but here we are looking at more general and universal forces. Pines (1982), for example, shows how the ties to her own mother can make it difficult for the mother to separate herself in her mind from her baby: 'The inevitable regression occasioned by pregnancy and motherhood may be a painful and frightening experience' (p. 318). Confusingly, the mother may have opposing wishes to merge with her own mother and to pull away from her. Pregnancy thus throws a mother back into powerful links with her own mother, and her attempts to extricate herself can get tangled up with her picture of how separate she is from her baby.

Mother's ambivalence and anxiety

Having conflicting feelings about being pregnant and giving birth is quite normal. In fact, anyone who cannot let herself know about feelings of *not* wanting to have a baby, at the same time as also wanting to, may have a harder time either giving birth or adjusting to the new baby. Difficulties and adversities of all kinds in pregnancy may have a later effect, in various ways, on the baby itself, including on its sleep. One way in which this might happen is that the mother's anxiety during pregnancy can raise her baby's cortisol levels, even in the womb (Gerhardt, 2004), and affect the rhythms that develop between her and the baby, thereby influencing its later sleep and other regulation systems. The mother's ambivalence can produce stress and anxiety in itself. Here I would add that it is the *unacknowledged* ambivalence of love and hate that is at issue. The mother's lack of self-knowledge about her own feelings carries over to a not-knowing about the range of her baby's feelings and rhythms. It is worth noting that the mother's state of mind is partly an effect of the support and resources she can draw upon, or not, and its potential impact on the baby may be tempered by the care of her partner and others in her family and support network.

The ambivalence a mother may feel about the irreversible change in her own life is acutely expressed in *Poem to My Daughter* by Anne Stevenson (1983).

> A woman's life is her own
> until it is taken away
> by a first particular cry.
> Then she is not alone
> but a part of the premises
> of everything there is.

The experience of birth and its difficulties

We can see that a mother may be confused about whether the foetus inside her is a part of her body or something separate, and her reaction to the impending birth may include being afraid and unwilling to face the next stage of separation that birth implies.

There is evidence to show that difficult labours and birth have a deleterious effect which can include severe sleep problems (Blurton-Jones et al., 1978). It is important here not to assume that separation or other psychological problems in the mother's own psyche are a cause of all birth difficulties. However, the *experience* of a difficult birth is described in such a way by some mothers. Birth experiences of course may affect either one or both mother and baby, and physical and emotional causes and consequences may be separate or intertwined.

Moore and Ucko (1957) discovered that some infants who showed unexplained sleeping disturbances, together with general unpredictability and over-reactivity, had had some asphyxia at birth. They suggest that asphyxia might also lead to hyperactivity later on. Trowell (1982) shows how unexpected caesareans can affect the relationship between mother and baby. The mothers have had the 'distress, crisis and sense of failure produced by an emergency Caesarean section . . . their labours were longer and they had more medication before and after delivery and were unconscious at the time of delivery' (p. 87). Trowell shows how these factors can impede the sensitive early stages of mother and baby getting to know each other. At one year, a group of mothers who had had caesareans reported more problems with their babies than did the control group. Crucially they reported leaving their babies to cry for up to five minutes before responding; the control group usually responded in two minutes. We see from this that there may be later effects from a birth where the mother has been unconscious for some time after delivery and where she also needs to be preoccupied with her own state while recovering from an abdominal operation. She is less ready to respond to the baby's signals, and it may take longer for mother and baby to feel closely in touch with each other. Trowell emphasizes the need for obstetric care which minimizes medication and allows the mother to participate as much as possible, both in giving birth and in caring for her baby afterwards.

We have already seen how the bonding process between mother and infant starts immediately after birth and that the setting up of this closeness affects the way in which the mother is able to influence the baby's physiological sleep/wake rhythms. What follows is an illustration of how the experience of birth and shortly after can influence the bonding and therefore the separation process.

A case example

With Matthew and his mother, it seemed clear that a difficult birth experience kept on getting in the way of this mother's picture of herself and her baby.

Matthew was nearly two and still breastfeeding; his mother was embarrassed by this, but she could not let go of him. In the first session she cried as she told me about his birth. She had prepared herself well, but when the time came it was all unexpected, rapid, violent; midwives and doctors came and went, only her husband was there throughout. She spent ten days in hospital and began to recover. On the last night, the hospital offered to babysit, and she went out to dinner with her husband. She came back and found her baby apparently neglected – crying, hungry, in need of a nappy-change. She felt she should never have left him and that this experience must have damaged him permanently. Since then he had had problems in getting to sleep except when held at the breast, fed and allowed to go to sleep from there. He had never been able to lie in his cot and fall asleep on his own.

We talked about how the first 'letting go' of him, his birth, had gone so wrong and that she could not trust herself to let go of him without doing him damage. I questioned her assumption that bad experiences were the only significant ones. She had pinpointed the moment in hospital when Matthew had been left hungry, dirty and alone. I asked her to put this in the balance with all the times his needs *had* been attended to and suggested that his cumulative experience of this could be equally memorable. It was as though Matthew's mother felt that good experiences must be obliterated by bad ones – and that letting go or separations were the same as bad experiences. We talked about how Matthew might be able to enjoy a feed, let go of her, and she of him, and then lie in his cot, savouring the memory of his feed and digesting the experience along with the milk. We noted that emotional as well as physical growth comes from this.

Matthew's father had always been enjoyably involved in the bedtime routine but had then handed Matthew over to his mother for the final feed. His mother now entrusted his father with sometimes putting Matthew in his cot. She left a bottle of milk and biscuits within reach and offered herself less quickly to Matthew in the night. The breastfeeding soon faded away and Matthew stopped waking up in the night. His mother then thought of the milk and biscuits as being too much of a direct substitute for her breast – she felt he would become someone always relying on food for comfort. She replaced the bottle with a musical toy, which Matthew loved and played to himself as he lay in the cot going to sleep and when he woke up in the morning. She made the leap herself, and presumably therefore enabled her son to do the same, of creating a symbol instead of a direct substitute for her breast.

I saw Matthew's mother over several weeks. She lost excess weight as she weaned him. In the last interview when she came to say goodbye, she had had a crisp new haircut. An outline that had seemed to merge with her child had regained definition as an individual. Her relationship with her husband improved – two years of Matthew's night waking had left little time for their sex life. She relaxed her tendency to exclude him from aspects of caring for Matthew through her idea that only the breast could send the baby to sleep. She became able to let Matthew's father help her with the weaning and, when Matthew was weaned, he could be an equal partner in caring for his son.

The musical box served somewhat belatedly for Matthew as Winnicott's transitional object, an idea intimately connected with separation. I often feel that what I am doing for mothers is providing them with something like a temporary transitional object through the medium of my words. I think with them about their position with the baby, then put into words what I feel is going on and leave them with these words to hold on to when they go back to their baby and renegotiate their relationship through the following nights. The words contain the combined thought of the mother and myself about the transition from one state to another.

Intimacy and separation

Matthew's mother equated separation with a bad experience, but some mothers find it difficult to acknowledge the baby's separate existence for their own sakes, not just on behalf of their baby. Let us now look at the ordinary routes by which mothers and babies first establish intimacy and then achieve separation from each other, using the overlapping frameworks of psychoanalytic thinking and development research.

From detailed observations of babies – both psychoanalytically inspired ones (Bick, 1964; Reid, 1997; Miller et al., 2002; Sternberg, 2005) and the research findings of developmental psychologists (Stern, 1985) – we see many examples of babies recognizing their mother by sight, sound and touch. In fact babies develop a preference for their mother's voice in the womb, displayed immediately after birth (Lee & Kisilevsky, 2014). The inference from this is that the recognition of the mother includes an awareness of her as separate from the baby's own self. Alvarez (2012) and Braten (2007) both see the baby as coming into the world ready to meet a 'virtual other'. Perhaps we may imagine the baby as able to recognize separateness at times and at other times lapsing into a sensation of merging. As adults we may have fleeting recalls of such merging in both sensual or aesthetic experiences. Pine (1986) has described graphically how the infant's body can 'melt' into the mother's body at times of falling asleep, whereas in a state of higher cognitive functioning there will be a clear sense of boundaries.

It may be helpful here to turn to some psychoanalytic ideas about togetherness, boundaries and separation and their links with the earliest mother and baby relationship. According to Klein:

> In the earliest stages love and understanding are expressed through the mother's handling of her baby, and lead to a certain unconscious oneness that is based on the unconscious of the mother and child being in close relation to each other. The infant's resultant feeling of being understood underlies the first and fundamental relation in his life – the relation to the mother. At the same time frustration, discomfort and pain which . . . are experienced as persecution, enter as well into feelings about his mother, because in the first few months the whole of the external world, therefore both good and bad, come in his mind from her, and this leads to a twofold attitude toward the mother even under the best possible conditions.
>
> (1959, p. 248)

Klein describes how a little child readily experiences things in extremes, all bad or all good, and can quickly switch from one to the other, all tears to all smiles. She stresses two very important processes in this, introjection and projection.

Introjection is the process whereby an experience of something from the outside world is taken in and influences the child's sense of himself, however minutely, in a long-term way. It is what happens in much emotional learning, of course. Projection, on the other hand, occurs when a thought or a feeling at first arising in the self is denied and located elsewhere. The belongingness to the self is obliterated and the thought or feeling is felt to belong outside.

We can see how Matthew's mother intuitively understood something of these processes of introjection and projection, though she saw it only as a malign process. She felt that the bad experiences Matthew had undergone would influence him and become part of his internal world. In contrast to this, Klein describes the way in which a mother's empathic understanding of the baby's bad experience can mitigate its effect, helping him not feel so bad. But Matthew's mother was too convinced that he must have been damaged to help him in this way. Perhaps she herself felt too vulnerable and at the mercy of this 'damage' as she saw it being projected back into herself.

The division into distinct good and bad experiences is referred to as 'splitting', and maintaining this splitting is important for an infant's feeling of goodness and ease. He can feel purely good in the presence of pure good things, unmuddled by an awareness of 'bad' things. The process of 'emotional purification' is much assisted by projection, where badness is felt to be outside the self.

This badness seems to have to go somewhere; mothers are usually on hand, so they often become the receptacle. If they do not do this easily, the rest of the world and the people in it can become increasingly 'bad' to the baby. Klein felt these processes were crucial in earliest infancy, and because of the importance of splitting and projection she called this state the paranoid-schizoid position. Alvarez (2018) has since refined this notion, separating out the potential for paranoia from the more split or even empty states of mind, which may arise from chronic dissociation or profound neglect. However, Klein pointing out our human proneness to this way of dealing with extremes of feelings is of vital value.

If all goes well, the baby certainly seems to move from a predominantly egocentric position, when he sees his mother mainly in terms of *his* states of being, to perceiving her as a person with feelings of her own. He becomes aware of the effects of *his* actions *on her* and has some *concern* for her. Klein called this new state the 'depressive position'. A simple example is the baby at the breast who has produced his first teeth. His pleasure in his power to bite may be tempered by the realization that he is giving pain to the mother who feeds him. A delightful and frequently observed game is where the baby 'feeds' his mother from the spoon he has just learnt to hold. Mothers perceive in this their baby's grateful wish to give something back for having been fed.

How does this connect with the ability to sleep or not? At an early stage of development the baby projects into his mother intense and passionate feelings of all kinds, including loving, hating and aggressive ones. To many mothers it is all in the day's work to 'receive' these feelings and 'give back' to the baby a sense of understanding and putting into perspective. However, a mother who, perhaps because of her own experiences, is frightened of what her baby is expressing will not be able to reassure him. He will be left unsettled and maybe unable to sleep. If a mother is able to help the baby to deal with his feelings, repeated instances of this relationally wire in Schore's (2000) psychobiological patterns, so that he begins to embody these responses and the feeling of being regulated, helping him manage later on his own.

The neurobiology bears out some psychoanalytic ideas about the transition to relative independence. We will touch on them here, including Winnicott's idea of the transitional object. First, I will touch on some ideas about good and bad, presence and absence in relation to feeding and separation. One approach suggests that at first the breast is felt to be 'good' when it is present and 'bad' when it is absent and needed (O'Shaughnessy, 1964). The idea is that a baby lying alone waiting for a feed will feel that the pain of hunger in his body is bad. Given the intensity of the baby's feelings and the need for the badness to go somewhere that I mentioned earlier, he feels that the feeding mother that does not come when he cries is leaving him to starve and must be bad. Gradually, as he has repeated experiences that the mother does arrive to feed him, his memories allow him to look forward in her absence to a 'good' feeding mother arriving.

Winnicott shows how the 'ordinary devoted' mother helps the baby develop this capacity to wait – and begin to bear to be separate – through her ordinary devoted attention right at the beginning, in a period he calls maternal reverie: 'The good-enough mother (not necessarily the infant's own mother) is one who makes active adaptation to the infant's needs . . . that gradually lessens according to the infant's growing ability . . . to tolerate the results of frustration' (1971, p. 10). This mother is able to help the baby by managing a very close adaptation to his needs to begin with, and then 'if all goes well the infant can actually come to gain from the experience of frustration, since incomplete adaptation to need makes objects real, that is to say hated as well as loved' (1971, p. 11). She does not need to be idealized and can bear taking the hate when she cannot put him first, as well as the love when she can. Her early almost complete attention establishes a secure foundation and helps with the task of gradually 'disillusioning' the baby and helping him cope with the frustrations of weaning.

Transitional objects are one way in which the baby gets through this stage of disillusion. This is how Winnicott describes them:

> There may emerge some thing or some phenomenon – perhaps a bundle of wool on the corner of a blanket or eiderdown, or a word or a tune, or a mannerism – that becomes vitally important to the infant for use at the time of going to sleep, and as a defence against anxiety, especially anxiety of the depressive type. Perhaps some soft object or other type of object has been found and used by the infant, and this then becomes what I am calling a transitional object. The object goes on being important. The parents get to know its value and carry it around when travelling. The mother lets it get dirty and

even smelly, knowing that by washing it she introduces a break in continuity in the infant's experience, a break that may destroy the meaning and value of the object to the child.

(1971, p. 4)

Many parents will recognize this essential and often grubby object. Winnicott sees it as belonging unquestionably to the child, and as being subject to severe cuddling and treated with a mix of love and mutilation. Nobody else must try to change it. It belongs not quite to the outside world, and not entirely to the inside world of the baby either, but somewhere in between, in a transitional space.

In essence, it helps the baby to feel separate while still in touch with the parent. It in no way replaces the parent. In fact, babies who have become separated from their parents lose interest in the transitional object if they do not have contact with them. The object loses its symbolic meaning if this is not reinforced by a further connection with the parent.

In Matthew's case the use of a transitional object did not happen spontaneously. Only his mother herself would do for Matthew. Did his mother confirm his belief? Perhaps it was unthinkable for her that he could manage without her. It is interesting that with my help in thinking it all through, Matthew's mother was able to allow him to have such objects and then was able to help him change the objects which stood in place of her. The bottle and biscuits were replaced by a musical toy; the direct physical substitute gave place to a symbol.

The developing sense of self

Recent psychoanalytic and developmental observations show that an infant's recognition of his mother occurs very early on, which means that at least some of the time from soon after birth he sees her as a separate being. As he begins learning to physically move away from his mother, first by crawling and then by walking, he is making 'first tentative steps towards breaking away, in a bodily sense' from the mother (Mahler, 1975). As the baby increasingly 'hatches out' into the world, there is the practising period, when his increased abilities in crawling, standing up and walking mean that he can take charge of moving away from his mother.

At this stage, as many parents know, the baby may suddenly become very intolerant of separations. A baby who can crawl out of the room away from his mother may be panic-stricken to turn around and find that *she* has moved out of *his* view. Some babies cannot let their mothers out of their sight even to go to the toilet. Perhaps their own moving away makes them fear that their mother will vanish. In this stage, when mothers and babies start to feel increasingly separate, a mother may take it as a good time to go out alone or even return to work. She then may be surprised to find that they may go through a kind of crisis of reunion when she gets back, where the baby cries inconsolably and may resist being put to sleep. Thus sleeping problems can arise around emotional anxieties caused by three different experiences coinciding: the baby physically moving away from the mother as he crawls or walks away from her; the physical and emotional separation of weaning; and the mother physically and perhaps psychologically too moving away from the baby.

In studying the moves towards the sense of a separate self, Stern (1985) describes four phases: the Emergent Self, forming from birth to two months; the Core Self, forming between two and six months; the Subjective Self between seven and fifteen months; and the Verbal Self after that. Once formed, each sense of self remains active throughout life. At each of the major shifts, Stern describes a forceful impression of change, of dealing with somebody altered. For instance, when a few-weeks-old infant starts to smile responsively and gazes into the parents' eyes, a different social feel is created. It is the altered sense of the infant's subjective experience lying behind these behavioural changes that makes the parent act and think about the infant differently. Further, Stern suggests that the change in the infant may partly come about through the adult interpreting the infant differently and acting accordingly.

In the forming of an organized sense of a core self, infants are seen to begin to have an integrated sense of themselves as distinct and coherent bodies, with control over their own actions, ownership of their feelings and a sense of continuity – always provided their relational experience fosters this gradual integration. They sense that they and their mother are separate physically, are separate agents, have distinct affective experiences and have separate histories. In discovering their own minds and a sense of their own subjective self, they then begin to discover that there are other minds out there as well as their own.

Stern makes clear that this development is experience-dependent, and even experience-expectant. He shows the interrelation of minds as formative, distinguishing the sense of self *versus* other from the sense of self *with* other. He relates how the infant with an 'other' can make something happen that neither could do alone. For example, during a peek-a-boo game, 'the mutual interaction generates in the infant a self-experience of very high excitation, full of joy and suspense and perhaps tinged with a touch of fear' (1985, p. 102). This feeling state could not be achieved alone; it is a mutual creation. 'The infant is with another who regulates the infant's own self-experience. In this sense the other is a *self-regulating other* for the infant' (p. 102, author's italics).

Security and attachment likewise arise out of patterns of relational experiences, ways-of-being-with (Lyons-Ruth et al., 1998). The relevance of this to sleep will be apparent. Even though it is the infant's own self-state that is changed, such as from sleepiness to sleep, another person is involved in the physical regulation of this self-state. So the rhythms of feeding, changing, rocking, being put in the cot, all of which are part of the experience of going to sleep for a baby, are also experiences of the way-of-being-with the other person. Going to sleep is a social event.

The physiological, neurobiological basis of introjection becomes clear; these repeated patterns and rhythms of ways of being with the person who helps (or not) the baby regulate his own states becomes represented in psychobiological patterns (Schore, 2000) in the baby's mind and body; an evoked companion who goes on being remembered, whether present or not, like Klein's internalized 'good' mother. This experience of being almost continuously with real and evoked companions is what leads to the infant feeling trustful and secure enough to be able to separate and explore his surroundings, or indeed, fall asleep.

This is at the heart of the question so often pondered by parents: how does a baby acquire the ability to be on its own? We see how the parent's initially very available presence gradually helps the baby learn how to manage his own states for himself. The baby's developing ability to do this himself in the interested presence of his parent is rather different from the idea that it is the parent who makes them do it. Penny's mother, whom we will meet in Chapter 9, had made this distinction when she said to herself of her baby, 'Why don't you *let* her go to sleep, not make her go to sleep?' The parents' reliable presence eventually enables the baby to feel sure of their connection and recall their support and thus the feeling of having it continues, even in their absence. Phillips writes of the baby learning to be on his own,

> Another opportunity for the baby to begin to form inner resources is during sleep. Sleep is not a stable state to which we just go into and then awake from. Many emotions and sensations go on . . . Saying no to the urge to rush to the baby who whimpers creates a space for growth.
>
> (2003, p. 28)

She talks about leaving a baby to wake up on his own with a moment of pleasure, 'to get a sense of himself on his own, free to take in the world at his own pace (p. 28).

As the baby develops the sense of a subjective self, from the seventh or ninth month, realizing that he has a mind and that other people do also, another of Stern's (1985) vital concepts, that of 'affect attunement', appears. We will see in various instances in the book how the satisfactory achievement of this tuning in, or the failure of it, influences the baby's capacity to sleep.

Tuning in is a rather complex and miraculous process, but it happens every day – more easily when parents have had an experience of someone tuning into their own state of mind. First, the parents read the infant's feeling state from her overt behaviour. Second, the parent performs some behaviour that is not a strict imitation but nonetheless corresponds in some ways to the infant's overt behaviour. For instance, if a baby is beating time with her hand on a toy, the parent may join in by singing to this beat or the parent may move her own body in time to the child's singing sound. Third, the infant must be able to read this corresponding parental response as having to do with the infant's own original feeling experience, and not just imitating the infant's behaviour. It is only in the presence of these three conditions that feeling states within one person can be knowable to another, and that they can both sense, without using language, that the transaction has occurred. In this way, minds develop, and with them a sense of having a mind of one's own and recognizing that of another. This is how human beings achieve a feeling of understanding each other deeply.

From the point of view of our particular interest in sleep, we can see how this process has implications for the whole sequence of a baby's bedtime. The routines of bathing, stories, little games, in addition to the basic experience of feeding, provide opportunities for parent and baby to achieve this state of feeling attuned, which lasts beyond the excitements of the actual interchanges. The feeling of being in touch with each other's state of being is a major part of what can allow the baby to 'let go' into sleep. The various games, of course, have many other subtle functions, such as negotiating a transition phase or being a way of mastering fears.

Stern's (1985) final sense, of a verbal self, takes us into the second year. He shows how language makes some parts of experience more shareable with other people and finally allows the child to begin to construct a narrative of his own life. But, says Stern, language can be a double-edged sword – it can make some experiences less shareable, creating a split in the self when experiences that are felt cannot be put into words. Parents and infants may find they have to live through a time when the infant's grasping for words sometimes creates a barrier of communication between them. The frustrations of this stage may lead to a state of tension in the infant which makes getting to sleep much harder.

Another factor in the ordinary development of a sense of self is that the baby's aggressive feelings begin to become more forceful and articulate. This can lead to a growing concern for what these impulses might do to the parents and also to a fear of retaliation. All of this accounts for some of the anxieties underlying fears in the night, with sleep disturbances following on from them.

Conclusion

We have seen how vital is the relationship between parents and babies in the development of the baby's own sense of who she is. What happens next is that this process gradually allows the baby to venture out and be on her own.

Several central and fascinating questions follow from looking at ideas about separation and the self in this chapter. How much do mother and baby need to enjoy being together as a prelude to enjoying being apart? How much does being together enable future moving apart or how much does it prevent it? There is also an important tension and balance between genuinely having reached the stage of experiencing the self as a separate person and tolerating separation for a time, while still feeling the need to be with the parent. I have tried to show that the ability to sleep is partly dependent on feeling secure, which includes feeling safe enough to be separate. So separateness arises out of security in relation to a protective and loving person, usually the parent. In order to achieve secure separation there must first be close, intimate contact with this loving, protective person. The intimacy gives the infant as she grows a feeling of self-worth and a feeling of being understood, which then lasts away from the presence of the parents and persists as she grows up. Physical closeness is one way in which this develops, and another is a well-timed response to the baby's signals of her needs.

Chapter 8

Separation and attachment problems

In this chapter, we will look at how the baby begins to move away from her parents, having begun to develop her own sense of a separate self, as we saw in the last chapter. The security built up inside her, from the experience of the continuous and reliable presence of her parents, enables her to try doing things for herself. At first, any moves away are quickly followed by a scuttle back into her parents' sight and presence.

The consequences of this stage are various. As the baby moves away from his mother, his bids for freedom and independence bring anxieties. We have already mentioned how sleep disturbances are one of the results of these. Moreover, the degree of separation must be kept in perspective. At this period, that is, from the end of the first year, babies only start to manage to be independent; they need to practise this independence in the near presence of a parent or carer who goes on being interested and available for much of the time. To put it at its simplest, a baby who crawls away from his mother into the next room needs, for most of the time at the beginning, to find his mother still in the same room when he crawls back again. The first wanderings off are *in relation to* the parent. This has strong bearings on sleep problems, since one of the principal contentions in this book is that sleep problems are a form of separation problem.

To young children time can seem endless and, remembering that children feel things in extremes, we can understand how at moments a separation might seem as though it is forever. If Mum is not there, will she ever come back? How can a child be alone without also being lonely?

Babies and young children have difficulty enough managing the stages of being on their own; sometimes it can be even more difficult for their parents to manage it, both in terms of their own separation from their baby and in the sense of bearing the separation on behalf of the baby. While for some parents separation is a prized goal, for others it can be unbearable. For instance, it may symbolize bereavements and other intolerable losses that the parents have endured themselves. In such cases the ordinary repeated separations of bedtimes cannot be experienced in an ordinary way; each one contains echoes of previous traumatic separations or rejections.

Let us now look at how the separation process normally develops and at the important process of the development of attachment between parents and baby.

Attachment

Bowlby's ideas about attachment are rooted in links between human behaviour and that of animals, taking evolutionary processes, survival mechanisms and biological systems into account. He saw attachment as 'a product of a number of behavioural systems that have proximity to mother as a predictable outcome' (1969, p. 223), prioritizing physical safety in the service of survival. 'All in all, it is held, of the various suggestions advanced for the function of attachment behaviour, protection from predators seems by far the most likely' (p. 278). It should be remembered that we spent four million years as hunter-gatherers during which this protection from predators was essential to our survival.

He shows how instinctive patterns of response by the baby – sucking, clinging, following, crying and smiling – serve the function of binding the child to the mother and getting her care and protection in return; the result of this is that the child stays close to the mother. This behaviour develops at each baby's own rate and increases as the baby herself becomes mobile. It shows most strongly in the second year, when babies are increasingly practising moving off on their own. As they move away, their mother's departure or anything frightening will activate alarm. The cure for the alarm is the 'sound, sight or touch of mother' (p. 223).

Security and the ability to explore confidently come from being in the presence of attachment figures, who may include the child's father and other older family members. It has become clear that children have different attachments to different figures, depending, as we might expect, on the qualities of those relationships. Attachment to a child's father is entirely separate and independent from that to his mother; it may be secure with one and insecure with the other. Babies with no secure attachments develop symptoms of disturbance; we will turn shortly to look at this troubling situation and at the different categories of attachment developed by Main (1989) and others. In thinking about children's need to make other wider and deeper relationships, we can see the benefits of an extended family or other network which a child can enjoy, while still having her mother as a base from which to get to know the other members.

Attachment to parents continues throughout life in different forms. During adolescence, other adults also become important, and friendships and sexual attraction to peers may take precedence. In adults, many of the attachment functions of the parents will be taken over by marriage partners. In old age when attachment behaviour can no longer be directed towards an older generation, it may be directed towards a younger one. Attachment in adult life is a continuation of such behaviour in childhood, so that in sickness, danger or disaster an individual will seek proximity to a known and trusted person, and this behaviour is not a form of regression. Even in adult life, Bowlby argues, we do not become totally self-reliant but need a companion to help us deal with difficult situations. Adult fears need not be rationally based and can be assuaged by company.

> How many of us, it may be asked, would relish entering a completely strange house in the dark, on our own? What a relief it would be were we to have a companion with us, or had a good light, or preferably both companion and light.
>
> (1979, p. 120)

A major facet of Bowlby's work is concerned with the effect of the *loss* of attachment figures, and we will see later examples of this, such as hospital stays for children or the influence on a mother's parenting of the death of her own mother. Bowlby describes what goes on when a child needs his mother. He cries, receives her response and is satisfied by her reappearance and her touch; the alarm is switched off. We will turn now to look at what happens when this process goes wrong.

Attachment studies

Main (1989), whose work stems from Bowlby's, describes how an infant can be affected when parents are averse to physical contact with their babies. She explains that when a baby seeks contact, most parents adjust their bodies to an open posture and accept the infant in ventral–ventral contact. Others adjust their bodies so that the infant is barred from access, or turn the infant's body so that the infant's ventral surface does not touch that of the parent. Others simply push the infant away entirely. When parents push their children away, a self-perpetuating conflict occurs. A physical rejection from the mother activates the attachment system and when this is activated, only physical contact with the attachment figure is able to switch it off. We thus have a vicious circle: fright without resolution.

Here we can see the scene set for that angry confusion which builds up between some mothers and babies in the night, when the mother is unable to offer physical comfort to their babies. The origin of this inability is often in their own experience of parenting. They go to their baby but are unable to satisfy him; moreover, their presence is even a stimulant, causing the baby to need them even more. Mother and baby are thus in a continual state of activation without end, which is damaging in all kinds of ways for the baby's developing systems, leaving him on red alert.

The Strange Situation Test (Ainsworth & Wittig, 1969) is a way of assessing attachment patterns through looking at one-year-old children's reactions to reunion after a short separation. It has produced so much material that it is worth describing in some detail. Mother and infant are put together in a pleasant but unfamiliar room. The infant is then subject to a series of minor stresses in which a stranger enters the room and talks first to the mother and then to the infant; the mother goes out and leaves the infant in the company of the stranger; the mother returns and the stranger departs; the mother goes out and leaves the infant alone; the stranger returns and the mother returns again for the final reunion. All this is carefully recorded. Each episode lasts three minutes unless the infant is very distressed. The test was intended to be no more disturbing than normal situations encountered by a baby.

Interestingly, the telling moments are not so much during the separation but during the reunion. Based on the reunion behaviour, the infant's attachment could be classified into three categories – B secure, A insecure (avoidant), and C inse-cure (ambivalent). Main and Solomon (1986) identified a further category (D) of babies with disorganized-disoriented responses. Those with a secure attachment, about 60 percent of children, turn at once to their mother when distressed and alarmed. They express anger and distress openly, are easily comforted by her and quickly resume an interest in play and exploration. Observation of these securely attached babies in their homes during their first year showed that they had mothers who were sensitive to their needs, emotionally available and ready to offer close physical comfort when the baby was distressed.

About 20 percent of babies in the test sample had insecure-avoidant attach-ments (A). These children actively avoid and ignore the parent during reunion epi-sodes, turning away from the parent and asking to be put down when picked up. They may show no distress during the parent's absence and continue to explore the room and toys. There is apparently an absence of fear, distress or anger, though later studies (Zelenko et al., 2005) showed increased heart rates, belying their calm exterior. Main et al. (1985) have shown that the mothers of avoidant babies tended not only to be insensitive to their babies' signals, but also to have marked difficulty in responding to them. Many of these mothers were found to be themselves averse to physical contact and emotionally unavailable. Not surpris-ingly, the origins of this inhibition have been found to spring frequently from the mother's own childhood.

Babies who have an ambivalent insecure attachment pattern (C) represent another 10 percent. They may be upset even before the first separation and are often fearful of the stranger. They express extreme anger with the mother and are distressed, clinging and not easily comforted. Their mothers are found to be very inconsistent and insensitive and often intrusive. In terms of the likelihood of babies having sleep problems, both sets of insecure babies are obvious candidates. The secure babies, as we will see later, are often able to sleep well, knowing that their mothers are available and responsive if needed.

Crying

Crying is one of the main ways by which babies signal their needs to their parents, who respond to the signal with varying degrees of success. Babies cry less at a year old if their mothers responded to their early cries promptly and appropriately. They say, 'by the fourth quarter infants whose mothers had responded promptly and appropriately to their crying early on now cried less'. They also show that maternal sensitivity to infant signals during feeding, play and episodes of close bodily contact in the course of the first three months also turns out to be correlated to the infant's behaviour at 12 months; babies who had been sensitively responded to early on had fewer problems later on.

However, it is relevant to note that babies in residential nurseries cried *less* with the nurses who responded less quickly to them and more with the nurses who responded more quickly. Their expectations of whether they will be responded to colours their expression of need and affects their future hopes of being listened to when in need. They have often gone beyond protest and despair to detachment. In a more ordinary home setting, the opposite reasoning may also pertain: a baby who has been responded to may seldom cry because he feels secure, while a baby who has not been responded to may cry to voice his hopelessness, even despair. Crying can have many meanings and so also can not-crying.

It is also important that babies in some institutions sleep for unusually long periods. I would surmise that such a baby is escaping into an internal world, a sort of self-consoling situation, or collapsing into a state of despair when there is no adult who looks forward to the baby being awake in order to be able to feed, play with and cuddle him, in the way that parents usually do. If there is no one who actively delights in a baby's company, there is nothing much for him to wake up for. Foster carers of babies from institutional settings report that they often sleep excessively at first and then begin to sleep for fewer hours in response to individual care.

Leaving a baby to cry

Bell and Ainsworth (1972) stress the importance of responding *appropriately* to a baby's cries. This need not mean always picking up a baby who cries. It also need not mean that a baby who cries for a few moments when put down after being attended to should always be picked up again. Parents who are unable ever to put a baby down and leave him to protest may be ostensibly worried about the baby's feeling of being left. It could also be that they are upset by the way his cries express a difference of opinion. Turning this around somewhat, parents who can never tolerate their baby crying about being put down may be practising very heavy emotional 'blackmail'. In such a case, picking the baby up every time he cries may be a way of insisting that he should have the same view as themselves about being put to sleep, that is, that they are 'kind' in not putting him to bed, but it actually means that no mixed feelings or protest can be tolerated. Parents of course have to be sensitive to what a baby's crying means and to the real needs that he may be expressing. Allowing a baby to be separate includes allowing the baby to be angry and to express this anger. Unadmitted anger can underlie extreme fears of separation, particularly, as we will see in this chapter, fears whose logical conclusion is that the baby will not survive the separation. Bound up with this may be the apparent opposite. A mother may be angry at *not* being able to separate from her baby, and her over-reactive response of keeping the baby too close may be to protect him from her wish to be off and away. Many mothers who cannot leave their babies say, half-jokingly, 'If I went away from him I'd never come back'.

Others cannot think what they would do if they regularly left the baby with a friend or family member for half a day and had some free time. Depending on the baby's age and stage of development, this inability to think of what to do separately from the baby may be partly a slight over-indulgence in 'primary maternal preoccupation'. In other cases, the mother may feel unadmitted anger at having to plan for such limited precious freedom.

Other mothers may be suffering from some degree of postnatal depression. They may feel depressed much of the time, with or without the baby, but have some sense of purpose while with the baby which disappears when he is not there. Such a mother may have no sense of self when the baby is out of sight. In extreme cases, we can see how the origins of agoraphobia in mothers, and school phobia in children, may be foreshadowed or stirred up by these early difficulties in separating between mothers and babies.

Death wishes and death fears

Conflicts about 'holding' a baby or putting the baby down can represent deep-seated conflicts about having a baby at all. Some parents have great difficulty in preparing themselves during pregnancy for the arrival of the baby. One such pair of parents described the idea of buying equipment for the baby as being conventional and 'consumerist'. Instead of a cot or cradle they would put the baby in a drawer. Their doctor, telling me of this added, 'and shut it away'.

These feelings can persist after the baby's birth, sometimes as the predominant feeling about the baby, sometimes just as a fleeting thought about a baby who is crying and refusing to go to sleep. Negative and hostile thoughts about a baby can come either from the parent's own emotional lack of readiness to have a baby or they can equally come from a situation where matters have gone wrong in the immediate present between parent and baby. When a baby cries and cannot be consoled, the parent is, quite naturally, likely both consciously and unconsciously to wish to be able to put the baby down and walk away from it. Parents who are conscious of such wishes and can 'own' their angry feelings towards the baby are those in the best position to deal with these feelings, to moderate them and go on working out how to attend to the baby (Parker, 2005). When, on the contrary, parents do not acknowledge their own feelings, when they project them, attributing them to others or getting rid of them in some other way, they lose the power to confront and change the feelings in themselves. Parents who are shocked by their own wish may go on holding the baby excessively as a counter-reaction to it. The extreme logical extension of putting a baby down and getting rid of it is in fact for the baby to die. Fleeting thoughts like this may underlie tensions and hostilities in all relationships. Usually they disappear into the jumble of strong emotions that characterize family life and are counterbalanced by equally strong loving feelings. When things are not going right emotionally, these hostile feelings, especially unacknowledged ones, can get fixed as 'death wishes', which themselves can get translated into death fears.

All parents have such fears at moments about their babies. They are indeed part of the background to making things safe for a baby. However, when these fears persist and have an obsessional quality to them, then something is going wrong between parents and baby. When straightforward channels for communicating feelings, especially angry ones, between parent and baby have gone awry, parents are perhaps obliquely expressing such feelings through their fears. They will also be rejecting in their behaviour to the baby, who will turn away from the unacknowledged impact of the rebuff.

Transitions

Where death fears exist they may also colour the parents' picture of what going to sleep entails and of the transition from wakefulness to sleep. Going to sleep is in itself a transition. Managing this state of change depends partly on the picture, the anticipation, of what the new state will be like. Is 'sleep' a place of safety or a place of danger? Each individual has their own, albeit fluctuating, picture of it. The parents' picture has some bearing on their child's ability to fall asleep. Not only is there the problem of achieving the new state of sleep, it is also necessary to manage being in transition.

A seven-year-old girl in therapy had great difficulty in getting to sleep. Her mother had similar problems. The girl said to her therapist, 'What will I do if I can't get to sleep?' This poignant question seems to be not about lack of sleep, but of *where to be* during the fruitless transition period. In the extended family of this little girl, a baby had recently died and perhaps there did not seem to be a safe place for her to be, either in her own mind or in her mother's.

All cultures have ways of dealing with the passing from one stage of life to another; we call them rites of passage. Rituals are likewise used in helping to pass from wakefulness to sleep. We have seen from Winnicott how transitional objects can help infants deal with being away from their mothers, how the object can represent the relationship. What these objects can also represent is the ambivalence that mother and baby have about each other. The object is fated, Winnicott (1971, p. 5) says, to be hated as well as loved, and this derives from the hatred the baby feels for the mother who has dared to put him to bed. Part of the function of the object which is cuddled and mauled is to *survive* this love and hatred.

Klein (1932) suggests another function of the toys that a small child takes to bed. Her patient Rita, aged two, had an elaborate ritual to go through before dropping off to sleep. She had to be tightly tucked up in bed and her doll had to be tucked up beside her. This doll represented the 'super-ego' or 'conscience' and was there to ensure that the little girl did not get up in the night and disturb her parents' time together. Fraiberg (1950) shows how a little girl Kathie, aged 18 months, suffering from a sleep disturbance, was in a state of conflict about her own impulses and about her relationships. She particularly had mixed feelings about being toilet-trained. Kathie began to take two toys to bed with her – one, a teddy, was cuddled and offered endearments; the other, a doll, was battered unmercifully, flung about and scolded. We can see how two sets of feelings about herself as well as about parents or others were expressed through her treatment of the two toys. As she played this out, her sleep started to improve.

Winnicott has described how the infant deals with intermediate experiences. In theoretical formulations, and also in poetry, the intermediate state of going to sleep is variously described: from the somewhat coy 'into the arms of Morpheus' to the powerful image of Dylan Thomas's 'Do Not Go Gentle into That Good Night', often recited at funerals. With the symmetrizing logic (see Rayner, 2019) typical of them, sleep and the unconscious know no gradations, no similarities between things, only sameness. At such levels of imagination, death is sleep and sleep is death. So fear of going to sleep may include a fear of dying and for a parent this may extend to death fears for their baby.

When parents recount these fears to me, I am shaken each time by the genuine life and death quality of the story I am told. There may indeed be some external cause for anxiety – difficulties in birth, such as Matthew's mother experienced (see Chapter 7), or other problems in the early weeks that the mother has not recovered from and not properly absorbed. Even without such personal experience, these fears can be based on reality in that everyone knows or has heard of tragic deaths of babies. Similarly mothers, even in these relatively advanced days, may fear the possibility of death for themselves when they go into labour. The risks are very small, but they exist. Looking at the possible real bases for these fears does not, however, take us very far in understanding them. To use an analogy, all forms of transport have their risks of death, but we still think of someone unable to travel as having some particular unrealistic difficulty or being phobic. We might also expect that, usually, the thrust of life-forces involved in the process of giving birth has an overriding effect that allows a mother to set aside such fears.

For each mother the actual experience of herself and baby surviving may or may not have a degree of reassurance that all will continue to go well. For vulnerable mothers, talking through these fears and experiences may make them more manageable. In working with such mothers I often also feel that what I am doing for them is directly containing their anxiety, so that they can go back to the baby and contain the baby's feelings. When a mother then meets her baby's anxiety in the night, it no longer connects with her own infinite experience and she can respond to it appropriately. Some mothers also, poignantly, feel they have never had a 'blessing' bestowed on them with their babies. Their right to have a live baby has not been confirmed either by their own mother or by another significant person. This idea is developed in Chapter 10 on parents' own childhood experiences.

A case example

Peter's mother had fears with a life and death flavour. When I first met Peter and his family, they were all in a desperate state of sleeplessness and mutual fury. Peter was almost a year old, woke up repeatedly during the night and had to be breastfed each time by his mother. He cried so persistently that the family were all disturbed; his father often escaped to sleep in a room downstairs; his mother rushed to attend to Peter before he woke his three-year-old sister, Sophie.

Two powerful themes arose in our work together: first, the fear these parents had that there must be something wrong with their baby, so that he had to be attended to at once and could not be asked to wait; and second, a difficulty in dealing with his anger and their own. Both of these themes were vividly represented in the meetings between the parents and myself. In the early sessions they angrily recounted the endless wakings of Peter in the night and the moves in and out of beds and rooms. I could not understand or make any pattern of it in my mind, although I was aware of the parents' angry disappointment with my inability to share their experience or to help. In one early meeting, Peter's father stormed out of the room, taking one of the children who was somewhat restless out with him; after a brief walk he came back in a friendlier mood.

In spite of my perplexity as to what was going on, I encouraged Peter's mother to start to wean him, and she did so with his father's support. It seemed as though this helped both mother and baby to feel more separate in the night and Peter woke fewer times. I then realized that the parents, and particularly the mother who came to some appointments on her own, were usually late. They also often left early, apparently because both had very tight working schedules. One morning while I was waiting for mother's late arrival, her health visitor told me that the family had called the doctor three times the previous weekend for advice because of an ear infection that Peter had. As I waited, I started to put all this together.

When Peter's mother arrived, I told her of the conversation her lateness had provoked. She took this in good part and seriously examined the implications of the information with me. I compared her inability to wait to talk to the doctor in surgery hours with her inability to make Peter wait until morning for a feed. I asked her if she could remember the feeling of 'waiting' herself when she was a child. She immediately thought of what long hours with a housekeeper felt like while her own mother was out at work. I connected this also with her lateness in coming to see me; perhaps she wanted me to know what it felt like to wait. But more vitally I pointed out she was communicating to me that she was never seen when she needed to be; the times that I saved for her did not fit with the times she really needed help. The times she really needed me were when she felt desperate in the night.

We also thought about what happened to her own judgement of how bad her son's ailments actually were; on the visit from the doctor and the subsequent telephone conversations with him at the weekend, little actual 'medical' interventions were either needed or given. We thought about her inability to act on her own experience; Peter is her second child, and although her confidence was much greater than when her first child was born it tended to evaporate at times of illness. It seemed to this mother, thinking about it all, that her lack of confidence now was a legacy from the feeling as a little girl that her own mother's interest and excitement were directed mainly towards her work. As a little girl she had felt that she wasn't really worth talking to and spending time with.

Peter's mother was then able to put my comments on her time-keeping into immediate effect. She came on time to future appointments, humorously wondering if this was a compliance, being 'good' to please me. More importantly she was able to think about helping Peter to use her at the 'right' time, that is, during the day. This was complicated, as she was away at work for much of the day. However, she was trying to face up to the fact that she was doing with her children what she had so much resented in her own mother. Her seeking to attend to Peter in the night was partly a well-meant wish to make up to him for her absence. But this continued a kind of chain of reproach passed on from one generation to another and seemed to leave Peter no more satisfied than she had been herself as a child. However, as she became less eager to meet his needs at night, he woke up less.

Peter's father meanwhile was thinking hard about his role in all this – he had tried to help his partner cope with a very demanding baby who could not be kept waiting; he also had felt the brunt her feeling of being kept waiting for him to come back from work and help out. Now he too started to think about how to help her question the baby's demands and how also to help her feel his support and confidence in her ability to cope when he wasn't there.

As Peter's parents came to know and trust me, we were able to look more clearly at their anger. I suggested that this inability to be ordinarily firm with Peter might connect with a worry about going too far. If they started to get angry with him, would they know how to stop? A crucial problem for many parents is dealing with a baby's anger in the night, while at the same time feeling their own anger at not being allowed to sleep. Many parents are particularly afraid of battering their baby in the night. The fears of going too far may stop them from being reasonably firm. Experiencing anger within bounds may be as much a relief to the baby as to the parents. Babies who go on crying in the night undermine parents' belief in the quality of their parenting and in their judgement.

With Peter's parents we had an intense version of this problem. They were now able to confide in me examples of their worries about their own aggressiveness. Peter's father told me how nervous he sometimes felt when he was driving – he felt he might kill someone. This was a chance for us to talk about the problem of keeping anger and aggression in check when dealing with a vulnerable baby. This in turn enabled us to turn our attention to Peter's mother's problem of never being sure how ill her children were: each time they had a high temperature she thought they might die; that was why she had to keep calling the doctor. We started to understand how unsure she was of herself as a mother and unsure of her own judgement, so that it felt to her that she was unsure of her ability to keep her children alive.

To both these parents it came as a great relief to share their fears with me and with each other. Putting their fears into words and making connections with their own childhood emotions made them begin to seem manageable. You could say that they started to like themselves better and, as this happened, their natural humour appeared. Peter seemed relieved at his parents' new assurance, he slept better and the parents started talking with me about their marital relationship. I continued for a time working with them on family problems and then referred them on for more intensive marital work.

At this point I thought back to the way that these parents had, for several weeks when they felt most desperate, dosed Peter almost nightly with sedatives of various kinds. I then realized the incompleteness of my work with them. At the point where Peter's mother had been able to tell me about her extreme lack of assurance of her ability to keep the children alive, I had let the subject slide, believing that we had 'aired' her fears sufficiently. I had not, however, really helped her look at the implications of what she was owning to. This mother's fear was of a 'sin of omission', not of actively doing something to kill her baby, but of failing to do something to keep him alive. By forgetting him, she would bring about what lurks ambivalently in nearly every mother's mind, the wish to get a troublesome baby out of the way. Other mothers have similarly told me of sterilizing their baby's bottles more than once because of their fear of not getting it right and inadvertently allowing the baby to be poisoned by the 'germs' in the bottle. By calling so frequently on the doctors, the mother was in a sense making a valiant and sincere effort to counteract this unconscious wish to 'forget' her baby and sedate him. Instead of trying to understand the cause of the sleep problem, she was perhaps trying to alert the doctor, and myself, to this conflict in herself about wanting to 'get him out of the way'. *Our* sin of omission was in not properly noticing this.

These two parents had told me, very movingly, of a range of fears that their kind of parenting was harmful to their children. My belief, from thinking retrospectively about what they told me, is that *not* taking up the implication of this sufficiently was a failure on my part. This belief in itself requires an examination of what good it does to discover deep fears, such as these parents possessed. Sharing these fears should make it easier for parents not to act them out towards their children, though as professionals we often worry about whether bringing them to consciousness might make it more likely for parents to act on them. With Peter's parents, I felt that only partially discovering their fears left them in a state of perpetuating the problem.

Fraiberg (1980) has described the inherent difficulty when patients, afraid of abusing their own children, start to connect this in therapy with what happened to themselves as children. In the chapter 'Ghosts in the Nursery', she says of a patient:

> She remembered factually the experience of childhood abuse. What she did not remember was her suffering. Would the liberation of affect in therapy increase the likelihood of acting out towards the baby, or would it decrease the risks? . . . It is the parent who cannot remember his childhood feelings of pain and anxiety who will need to inflict his pain upon his child. And then I thought, 'But what if I am wrong?'
>
> (1980, p. 182)

Looking back at Peter's family's problem, what stands out is his mother's experience of neglect by her own mother. Like her mother, she also went out to work and of course for many mothers with a year-old child this is not a problem. This mother, however, was doing to her child what she had not been able to bear for herself as a child. Her flustered attentions to Peter in the night stemmed from this dilemma.

She seems to have felt that her mother did not take responsibility for her, either when present or not. We do not of course know whether her mother was in fact unduly absent, or whether she was unable to bear what another child might manage. In either case the feeling got passed on, that she as a mother did not know how to be responsible for her children. Keeping them alive is the ultimate way of describing what this responsibility entailed. Her repeated frantic calls to the doctor, and her use at times of me, were perhaps part of an attempt to get someone else to take over this responsibility. In conclusion perhaps no one, neither her mother nor any other person, had let her know that she really *deserved* to have live, healthy children.

Sleeping together or alone

I change direction here to look at another facet of the gradual process of separation: the question of children sleeping alone or with their parents. In Chapter 5, we considered it in terms of the regulation of the baby's physiological states, but here we will look more closely at the psychological impact on the child and family in their cultural context. In the previous chapter we thought about separation and individuation and two questions come to mind about this: first, how much is separation prized in different cultures and second, how much is it necessary to be alone to feel oneself to be a separate individual? I will bear these questions in mind in addressing the subject of co-sleeping.

To begin with, whose needs are being met by taking the child into the parents' bed? Lozoff et al. (1985, p. 482) point to the complexity:

> Sleeping with parents may occur in reaction to the child's sleep problem and/ or to the mother's awareness of her partial emotional withdrawal from the child. Such bedsharing may be one avenue via which an ambivalent, stressed mother expresses both her positive feelings towards her child, and her own needfulness.

It appears that co-sleeping as a normal cultural practice is independent of stress; but where it goes against the cultural norm it indicates, by definition, that family functioning is out of the ordinary. From the point of view of the individual child with a sleep problem, Lozoff et al. (1985) imply that co-sleeping may postpone grappling with the problem and that the proximity itself may prolong the problem. Conversely it may sufficiently answer a need in both mother and child to then allow the child to sleep. What is *not* addressed by this study is the wider issue of separation. We see the effect that sleeping with parents has, adversely or not, on children's ability to sleep. We do not see the effect it has on their ability to be on their own. Without knowing the personal details of any of these families, we might still guess that some of these parents have unresolved problems with their own parents about being kept separate in the night. Since some co-sleeping children do not sleep even when they are allowed to be with the parents, perhaps what is communicated to the children is not so much that a gratification of a need is being offered, but rather that the issues of separation in the night are complex and insoluble.

We are still left with the problem of how parents and babies ultimately achieve a state of separation necessary for adulthood. The study highlighted earlier vividly shows us the differing cultural assumptions that families may have of the degree of separation there should be at night between parents and babies. There is a dilemma in putting this together with a Western ideal of individuality, of the importance of differentiation and of individually recognized achievements. The baby who is given her own cot, her own specially decorated room, which is recognized as her own space, is the inheritor both of material 'progress', but also, if McKenna (1986) is right in seeing sleeping separately as a form of deprivation, of a certain poverty in this approach.

It is essential always to differentiate the needs of babies at different ages. Perhaps there is a *universal* need for parents and babies to be in close contact in the first days or weeks. Perhaps the time to separate then depends on the concept of separation and individuation that obtains in each family or culture. McKenna's argument, empirically based though it is, that nocturnal separation can in some circumstances be one of the converging factors leading to cot deaths, also connects with the pathological phobic perceptions of some parents that their offspring will die out of their sight. It is not easy to work out where realistic anxiety in parenting and phobic concern begin and end. Parents teaching their child to cross the road alone know this only too well.

Winnicott is helpful in describing the psychological processes involved in separating. In *The Capacity to Be Alone* (1958), he shows how the infant's first experience of being alone is in fact in the presence of the mother. The infant achieves the awareness of 'I am' protected by a mother who is preoccupied with him and with his needs. She is also able to identify with his being ready to change. Following 'I am' comes the thought 'I am alone'. Winnicott tells us that 'I am alone' is a development from 'I am', dependent on the infant's awareness of the continual existence of a reliable mother whose reliability makes it possible for the infant to be alone, and to enjoy being alone, for a limited period (1958, p. 33). His view that the capacity to be alone depends on the existence of a good object in the person's psychic reality is confirmed by the development research. This belief comes from a repeated experience of having instinctual needs met, Stern's (1985) representations of interactions that have been generalized (RIGs). Infants first need their mother's reliable presence before they can have an internal picture of her which can remain enjoyably with them in her absence.

The parents' relationship

How does the parents' own relationship fit into this? Winnicott points out that a healthy child will have an imagined idea of the parents' relationship and a sense of it as sexual, whether actually having perceived it or not, and will find a way of dealing with the feelings of jealousy and exclusion stirred up by it. McDougall (1974) looks at it from another point of view – a mother not invested sufficiently in her own love life will be over-involved with her child.

Other writers have described the effect that children in the parents' bed have on parents' sex life. Lozoff et al. (1984) comment that co-sleeping and letting the child fall asleep in adult company and not in his bed 'reflect an emphasis on nurturance in family life, rather than on the relationship between father and mother' (p. 180). Are babies in the bed a bar to sexual intercourse? There are, of course, usually other rooms in the house. Glasser, recalling his childhood in Glasgow in *Growing Up in the Gorbals* (1986), describes memories of being lifted out of the parental bed and then put back in. However, these experiences still imply that the family/parental relationships take precedence over the marital one. The child is reared 'in the bosom of his family'. Families with limited accommodation may feel distraught at the lack of privacy or be quite tolerant of the situation. But what different view will a child sleeping in the same bed as his parents have of them, and of himself, from the child sleeping alone in his own bed or in his own room?

Parents who come to discuss their children's sleep problems sometimes report 'success' in dealing with the problem as getting the child out of sleeping in the parents' bed to sleeping in another bed in the same room. In some of these cases it would seem as though a child in the parents' bed is experienced as breaking up the parents' relationship. As we will see in Chapter 11 on parents' marriage, a toddler who gets into the parents' bed and then either keeps the parents awake by kicking or actually ousts one parent is acting out her dissatisfaction about how she fits in with the parents' relationship. A child in the same room, but not in the same bed, may be needing some security of being in the parents' presence, but expressing this in the context of accepting the parents' relationship with each other and feeling protected within it.

Distance from parents

Separation has to happen in some form when a baby falls asleep; it is *her* organism that changes its state, however close she might be lying to her parents. Paret (1983), in a study I mentioned earlier, looks at the connection between sleep problems and the distance the baby keeps from her mother. Citing the rise in frequency of sleep problems in the second half of the first year, she reminds us that sleep disturbances can be transitory difficulties due to both the external and internal stresses of this developmental phase. As attachment to her mother increases during the first year, this can then interfere with the baby's ease in falling asleep. The anxiety produced by awareness of her attachment and her new ability to move away from her mother may produce stress. This may be reflected in the daytime behaviour of the nine-month-old baby, who cannot venture too far or for too long without checking back and 'refuelling', reading her mother's signals in order to feel safe.

Of the 34 babies in this study, there were 11 'wakers' and 23 'sleepers'. In looking at the differences between these groups, Paret found that the 'sleeping' babies were further along with weaning and that they did not need to be moved or rocked to get to sleep. She also discovered that more of the sleepers used transitional objects or sucked their thumbs. She suggested that although these babies may wake up at night, they are able to *put themselves* to sleep again, whereas those in the waking group will require the physical presence or even the breast of the mother. Paret speculates upon what in the interaction of the mothers with the 'sleepers' encouraged the capacity of the baby to comfort himself, put himself back to sleep and create a transitional object. She then tried to correlate a measure of how well the child slept through the night with a measure of the child's physical distance from the mother during the period of observation in the day. She noticed that 'wakers' stayed close to their mothers and were more likely to be held on their mothers' laps and to be touched by their mothers. Good sleepers showed a tendency to travel away from the mother earlier in the observation, to go further and to look at the interviewer more. The babies who maintained the greatest mean distance from their mothers also sucked their thumbs more. Their mothers showed a tendency to interact with them by looking at and talking to them during the interview. A really striking connection arises from this: 'These babies, the thumbsuckers who played at the greatest distance from the mother, were the babies who slept through the night' (Paret, 1983, p. 175).

The filmed evidence was that all the babies woke up in fact, but they did not all disturb their mothers. Perhaps the so-called good sleeper does not demand the presence of his mother during the night because he has already taken qualitatively different steps in ego development, he has the capacity to reduce tension and comfort himself, to enjoy exploring and mastering the new environment on the floor, to assert comfortable control over the physical distance between himself and his mother while still maintaining contact with eyes and ears. The baby's mother is able to tolerate – perhaps one can say encourage – such developments by her willingness to reduce his dependence on her (weaning), permit gratification (thumb sucking, transitional objects, other than those she personally provides), enjoying his distancing of himself and his interest in new things and people and respond to rising tension in her nine-month-old baby by reassuring with looks, smiles and gestures in addition to holding or feeding.

From this we can see that the sleeping babies who can travel from their mothers are not, however, also emotionally distant from their mothers. For these babies, independence seems to be based on having a secure idea of a relationship with their mother. According to Paret's observations, mothers and sleeping babies stay in contact with each other through looking and talking. This is very different from the attachment category of 'avoidant' babies, who after a short separation are unable to greet their mothers and turn away and occupy themselves with toys, seemingly *in place of their mother* and not in addition to her.

Tomson (1989) made a similar discovery to Paret's about the connection between the distance babies are able to travel from their mother and the ability to sleep well. He and a health visitor colleague worked with a group of four mothers and infants with sleep problems aged between 9 and 22 months. All these babies fell asleep at night only in their mother's arms. They noted that during the first group meeting *all* the babies sat on their mothers' laps. As the group went on in later weeks, the babies began to sleep better at night. At the same time, they became able to separate from their mothers and to move away from them across the room when the group met. As their babies started to sleep, the mothers' clothes became smarter and they also used more make-up. It seemed as though the mothers' sexual identity was able to come back into focus, as their closeness to their babies lessened.

The babies who can best manage separations from parents are perhaps those whose parents are known to be reliably available when needed and those who signal their comings and goings. One important route for the mastering of separations is learning to say 'goodbye' and, following from this, playing games about separation. Freud (1920), in a famous, and for him rare, observation of a child's play, observed his grandson aged 18 months playing a game with a cotton-reel on a string. In this game the child held the reel by the string, threw it into his cot, so that it disappeared into it, and uttered the sound 'o-o-o-o'. This was his favourite expressive sound, which his mother thought represented the German word 'fort' (gone). In the game the little boy pulled the reel out of the cot again by the string, with a joyful 'da' (there). Freud interprets this game as being the child's way of dealing with his mother's absences. By himself staging the disappearance and return of the objects within his reach, he was taking an active role, rather than being a passive recipient of her absences. The implication is both that the little boy, instead of being helplessly left, could feel as though he was in control of his mother's goings and comings and that the completed game would *ensure* that she did return after each leaving.

I saw a similar game, when looking after a friend's child of the same age while she went shopping. This child, lying on my lap, cried desperately for a few minutes after his mother left. Then he quietened, climbed down, took a wheeled toy and pushed it to and fro away from him and back towards him, over and over again for several minutes. Unlike the child Freud observed, he at first played in dogged silence. After a while he allowed me to make a verbal game of 'gone' and 'come back' and then went on from this to play a more varied game of moving little cars around. Here we see equally vividly this child's recovery from the desolation of his mother's having left him by a game where *he* makes something 'go' and 'come back'. It is also crucial that he could express anger and despair *first*, before marshalling his resources to deal with the separation. If I had tried to jolly him into such a game as soon as his mother left, it would have had much less meaning for him (or if his mother had slipped away unnoticed).

Similarly, Fraiberg (1959) recounts teaching a baby who was waking in the night to play the game of peek-a-boo. By playing this game of disappearance and reappearance, the baby got some control over the idea of her mother 'disappearing' in the night. The peek-a-boo game was a way of playing with ideas about separations and thus becoming less vulnerable to them. In my work with parents and children on these problems, perhaps the parents and I also play with these ideas about separation, so that the parents get some mastery over the ideas.

Conclusion

The underlying theme of this chapter has been of communication between parents and babies about signals given out and then picked up or missed, of the needs of the baby being responded to or not heard, of shared states of understanding or of misunderstandings. One of the vital communications is about changing needs and the baby's need to be looked after differently as she matures, and begins to separate from her parents.

We have seen how separation is about moving apart and becoming reunited. It does not necessitate feeling emotionally distant, in fact the opposite applies. Intimacy between two people, parent and child, depends on being separated out in order that a relationship between the individuals can happen. When the separations of the night seem really impossible, we guess that the difficulty is as much for the parent as for the child and that this ordinary parting is coloured by unbearable bereavements or losses of some kind. Similarly for working parents the separation from their baby during the day can leave too much painful residue to allow peaceful partings at night-time (as happened for Peter's parents). We have also seen how children with insecure attachments do not feel the protection of their parents through the night and cannot settle to sleep. Throughout the book, these themes recur.

Chapter 9

The connections of sleep problems with feeding and weaning

Feeding and sleeping are closely linked. In the first few days and weeks, babies sleep much of the time and wake mainly for feeding. The setting up of the timing and rhythm of both feeds and sleep are really part of the same process.

Newborn babies often fall asleep at the breast so that the end of a feed and going into sleep can be almost the same experience. In such a case neither the end of the feed nor going to sleep may be experienced as a separation from the mother. If this continues after the first few weeks, then the baby actually misses out on what could be thought of as an emotionally maturing experience, that of at least sometimes digesting a feed while awake and away from his mother's arms. If a baby only goes to sleep while being held by a parent, then if she wakes later on alone in her cot, she may feel that only the parent can help her back to sleep. Furthermore if going to sleep is associated only with breastfeeding, she may demand a breastfeed to help her deal with each arousal. When babies have only been able to fall asleep directly from a breastfeed, weaning can feel like a desperate problem for a mother and baby about to lose their one known way of the baby getting to sleep. With bottlefeeding, some of these issues also apply, though the fact that fathers or others can also give the baby a bottle may help to disperse problems that might have arisen specifically with a mother and baby couple.

Difficulties in weaning may highlight unresolved problems in the feeding relationship, and there is an interesting connection at this stage where success in weaning can correlate with ability to sleep. Playing at the breast, during or after a feed, also connects with good sleeping. This leads us to think about the need for mothers and babies to play with ideas about their relationship in order to enjoy and manage feeding, transitions and separations.

Leaving the clinic after our first meeting, six-month-old Penny's mother went into a shop, bought a packet of chocolate biscuits, put them on top of the pram and ate her way through them on the way home. Surprised at herself, normally a sparing eater, she thought, 'Food for comfort'. It seemed as though the consultation with me had been hard going! She was in fact dramatizing the theme of our talk together. She had told me that Penny needed feeding on and off throughout the day and also the night. She could not take solid foods and was solely dependent on the breast. We had talked about her mother's assumption that Penny *had* to be fed every time she woke and cried. Penny had in fact lain asleep in her pram during this first meeting and woke near the end. Her mother held her up to me and I met Penny's steady, dignified gaze.

Next week her mother came back beaming and showed me a chart of Penny's waking and feedings during the night, now strikingly fewer in number. She told me the anecdote of the chocolate biscuits as a way of introducing the theme of her thoughts during the week about herself and Penny. 'Food for comfort' was her interpretation of her own chocolate biscuits. She had then reflected that she did not have much imagination about how to comfort her daughter – it had to be the breast each time.

We discussed whether the breast really was always needed to comfort Penny and indeed whether the source of comfort had to come from her. It was also relevant that in spite of a very difficult birth, Penny had slept well in her first few weeks – the traumatic wakings had started after a trip abroad, and her mother and I discussed the possible stresses contained in this visit.

Somehow Penny and her mother had become hopelessly enmeshed. In this week of reflection her mother had said to herself, 'Why don't you *let* her go to sleep, not make her go to sleep?' As we talked, Penny woke up. Her mother picked her up and, in order to prove to me the progress the week had brought, did not immediately start to feed Penny. I was able to see for myself how painful it was for this mother and baby not to have their instant reunion at the breast. How could they be together and at the same time separate? Penny's mother told me that she now wears night-clothes, so as not to stimulate her with her naked breasts when she picks her up in the night. She felt this was a large factor in helping them both cut down the night feeds. Penny fussed and her mother said, 'You're sleepy, go to sleep by yourself'. She handed her teething rings, which Penny first pushed away and then took hold of. Penny cried fussily again. Her mother noticed that she had been holding Penny closely in the position for breastfeeding and remarked that this was not fair to her. She put her back in the pram. Penny kept up a low wailing sound and her mother tried to ignore it. I suggested, perhaps fancifully, that the noise was Penny's way of keeping a connection going between herself and her mother with her mouth and voice, keeping the link to replace her mouth on her mother's nipple. Right or not, my comment helped her mother listen to the noise for a while without feeling obliged to *do* anything.

For Penny and her mother, the feeding had got out of proportion as an aspect of their relationship. Let us now look at the way in which feeding usually is established between mother and baby.

Feeding and closeness

Feeding and sleeping have a major factor in common. Both are somatic states involving a change in neurophysiology which, as Stern (1985) points out, 'require the physical mediation of an other'. Achieving a rhythm and pattern for both these basic physiological needs is the main preoccupation for mothers and babies in the early weeks – working out the realities of the baby's own needs and rhythms and finding a pattern that is understandable by both mother and baby. The negotiating of this, as much as the achieving of it, influences future relationships. Many writers have linked problems in one area with those in another. Winnicott (1947, p. 90) describes the setting up of breastfeeding in poetic terms (I am indebted to Davis and Wallbridge's very clear presentation of Winnicott's thinking):

> Imagine a baby who has never had a feed. Hunger turns up, and the baby is ready to conceive of something; out of need the baby is ready to create a source of satisfaction, but there is no previous experience to show the baby what to expect. If at this moment the mother places her breast where the baby is ready to expect something, and if plenty of time is allowed for the infant to feel round, with mouth and hands, and perhaps with a sense of smell, the baby 'creates' just what is there to be found. The baby eventually gets the illusion that this real breast is exactly the thing that was created out of need, greed, and the first impulse of primitive loving. Sight, smell and taste register somewhere, and after a while the baby may be creating something like the very breast that the mother has to offer. A thousand times before weaning the baby may be given just this particular introduction to external reality by one woman, the mother. A thousand times the feeling has existed that what was wanted was created, and found to be there. From this develops a belief that the world can contain what is wanted and needed, with the result that the baby has hope that there is a live relationship between inner reality and external reality, between innate primary creativity and the world at large which is shared by all.
>
> (1981, p. 44)

We see from this account how the physical and mental experience of feeding produces much more than satisfaction of hunger. In a parallel with Stern's (1985) RIGs and Schore's (2000) psychobiological patterns, Winnicott sees it as the basis for optimism and the freeing of creative thinking in the present and in later life. Also engendered by a reliable feeding relationship is the building up of trust and of intimacy between the feeding baby and mother.

Winnicott has described this building up of trust and intimacy in terms of breastfeeding, but bottlefeeding can also be close, intimate and satisfying for both mother and baby. Breastfeeding is an efficient way of promoting intimacy, as mothers and babies have to be physically close during the feeding. Many settle easily into this intimacy; for other mother-baby couples who have had an uneasy start intimacy may at first seem daunting, but the task of feeding may be a route for learning to manage it; for some other couples breastfeeding never seems to work properly, with mother and baby not being able to find a mutually satisfactory position, rhythm or pace. Bottlefeeding can equally be carried out either as an intimate physical closeness between mother and baby or in a way that illustrates an inability to be close.

It is not therefore the method of feeding that determines the relationship that grows between mother and baby, but that the use of the opportunity for intimacy develops from the feeding. Perhaps, however, an intensity and range of feelings can be expressed more easily in breastfeeding than in bottlefeeding. The excitement of the experience and the expression of loving and aggressive feelings can be witnessed more openly when the baby is dealing directly with the mother, without the intermediary of the bottle. Winnicott says, 'the survival of the mother is more of a miracle' in breast than in bottlefeeding.

Bowlby (1969) suggests that it is not the physiological process of feeding which is the essential basis for the relationship, but the comfort given by the contact with the mother. Harlow's (1961) experiments on rhesus monkeys show that baby monkeys will cling to a cloth 'mother' rather than a wire one, irrespective of which model provided the food. Harlow and Zimmermann (1959) use this work to show the 'critical importance of contact comfort in the development of affectional responsiveness to the surrogate mother' (p. 262). We can infer from this that in normal mother-child relationships, being held closely and regularly by the mother is an important experience in itself and not just part of the background of feeding.

A study reported in the *Lancet* (Cunningham et al., 1987) concluded that 'carrying a baby close to the body in the first few months of life has a more positive effect on the mother-infant relationship than does breastfeeding' (p. 379). They note that babies who are carried more in the early months tend to cry less and show less distress. These results tell us that secure attachment is promoted by mothers and babies being close to each other for long periods and thus having the chance to respond to each other. We can see that for mothers and babies the opportunity for mutual exchanges creates an emotional climate. As we saw in Chapter 8, we would expect that closeness would in time allow the development of independence in the baby.

Penny's mother realized she had become stuck on the idea of 'food for comfort' and that she could have other ways of comforting her baby. What this study, looking at security of attachment, did not encompass is seeing whether direct expression of feelings is facilitated more in breastfeeding than in bottlefeeding. It may also be that the baby's closeness to mother in the snuggle carrier likewise promotes this and overrides the different feeding experiences.

Over-feeding and sleep problems

Working out the baby's physiological needs is one of the main tasks for mothers in the early weeks. Breastfed babies need to be fed more often than do bottlefed babies. Since human milk contains fewer proteins and calories than commercially produced milk does, the bottlefed baby will get more per feed and be likely to sleep longer. Advice given about length of time between feeds needs to address this difference, so that breastfeeding mothers do not think that their babies' 'short' sleeps are a failure on their part to provide enough milk, rather than a reason for giving more frequent feeds. In this context, shorter sleeps are not necessarily a problem. Klaus and Kennell (1976) put this case more strongly:

> Among mammals one can predict the frequency of feeding for any species from the ratio of fat, protein and carbohydrates in the milk. On the basis of the

composition of human milk, human new-borns should be fed every twenty to thirty minutes, as was once the custom, rather than every three or four hours, as is present practice.

(quoted in Stern, 1985, p. 237)

These findings are somewhat extreme and do not fit in with the observations of most mothers, even of newborns, of their baby's needs. I have not found any evidence of adverse effects from longer feeds with lengthier intervals between them. In any case, however frequent the newborn's feeds may be, the older baby increasingly can go for longer periods between feeds, with the consequence that he can also sleep longer.

Feeding and sleeping go closely together, and the baby's ability to sleep may be heavily influenced by her mother's beliefs as to how often she needs to be fed. Ferber (1987) summarizes how the mother's misunderstanding of what the child needs can actually cause or perpetuate a problem:

> Although an infant at six months of age certainly has the ability to obtain satisfactory nutrition during the daylight hours and to sleep through the night without sensations of hunger, repeated feedings during the night only condition the child to become hungry at these times. Therefore it is likely that some of the extra wakings are actually triggered on this basis. Some wakings may also be in response to the unusually wet diapers. Finally the intake of liquid nutriments during the night prevents the appearance of a more mature circadian pattern. The child's sleep and hunger feeding patterns remain infantile. Instead of the digestive/endocrine – sleep/wake rhythms adjusting to a day/night cycle with consolidated sleep and no feedings during the nocturnal period, they remain 'set' for recurrent interruption and intake. Consolidation of night-time sleep is prevented and frequent wakings persist.
>
> (p. 152)

We see here how feeding at night in itself causes the baby to wake to seek food. Often parents and babies have got into such a tangle for reasons to do with the emotional issues going on between them, and then get stuck in them for the reasons given. In such cases mothers and babies may find that they have to sort the problems out first during the day and that the sense made of feeding patterns then carries over to a more comprehensible situation in the night.

One baby, Agnes, whom I saw at 15 months, had a physical origin for her night-time feedings. She had been severely jaundiced at birth, following a very difficult pregnancy. Mother was instructed to give her fluids three hourly, day and night. This was obviously a necessary procedure medically, but one consequence was that it restrained the baby from settling into longer sleep periods. It also of course kept the mother on the alert through the night, waking herself to the alarm clock, not even to her baby's cries. In addition, the mother had been justifiably anxious for her baby's survival during the pregnancy and in the first few weeks. Having lost their chance of working out the baby's sleep rhythms early on, a year later both Agnes and her mother were still jumpily unable to settle into long and deep periods of sleep.

One worry for many parents, including Barnaby and Clare's parents (see Chapter 2), is whether what they have given their baby is good enough. Health visitors, nurses and doctors see innumerable mothers who wonder whether their milk is 'good' (Kahn & Wright, 1980). Such a mother may find it very hard to let a baby know clearly that she believes he has had enough food and care and can manage on his own in the night. When he cries, is he reproaching her for not giving him enough 'good' nourishment? Many mothers' uncertainty at night seems to be a continuation of this unsureness about feeds.

The example of Luke and his mother that I mentioned earlier, in the section on parents' dreams, shows how issues in the mother-baby relationship can get in the way of sorting out feeding. Luke was six months old when his mother came to me in a panic about having to wean him in two months' time, because she was going back to work. She was feeding him constantly, night and day. We looked at how her grief at the coming separation, which felt like a forced one to her, had left her unable to discriminate between when Luke needed her and her breast and when he needed to be away from her. He fed often and was often sick. She muttered that her milk was poisoning him. I asked about her own upbringing and she told me about her mother's uncertainties in her marriage and in her sense of herself as a mother. Returning to herself with Luke, it seemed that her sense that she and her milk might be really 'bad' for Luke, together with the parting to come, were interfering with her ability to see how he was really using her. Luke meanwhile played in my room, bringing toys to his mouth and then blowing bubbles and uttering little 'talking' sounds. I showed his mother how the use of his mouth and the pleasures he could get from it were developing and that we could hear the beginning of speech from Luke's use of his mouth to communicate at a distance from her. None of this happened when just clamped on to her breast.

Next week Luke's mother came back to say that he had slept right through the previous night. At first she could not remember whether anything different had happened that day; then she recollected that she had not breastfed him during the day – she had stayed out with him in his buggy as long as possible and kept moving. She had fed him once in the morning and once at night. As she talked, Luke pulled himself up and bit at the straps of his buggy. His mother said she had just realized he had a tooth when he had bitten her breast. We speculated that by not being allowed at the breast on and off all day, Luke had calmed down from a continual state of excited arousal. He was free to use his toys and experiment with his aggressive feelings without worrying about hurting his mother. His sense of self could develop both emotionally and cognitively. Similarly, his mother was free to own more of her feelings towards her baby – it occurred to her that the separation to come had masked her natural feelings of *not* wanting to be with her baby all the time. We saw her dream about this in Chapter 6.

What the examples of Penny and Luke show vividly are the problems for mothers who always interpret their babies' wakefulness in the night as the need for a feed and who have always allowed the baby to go to sleep at the breast. Neither of these babies had experienced being put into their cot while still awake and being able, while semi-alone, to digest sleepily the emotional experience of the feed along with the milk. (In Chapter 8 we looked at the question of how much emotional maturity depends on the mutual capacity to manage well-timed separation.) A specific consequence of this situation can be that after the baby wakes in the night he has then no experience of how to get himself back to sleep. As far as he knows, only his mother and the breast can do it. Ferber's (2013) chapter, *Sleep Associations: A Key Problem*, is useful in this connection.

Several families with this particular problem of night-time feedings have referred themselves for help at a point when the mother is thinking of weaning the baby. It seems impossible to lose the only known way of getting the baby to sleep. Simon's parents came, shortly before his first birthday, in this dilemma. The parents were young, lively and good-looking, each working part-time and sharing in Simon's care. They had recently moved him from a playgroup where he seemed to be unhappy to a morning nursery, and both parents were worried about making a change like weaning while he was getting used to the nursery.

Simon's mother's pregnancy and his birth had both been easy, but the first few months were miserable. They were isolated in a district where his mother knew no one, the local health visitor was herself on maternity leave, the mother had a difficult relationship with her own parents and felt herself to have no support. She had suffered from eczema as a child, brought on initially as a milk allergy. Stress, however, could also activate the eczema and did so now. In later meetings she increasingly attributed the onset of her eczema to the fraught relationship with her mother. When her eczema was bad, holding Simon was difficult. Perhaps when the eczema subsided, she made up for it by holding him 'too much'. In any case, the pattern of holding was not consistent from Simon's point of view.

The problem that brought the parents to me was that Simon woke repeatedly in the night, cried, was fed by his mother and took sometimes an hour to get back to sleep. While she told me all this over two or three weeks, she and her husband worked out together at home how to change things to help Simon. They thought he was frightened of the bars of his cot and bought him a bed. At first he was delighted, but soon found it as hard to stay alone in this as in his cot. He cried for his parents or came into their bed, but still disturbed them when he got in with them.

They decided that Simon's mother would wean him, so that both parents could equally attend to him if he woke in the night. This was a courageous step, as they were losing the means by which he and his mother dealt with his waking. However, he took easily to the bottle. The day after this weaning was completed Simon, sitting in the back of the car, said clearly for the first time, 'Mummy' and 'Daddy'. Simon's parents realized that this step of separation from his mother had given a boost to Simon's rudimentary ability to conceptualize and to relate to both parents through this new medium of talking. Even so, Simon was still waking up repeatedly; his parents felt I was not being useful and for a time we stopped meeting.

We resumed, however, a few weeks later with new energy and, significantly, Simon's father agreed to attend whenever work permitted. Now a new theme emerged – how people could be angry with each other. Simon's mother came one week to tell me she had felt angry with me the previous week, when I had asked her to define her ideas of what her child should or should not be allowed to do. We had seemed caught in a nebulous misunderstanding of where we were aiming for with Simon and I had asked her to clarify her thoughts. As Simon's mother talked about *her* anger, Simon, for his part, cried angrily all the time. His mother held him, unsure of what to do. I said I thought he was listening to what we were saying and was showing *his* anger about us trying to change what happened at night. The next week both parents came. As we talked, Simon brought me toys and then hit me. Again it seemed a justifiable comment on our conversation, as Simon was listening to the three of us discuss plans to keep him in his bed! Simon was still unable to get to sleep on his own. Since his weaning, his mother or father had to sit by him, stroke him or hold his hand until he fell asleep. Each time he woke the process had to be repeated.

I suggested that his parents sit by him, stroke him for a while and then go out for a few minutes, telling him they would come back soon, and to be sure to come back, whether he cried or not. They did this and to our joint astonishment found that Simon was sleeping several nights a week through the night, though he still kept getting out of bed during the first settling period. I suggested that they let themselves be angry with Simon and tell him not to get out of bed; the parents were politely incredulous that this could have any effect. I spent the next week pondering to myself how anyone ever got anyone else to do what they were told! They came next week and again surprised me by saying Simon was staying in his bed when told to. The parents would go out and come back as promised. His mother had started with a promise that she would 'come back to see if you're all right'. After a few days she changed this to a promise to 'come back to see if you're asleep' and Simon was managing to fall asleep in her absence. Simon's father realized that his method was less confident than his partner's and each voiced criticism of the other. As his parents cleared the air by coming out with their conflicting opinions, Simon illustrated the mood of the conversation by banging his toys. Simon had a special teddy that he took to bed. During the day he played at putting Teddy to bed and sometimes told him he was 'naughty'. It looked as though he was mastering his own situation as he played with Teddy.

The theme of all this seemed to me to be the evasion of direct conflict. Simon's mother and her own mother had never been able to have things out together. As I shall suggest in Chapter 13, perhaps this mother's own eczema was the physiological expression of her dilemma. In any case, she and Simon had to go on with breastfeeding when it did not really suit either of them any more until both parents' combined firmness released mother and baby from an impasse. Like Luke, Simon was also freed to speak and to play symbolically.

Colic

Colic is an interesting symptom which bridges physiological and psychological thinking. Weissbluth (1987a) reports that it affects a fifth of all infants and describes it as violent and unexplained screaming attacks starting at about two weeks, with infants crying for about three hours per day, usually at a regular time. The attacks disappear in most infants by two to three months.

Weissbluth says that colic is more than crying. In his book *Sleep Well* (1987b), he suggests the crying spells may be set off by physiological disturbance, sleeping patterns out of synchrony with other body rhythms, or abnormal hormone levels. His view is that colic is related to such physiological factors along with qualities of temperament.

These babies also tend to have irregular sleep patterns with frequent wakings. They have brief and irregular daytime sleeps and tend to miss periods of quiet sleep during the characteristic evening crying. From three to eight months infants who cry frequently during the day or night are more likely also to cry during sleep/wake transitions. Weissbluth vividly describes the uninhibited motor activity which occurs during the colicky crying spell, such as stiffening of the body, with fists tightly clenched, legs flexed rigidly over the abdomen, twisting or jerky movements. He says that 'facial grimacing coupled with the crying suggests to the parents that the intensely energetic, excitable wound-up infant is in severe pain' (1987a, p. 131).

There has been the view that colic was thought of mainly as a gastro-intestinal problem caused by, for instance, allergy to cow's milk in bottlefed babies or wind in the mother's milk, due to her diet, in breastfed babies. Many parents describe the condition as being due to their baby's failure to bring up wind and surmise at pain in the abdomen, when the baby draws up his knees. Others think this pain may be the *result* of taking in wind during the crying, not the initial *cause* of the crying. This is a useful idea, but it seems to me that this begs the question that too much wind could be produced by the manner in which some babies feed and that uncomfortable relationships between mother and baby lead to uncomfortable positions for feeding. Some such feeds could be experienced as 'indigestible'. Taking in wind while feeding at breast or bottle might be a consequence of an uneasiness or awkwardness in the way the baby is sucking.

Colicky babies often appear to be inconsolable. Kirkland (1985) writes of the varied ways in which parents hear a baby's cry. He says that not much of a baby's cry is needed to remind parents of previous horrors. The implication is that parents' panic does not help the baby in settling his mood and continual crying in any case can make colic worse. The irritated feeling in the baby's body is illustrated by an irritating cry, which makes the parents feel full of an irritating or persecuting pain.

All this is not intended to make parents feel even worse but to help them locate where to start to make things better. The old wives' remedy of holding the baby upright, tightly against the parent's body, sometimes works. The baby may feel held together both physiologically and psychologically by this. She may also feel that what she is going through in her body can be felt in the body of the parent holding her. It is crucial here for the parent to hang on to the knowledge that this is the baby's pain, that she needs help for it within herself; it need not be experienced by the parent as though it was his own pain. A baby who is kicking and thrashing about all over the place may be relieved by firm holding, although some babies may not be able to bear it.

It is also crucial to keep in mind another way of describing the baby's experience. In psychoanalytic terms, the force of unconscious processes may at times lead a baby to feel as though he is psychologically falling apart and can induce this feeling in his parents. Crying may be an expression of this feeling and a need to be held physically would follow. Sucking is another way a crying baby can comfort itself and again we can see the psychological parallel to a neurological process. The baby who feels emotionally fragmented gathers himself together through the focus of his sucking mouth.

Some case examples

Justine was a baby who cried, it seemed, endlessly. Justine's mother had given birth to her on a date very near the first anniversary of her own mother's death in an accident. In one visit to me, her mother walked around with her and suddenly handed me the baby. I very rarely hold babies while doing this work, seeing my job as being concerned with a mother holding her own baby and showing me the difficulties and pleasures. As I held Justine, I was taken aback by the absolutely rigid feel of her body, particularly the knotted-up feel of her little stomach. It seemed to me that there was a connection between her mother's bereavement, reinforced by the near coincidence of dates, that had not yet been absorbed and her inability to absorb and receive the pain her baby experienced. Justine's rigid body might also have been like her experience of a rigid, unyielding mother, too full of grief to take in the ordinary needs and pains of her baby; perhaps in this way the baby was also suffering some of her mother's pain.

When I started to put some of this into words, Justine's mother took her from me and stood with her back to me as she listened. I graphically felt how unbearable this whole subject was. However, it seemed as though something in all this worked. Her mother reported next week that Justine cried much less. Perhaps my brief holding of Justine, followed by my trying to understand the significance of her rigid body, felt to her mother like the kind of motherly holding that she herself had lost with her own mother's premature death. Babies who cry inconsolably may be expressing some grief of their mother's (Goldsmith & Cowen, 2011). Perhaps by talking to me about her mother's death, this mother's unresolved mourning was able to shift, freeing Justine as well as herself.

Patrick was a baby with colic. Perhaps he was physiologically vulnerable in some way, but the repercussions on the relationship between him and his parents were devastating. Patrick's mother brought him to see me at three months. After an easy birth he had always slept badly, with long spells of frantic crying from the beginning. He frequently had very explosive bowel motions and his mother was sure that his crying stemmed from a build-up of wind, only released through his bowels. As I mentioned in Chapter 2, she came in to the first visit angry, suspicious of anything I said and critical of all the help doctors and health visitors had given her in the previous weeks.

It seemed to me that the pain in Patrick's belly was experienced as overwhelming by his mother. When he had the pain, so in a way did she. Not only could she not help him deal with it, she was equally at its mercy, and when she frantically went to the doctor she, so to speak, took it with her. This pain was perhaps also an 'accusing' one; she felt 'accused' by her baby of causing it or, at the very least, not making it better. From this point of disadvantage whatever advice she was given by professionals felt like yet another accusation that she had again not got it right. I put some of my thoughts about this process into words and Patrick's mother was at first full of fury at what I was saying; gradually she became intrigued and leant towards me as I spoke. She started to confide both the details of Patrick's birth and the agonizing unsuccessful attempt she had made to leave him and return to work when he was six weeks old. It was likely that there was a connection between the prospect of this premature separation and the troubles between them, but to make too quick a formulation would have been in itself premature.

The following week, Patrick's mother told me that he had been sleeping through much of the night. She had gone to the chemist and bought some medication which had cured his wind. A medical colleague later authoritatively told me that this preparation 'doesn't work'. But something *had* made a difference. I felt that my descriptions to his mother of the effect Patrick's pain had on her released her from some of its consequences. She had felt like a mother who could not cure her child's pain. Each time she sought advice she had in a way reproduced this situation; she had taken an insoluble problem to each professional. By describing this I had broken the chain. In particular I had *believed* this mother's description that unbearable pain existed. She began to have some confidence in her own judgement and then in her capacity to do something for her baby. I think that she went to the chemist in the belief that something she did for her baby could make him better. In this spirit she gave him the medicine and it cured his discomfort.

The following week when I said some of this to Patrick's mother, she was dismissive of such thoughts. She said talking did not make a difference; the medicine had cured Patrick. I ingenuously asked why in that case she had not given it to him long ago. It again took a confirmation by me that she had had a very difficult time with Patrick before she could trust me to know a bit more about what she and he had been going through. She started to think about why Patrick had had so much wind. She described a very easygoing pregnancy when, unlike her usual self, she had had no anxieties. The shock of Patrick's birth and his frantic crying since had been tremendous. I thought that here was a real clue – through this 'easygoing' pregnancy, this first-time mother in her mid-thirties had not been psychically preparing herself for the birth and the impact of a baby. Patrick's mother then confided in me the disturbing dreams she had had in the early weeks after his birth about breastfeeding. In these dreams babies, animals and parts of the body were all shockingly interchanged. It appeared that breastfeeding was not pleasurable and was a shocking new experience to absorb. As she told me of this, she herself started to wonder how much of this had got through to her baby. Maybe, she suggested, her awkwardness about all the images stored up in her mind by breastfeeding had actually affected how she held him during feeding. As she thought about this, Patrick cooed and smiled at his mother from his pram; she smiled and talked back to him.

Patrick's mother told me all this against a background of another impending separation – at four months she would have to leave him to return to work. It occurred to her that it made her feel as though she never really had had him as *her* baby. She then recalled with some bitterness all the family visitors who had come to see the new baby in the first few weeks. Instead of finding the visits gratifying, it seemed as though she felt their visits had claimed him as the family baby, not as hers. She postponed her return to work and, with a long waiting-list, I changed our meetings from weekly to fortnightly. After the first longer gap, I was also five minutes late in starting the session. She told me that Patrick had slept through every night until last night, when he had woken up often. I half-jokingly said it sounded as though he could not last out the whole fortnight. I said I thought she had perhaps also felt like that when she had to wait five minutes to see me, after waiting for two whole weeks. She looked surprised, then laughed and said, 'I've always felt I want it now!' She then told me again something she had told me in an earlier session, that she had been a voracious eater as a child but had remained very thin. Until she was 16 her mother had left sandwiches and a drink for her to have in the night. I said that it sounded as though *her* mother had not been able to believe she could last the night without food. It was no wonder she could not believe that Patrick could manage either. She thoughtfully considered this. Patrick's problems were of two kinds: his colicky pain and his inability to sleep for long stretches in the night. Both were connected with the feeding relationship with his mother. The colicky pain, his mother felt, was due to her way of feeding him, and it took the sorting out of both her own disturbing experience of breastfeeding and her processing of her baby's pain before he was released from that.

The sleepless nights were also related to feeding. When Patrick woke in the night, his mother was irrationally sure he was hungry and immediately fed him. We have seen how in her childhood her own mother had not been able to conceive of her waiting till morning for food. One night while suffering from flu, she slept heavily, woke in the morning and realized she had not heard the baby cry through the night. He was peacefully asleep. She realized that she might have been arousing him by her usual immediate response to his cries. It seemed that he could, at five months, go for several hours without a feed. Parents of babies who have had severe colic often fail to adjust to their babies' changed needs after the colic has disappeared.

The next time they came in, Patrick, now five months old, looked around the room; his mother sat in silence as he turned to look at her, at me and at the window. She said to him, 'Have you sorted out where you are?' before telling me of the intervening fortnight. It is worth noting here that from about four months, mothers tend to begin to talk to babies of external matters of interest, not just of the emotions between themselves and the baby. As Patrick started to sleep through the night, he and his mother were freed to enjoy such conversations with each other. In fact the sleep problem was solved when his mother became able to step back from Patrick sufficiently to let his father in to help both of them with it. She asked her partner to go in to Patrick in the night instead of herself. Within a few days of this change, Patrick was sleeping through the night.

The experience of feeding

In their study, *Night Waking in Early Infancy*, Moore and Ucko (1957) looked at many variables to find what distinguished the babies who slept from those who woke at night and found that babies that received least extra play-time after a feed had the greatest tendency to wake, those that received a great deal of time after a feed were the next most wakeful group, while those that had between 10 and 20 minutes playful attention after their feeding time settled best. We are now in a position to take this argument a good deal further. It is no accident that Moore and Ucko identified this important contact time between mother and baby as being connected with feed time. The amount of time and the whole tone of the time around feeds is when key emotions between mother and baby are stirred up, experienced and dealt with. Both mother and baby are dealing with a microcosm of life and death fears, anxieties and fantasies at every feed. With a successful feed they get through this; reassurance comes from the actual experience. What then is the resolution of this experience? One outcome is for the baby to fall asleep at the breast and be put down while asleep. The mother can then feel a unity with the sleeping baby, satiated by the milk she has given him, whether from her own breast or from the bottle. Another way a feed might end is when a satisfied but still alert baby wants contact with his mother in another way and wants to play with her. Even a baby who falls asleep at the end of the feed may seek and take part in play-time with the mother during pauses in the feed. What are the uses of such play-time?

A feed is a gratification of an instinctual need; it is also a sensual experience and a learning experience. As the baby satisfies his hunger, he is also touching, seeing, smelling his mother and her breast. He is putting together sensations, expectations and memories and building cross-sensory impressions of patterns (Stern, 1985). Taking this further, we see how in pauses during the feed or in play-time afterwards the baby is able to do several things: firstly, to go on exploring his mother's body, away from the urgency of taking in the milk; secondly, he can assimilate the experience and deal with the *idea* of having had a feed and the *idea* of a mother who is there to feed him but who also exists in addition to this function. Part of the idea that grows in this time is of mother and baby as two separate beings who have been wordlessly together and are now about to move apart. It could well be that how a mother and baby manage this time influences and is significant for how they will manage the separation aspect of the baby falling asleep. If on the one hand the feed is carried out only as a necessary routine piece of care, with no time allowed for exploratory playing, then there is no period of transition for the baby to change from the *idea* of being fed to the *idea* of the end of the feed. If on the other hand a mother plays excessively long, it may be because she is not able to face with the baby that 'all good things come to an end' and cannot bear the small separations that happen many times daily.

One mother of a baby girl, Elaine, found herself spending an excessive length of time over feeds. She was thinking of going back to work when Elaine was six months old. Although absorbed in her career she thought of this present time at home with her baby as very precious and was full of doubts about whether to go back so soon. Elaine slept badly and her mother had to feed her often during the night. An observer noticed how, during the day, she hardly seemed able to put Elaine down after a feed. She would play with her for long periods and even bathe her in the middle of the feed, so that to the observer it was almost like two feeds very close together. However, by this long gap in the middle it seemed as though she was spinning out the length of time she could be intimately involved with her daughter; Elaine's sleep problems seemed to be a further sharp illustration of the difficulties in timing separation.

A mother who gets this timing right seems to be offering a useful transitional time for learning and co-ordinating. I think there is a link here with the tactile, sensory qualities of the transitional objects discussed earlier that help babies to move away from their mothers. The need for them to be looked at, touched and smelt seems to follow from the baby's earlier need to look at, touch and smell the mother, who is then no longer occupied with feeding, though still immersed in the emotional quality of the feed. The quality of the mother's participation in the feed is vital. We have seen (and will explore further in Chapter 13) the effects of a mother's state of mind on her baby's sleeping. But nowhere is her state of mind so apparent as when feeding her baby. Babies are acutely sensitive at this time to how much their mother is able to be occupied with them, Bion's (1962) 'maternal reverie'. For example, a baby of only four weeks was being breastfed. His mother looked at the baby and talked to him gently. Then, while still looking at the baby, she started to talk to a visitor. The baby lost the rhythm of sucking, lost the nipple from his mouth and started crying. His mother returned her attention to him and he refound the nipple. Thus the baby needed to be thought about as well as simply looked at, as he fed. The vital foundational value of this for the baby is an important thing to hold in mind as smartphones become so prevalent and preoccupying. The importance of responsive face-to-face parent-child interactions is confirmed for a whole range of developmental achievements, including the capacity to self-regulate. The impact of the parent being preoccupied with a phone instead of the baby disrupts the emotional connection and seriously interferes with these developments (Radesky et al., 2015). The very real need to be sensitively available to the baby during feeding goes along with the need to be sensitive to a baby's sleep rhythms. Another way of putting it is that *managing* to establish a rhythm of feeding can carry over to a rhythm of sleep.

The relationship between breastfeeding and night waking

In the study of 'wakers' and 'sleepers' I mentioned earlier, Paret (1983) made some interesting discoveries about the relationship between the timing of weaning from breastfeeding and night waking. At nine months she found that 8 out of 11 babies described as 'wakers' were still being breastfed, while only 10 out of 23 'sleepers' were still on the breast. Among those still breastfeeding, the good sleepers had taken many more steps in the weaning process than had the wakers. Only one of the eight waking babies still being breastfed had begun the process of being weaned, whereas half of the ten sleepers still on the breast were already down to one feeding a day. Also in another larger sample of babies, whereas 12 out of a group of 26 wakers were still on the breast, only one of 20 good sleepers were being breastfed. She found that the good sleepers did not need to be nursed or rocked to sleep before being put down and in general were further along in the weaning process. Paret notes that the longer the mother continues breastfeeding the baby, meeting or anticipating his needs with her bodily presence, the longer the baby will be dependent on her at night as well as during the day.

Fathers

As we will see in Chapter 11, the father has a crucial part to play in helping mothers and babies, first in establishing confidence in feeding and later in helping them with weaning. One of the problems for sensitive, involved fathers is in working out how much good fathering of tiny babies should be a continuance of the way the mother is with the baby and how much he should offer something different in his own relationship with his baby.

An essential aspect of breastfeeding is its exclusive intimacy between mother and baby. The range of feelings induced in other members of the family, from vicarious pleasure to envy, is one of the ordinary dramas of family life. Weaning means that both mother and baby become emotionally and physically more available to the rest of the family. Fathers can be felt either as supportive of this new stage or as destructive of the previous intimacy, according to the dynamics of the family. Equally a mother who clings on belatedly to breastfeeding may be jealously guarding her own relationship with the baby at the expense of the rest of the family or be showing her own difficulty in managing a more than two-person relationship.

Bottlefed babies and their parents do not escape all these problems about feeding and weaning. If a mother has slipped into giving endless bottles, a father may find himself being used as part of a chain of feeding. Or by contrast he may be able to bring in a fresh point of view, that perhaps the baby could survive without all these bottles. Fathers, by being able to share in bottlefeeding, are often able to help mothers and babies out of an impasse. We will return to consider other aspects of the role of fathers in more detail later on.

Weaning as separation

A pattern of dissatisfaction between mother and baby in feeding can lead both to sleep problems and to weaning difficulties. Problems about ending a feed in order to go to sleep and ending the feeding situation altogether in order to wean may stem not so much from a highly valued situation which both sides are loath to give up, but from an ambivalent, unsatisfactory one that has never been quite right. The difficulty in stopping may be an illustration of a feeling of not having got it right yet.

Some mothers and babies get into a circular problem. If they need to be together, how can it then be right to separate? Conversely, if there has to be a separation, how can they be connected first? Alternatively, how does being connected contain the germs of separating out later? Does initial connection provide an experience that can last, as Klein and the development research suggests?

One mother about to return to work part-time kept angrily telling her nine-month-old baby not to suck his thumb. She was starting to wean him and it seemed as though the sight of him sucking reminded her of his vulnerability and his need still to suck at the breast. In a way she could not win; it was bound to be painful for her. Either she was reminded of how important sucking at the breast still was for him at the point when she was about to start weaning him or else she would have to bear the pain of feeling that her baby had found a replacement and had no further need of her breast.

The experience of weaning for mother

Weaning leaves a mother with a different experience of her own body in relation both to her baby and to her partner. During breastfeeding some mothers may use their babies as a shield to protect them from unwanted sexuality. By inadvertently allowing the baby too large an access to her own space, she can leave herself feeling that there is not enough to share with her partner. One mother told me that breastfeeding was as satisfying as sexual intercourse and a lot less trouble. When talking to a mother weaning her fourth baby, I said sympathetically, 'You want your body back'. She replied, 'I want my mind back'. Many mothers at this stage feel the same – they want to reclaim their own solitary mental life (finding time, for example, to read again) as well as their bodies. At the point of weaning a baby, a mother may not even have walked anywhere unencumbered for 18 months. She may not have been out since before she was pregnant without carrying a baby either inside or outside her body, pushing a pram or carrying shopping. So weaning may be experienced by some mothers as a regaining of their individualities and the free use of their bodies and to others it may seem like the signal to conceive the next baby and continue with the cycle of child-bearing. For mothers weaning what they expect to be their last baby, regret and relief may be closely intertwined.

The failure to wean

When weaning is described by a mother as impossible to manage and the mother and baby seem caught in something unbearable, then the cause may be quite serious. One reason for prolonged breastfeeding may be that the breastfeeding has become sexualized, and this can have a lasting effect on the child's development of sexual relationships.

One father, consulting about the family's problems, described himself as an addict for eroticized stroking by his wife, but was usually impotent when they tried to have sexual intercourse. He connected the beginning of his addiction with his own childhood, when his father, a coal-miner, used to get up at five o'clock in the morning to go to work. He, as a little boy, for several years would then slip into his mother's bed and for two hours his mother caressed and stroked his body and let him suck at her breast. Not only was he deprived of two necessary hours of sleep, including the REM time of the last part of the night, but he also became inextricably confused and guilty about the feelings stirred up by this stroking. In adult life he was still addicted to being stroked and inhibited from full sexual intercourse, because of the embodied connection it had with his mother's abuse of him, whether he knew it or not. Child safeguarding guidelines (Department for Education, 2015) make clear that sexual abuse need not necessarily involve a high level of violence and can take place whether or not the child is aware of what is happening. We can see one impact of it for this boy in his later sexual difficulties. What is painfully clear is that there was an abuse of his need for intimacy and closeness and a cover-up to keep it secret, so that no one else knew of it. As an adult he still woke early every morning and felt he never dreamt. It seemed that the process of symbolizing had been interfered with early in his life by his mother's abuse.

In less abusive situations, over-stimulation is the clue to when breastfeeding is continuing as an inappropriately eroticized experience. When mothers and babies come with this problem, both usually seem agitated and preoccupied with each other all the time. My impression is that it is more often mothers and boy babies who have got themselves into this state, though we can see that mothers and little girls might also be in a state of mutually aroused erotic feeling. One family demonstrated these sexualized feelings to me vividly. Firstly, their referral was dramatic and somewhat out of place. It came in a late-evening phone call to me at home from a psychiatric colleague. When I met them, the mother of the two-and-a-half-year-old boy, Jonathan, declared to me that it was impossible to wean him. Constantly during our meeting Jonathan lifted his mother's jumper with a proprietorial air and burrowed underneath to have a suck at her breast. His mother was embarrassed, but she also had a triumphant air. Jonathan's father tried to tell him that this was not the right time to feed. His partner impatiently brushed him aside and said that he did not tell Jonathan in the right way. This incident seemed to me to demonstrate that in this family Jonathan's mother had allowed or even encouraged Jonathan to supplant his father in having access to her. The parents in fact went on to tell me of their severe marital problems. Throughout this meeting Jonathan roamed the room restlessly, rarely able to settle to play. His mother reported that Jonathan woke continually in the night to have a brief suck at her breast, for which she seemed to disavow any sense of agency, which was perhaps projected inappropriately into Jonathan. It seemed as though he too, like the father in the previous illustration, was being used by his mother in a way that confused him rather than helped him clarify his relation to his parents, and where he belonged in the family.

It is important to emphasize that extremes of this kind are not always the reason for failure to wean. Often, as we have seen, it is simply an issue of difficulty or delay in separating, with a mother either deciding not to make this break between herself and her baby yet or feeling unable to tackle it. Both mother and baby may be satisfied by the continuance of breastfeeding without it doing harm to the child's future development, including the ability to separate emotionally later on.

We have seen how negotiating feeding and sleeping rhythms are among the most important interchanges between mothers and babies. Feeding of necessity changes as babies move from breast or bottle to solid food and drinking from a cup. These changes in the physiological ability to chew, digest and metabolize various foods also represent a change in the distance between mother and baby, which in itself has emotional repercussions. A baby sitting up in his high chair, biting at a rusk or banging his spoon on the table, looking at his mother and babbling to her, is in a different relationship to her from a baby who is held close to her breast, her nipple in his mouth. We can guess that his 'thoughts' about her have also developed into a different form. His thoughts as he lies in his cot awake or his dreams as he sleeps will include the images of these different experiences. A baby falling asleep or dreaming as he sleeps is thus in a state which is partly a response to his feeding and weaning.

Chapter 10

Parents' own childhood experiences

Nine-month-old Bruce made a great fuss about going to sleep when his mother put him to bed, though he settled easily for his father or the babysitter. His mother said to me challengingly, 'Don't tell me to leave him to cry'. After we had talked about this for a while I asked, 'Were *you* left to cry?' Bruce's mother burst into tears and told me of her mother's fixed views that babies should not be picked up when they cried. I remarked that her views seemed to be as fixed as her mother's, though their content was different. She was one of twins, and it sounded as though her mother had tried to solve the dilemma of which baby to attend to first, by delaying going to either. Whatever had in fact happened in the past, this mother's memory now was of herself as a baby being left to cry in vain. It seemed as though Bruce's cries sounded like her own cries then, as unbearable in her son in the present as in her memory of her own childhood. Perhaps also contained in her determination to act differently from her own mother was a reproach. It was as if she was saying, 'This is how babies *should* be treated'.

It is clear from this that parents' experience of how they were looked after help determine how they look after their baby. Raphael-Leff (1982) has described how the period of pregnancy is often used by expectant mothers to muse over their memories of their own childhood. Part of this preparation period is of course one of preparing psychologically to become a mother. Memories are drawn upon, and one consequence of this time may be what Breen (1975) describes as a recon-ciliation with the mother's own mother. The birth of a first baby is a significant moment of generational change. At this point it can be seen whether past legacies are handed on unchanged or whether there is room for something new to emerge in response to the challenge of a new family life.

Bound up with all this is the need for people to have a confirmation of them-selves as parents from their own parents. For Bruce's mother, this lack of con-firmation from her own mother was a crucial factor. When Bruce was born, her husband's parents were pleasantly supportive and visited almost at once, but her own mother felt unable to attempt the long journey and did not visit for several weeks. It seemed to me that Bruce's mother did not have the seal of approval from the person whose opinion mattered to her most at this time. Perhaps both grand-mother and mother missed a particular moment of reconciliation that might have happened between them about the shortcomings of the past. Perhaps also Bruce's grandmother's 'mistiming' of this first crucial visit re-evoked in his mother the bitterness she felt at her own mother's 'mistiming' of attention to her baby self in the past.

Gareth's mother, Maria, as we saw in Chapter 3, went through a traumatic experience at the time of her baby's birth, which affected things later. She had had a very good relationship with her mother, but two weeks before her baby was due there was an earthquake in her home country. She went into labour on hearing the news and for four days after Gareth's birth did not know whether her parents and the rest of the family were alive or dead. It is not difficult to see how unbearable this experience was for her. The family were in fact safe and Gareth's grandmother visited a few weeks later, but Maria said wistfully that all her sisters had had her there from the beginning. She told me regretfully how difficult the beginning had been. Her account is so gripping that I quote it again from Chapter 3: 'Every time I was changing him he was screaming. I didn't know what to do. I couldn't relax. My husband said I was like a machine. After my parents had been to visit, I realized Gareth had been aware of everything.'

It seemed as though this mother's realistic fear of her parents' death at the time of her baby's birth had not been dispelled until she actually saw her parents. Not only did she not have her mother's help and reassurance about her new baby, she had also had to deal with the shock of her parents' possible death. The preoccupation this caused in her got in the way of being able to notice and respond to the baby.

The examples of Bruce's and Gareth's mothers show how important is the mother's relationship with her own mother, particularly at the time of childbirth. Trowell (1983), writing on the effects of emergency caesarean sections, comments on factors that may partially determine whether this procedure is carried out, noting that the presence of a familiar woman can halve the length of labour. We can guess that this woman represents the mother's need for mothering during the actual process of labour, though it is important to recognize this need as being for symbolic mothering – the familiar female is rarely the actual mother. Further, it may be the quality of the internalized relationship the mother has with her own mother that affects her at the birth of her baby. The grandmother may in fact be absent through distance or death but be vividly present in the mind of the child-bearing mother. Equally important of course is the father's presence at the birth, both as a support to the mother and in his own right, as the father of the baby.

Gareth's mother's irresolution and lack of confidence about how to deal with Gareth at nine months old still stemmed from her disastrous experience in the first few days of his life. This was compounded by the fact that his father had had unhappy times in his own childhood. As well as the individual effects all this had had on them there were also disagreements between these two parents about how to solve the problems with Gareth. I suspect that quite often strongly held differences of opinion between husband and wife about how to deal with aspects of childrearing may stem from unsatisfactorily resolved experiences with their own parents. ('Getting hit never did me any harm', is the sort of example that springs to mind.) Parents are unable to negotiate with each other and work out the relative usefulness of each point of view, because their fixed reactions are based on a denial of what their own childhood was really like. Because they cannot argue out within themselves what the past was like, they cannot argue with each other about what to do now.

Amy's parents were a good example of this. Both parents had suffered mistreatment of one kind or another from their own parents. Amy's mother was cynical about her background, but her father clung to an idealized view that not only was his mother's neglect of him understandable in the circumstances (which it was), but also that it had not harmed him in any way. Because he could not look at the thought that it *might* have done so, he was unable to work at forgiving her. Amy's father was left feeling in a muddled way that his mother must have been right in her dismissal of her children's needs. He uneasily felt that he wanted Amy to have something different, but he did not know what. He and his wife had indecisive arguments about what to do for the best; neither had an inner certainty to bring to the discussions.

Parents with deprived backgrounds have a good chance of doing better with their own children, if they can remember their childhood clearly. They need to be able to recall the feelings about what happened, not just the factual circumstances (Fraiberg et al., 1980). Those who may be doomed to reproduce the behaviour of their own parents are those who have no memory of their childhood and those who idealize it (Main et al., 1985).

Stanley's parents had similar problems. Stanley could not get to sleep without hours of one or other parent sitting with him, and he woke often in the night. As we talked about the difficulties, it emerged that each parent had real torments at the thought of leaving him to get to sleep on his own. Equally they were at loggerheads with each other about any possible changes in the routine they had all three devised for themselves.

I discovered first that Stanley's mother's own mother had died suddenly when she was in her early twenties. The experience of this bereavement being unbearable still underlay her feelings, although she had achieved much in her life since. She was successful professionally, and her marriage, though full of complications, was a going concern. It seemed to me that the ultimate separation that was felt to be unbearable, her mother's death, coloured her attempt every night to put her baby down to sleep. She could not bear the separation from him; much more important she could not bear it *for* him.

Stanley's father brought other problems from childhood. After we had met three or four times, he dreamt that Stanley (who could not yet talk) said to him, 'Why don't you show me how to get to sleep?' This dream (as we saw in Chapter 6) evoked memories of himself as a little boy, also unable to get to sleep, and he now said that he felt *his* father had been unable to help *him*. We are again left with the dilemma so many people have: how to pass on to their children what they did not get from their parents. (We are reminded of the example that pet lambs, brought up away from their own mothers, do not make good mothers themselves.) These two parents both had problems about what to pass on to their child from their own parents. Stanley's father felt his father had not known what to do in crucial situations; Stanley's mother still felt the loss of her own mother.

The death of the mother's mother

Many of the mothers and fathers I see had their own parents die before the birth of their first baby; in their flounderings about what to do, this loss is often obvious. We will see later, in Chapter 13, that mothers whose own mothers died when they were young are vulnerable to depression, perhaps particularly postnatal depression. It is important to separate out the various consequences for a mother of her mother's death. In the immediate present we have a mother who lacks the chance to have her mothering of her baby confirmed by her own mother. She may feel her mother's death more acutely at her baby's birth than at any time since it happened. Becoming a mother puts her emotionally into contact with herself as a baby, as Pines (1982) has shown us. Not having a real mother there may leave her with her own infantile feelings stirred up; without a chance to have these symbolically satisfied by some attention from her mother, the feelings remain unresolved.

However, a mother who has lost her mother through death can be helped by having time to talk over her memories of her mother and of the mothering that she did get from her. If her mother died when she was young, then talking about her experience of growing up without her can help to bridge the gap from the time of the death to her own baby now and revive what memories she has of when her mother was alive. Talking about what her own mother would have thought of the baby seems to give the mother a chance to think of her mother as approving and confirming the new mother and baby's existence.

Talking in this way may then help the mother to feel more able to use other older figures – her father, stepmother, mother- or father-in-law or other relations – as supportive to her in her new role. It does appear that a father's death does not have the same specific high-risk effect on mothers undergoing childbirth as does a mother's death. However, any bereavement during the actual pregnancy can have a confusing and adverse effect.

Parents' deprivation

It is not too fanciful to reverse the idea of parents telling their children what to do and suggest that babies 'tell' their parents how to look after them. Parents in difficulties are often ones who have missed the cues from their babies. Main et al. (1985) have argued that adults secure about their relationships with their own parents are able to pick up signals from their babies about their needs. Insecure adults have to ignore the signals; otherwise, they put themselves in the painful situation of remembering their own unmet childhood attachment needs.

When parents start to tell me about their own unmet needs, it seems that even in this brief work one of the features that helps change can be to experience *me* as the parent who does not notice or listen. One mother told me very painfully of a frightening incident that had happened in her teens. She had never been able to tell her mother about it. The next week she was convinced that I had forgotten what I had told her. The therapeutic vehicle was not only that I was the sort of person who *could* be confided in, but also that I was felt to be someone who *could not*. Working out her distrust, based on the real experience of her mother, enabled her to take another step and separate out what *her* son thought of her now. She decided that perhaps she could let him know that she *did* listen to him and remember about him. With this idea of remembering in her mind, her little boy became less anxious in the night and slept better.

Judith's parents, both in therapy, provided examples of parents' childhood difficulties getting in the way of their relationship with their own child. Judith's mother came to see me, referred by her own therapist. Judith's acute sleeping difficulties were causing the whole family to have very disturbed nights. Both parents felt they could not stand it any longer and were furious with each other to the point that the marriage was in danger. On the first occasion the mother came with one-year-old Judith, she poured out a bitter account of her own difficult and deprived early life. It sounded as though her mother and an influential aunt had been both neglectful of her and also later on ambitious for her, in a way that made her feel that she was not valued for herself, but only for the prestige that she might bring to the family by being successful professionally. She came over as angry, unsure of herself, untidily dressed, obviously *very* tired, but also as intelligent, very warm to her baby and surprisingly open to new ways of thinking after an initial quibbling response to every remark of mine.

At the parents' own suggestion, Judith's father also came the second time. He was suffering from the recent death of his analyst, but a consultation with a psychiatrist had helped him deal with some of his feelings about this. He felt that in this process he was also retrospectively mourning his parents properly for the first time. He also had a tale to tell of neglect and misunderstanding in his childhood. I saw these parents three times before a holiday, and there was an immediate improvement in the baby's nights. In fact this improvement had started with the referral, and it seemed as though even the prospect of support in their problems enabled them in turn to start to help Judith. The problem was that Judith cried out repeatedly in the night and one or other parent, usually her mother, would go in to comfort her, often give her a bottle of milk and stay till she settled down again. These parents were sensitive to the fears they felt she was expressing and were perhaps especially open to her emotional state. Because they themselves were personally open and vulnerable at this time, having explored their own infancies in their therapy, they were well able to understand Judith's fears. However, it seemed as though they were less able to contain and mitigate these fears. The brief, focused work with me could respond to a different timetable from the longer-term work of their therapy.

In order to give them something to hold on to between sessions, I suggested that they read Winnicott's (1964) *The Child, the Family and the Outside World.* In the last session before the holiday, I had lost my voice. I decided not to cancel the session, as I did not otherwise feel ill. It seemed important with this family not to disappear when crucial work was going on. (It is difficult to decide whether this 'the show must go on' policy is helpful in the end to patients or not.) In any case I had to whisper and Judith's mother was able to voice her fears that her destructiveness and exhausting of possible help was the cause of my disability.

We started again after the holidays with a new contract that both parents would be part of all sessions, so that they could work as a family. The focus shifted from the fears that Judith might be feeling. It seemed as though the parents had first had to be sensitive to these fears, in a way that their own parents had not been for them. With no memory of their own fears being listened to and understood, they did not know what to do next when they received the impact of Judith's fears; they simply felt overwhelmed by them. Repeatedly going in to her in the night was less a comforting response to Judith than a panic reaction of their own. As we talked about all this, they started to feel more in control. They thought about a setting of limits and Judith's mother having rights herself, that is, to stay in bed and to sleep. We were able to start looking at her negative feelings towards Judith. As she started to acknowledge these feelings, she realized that previously she had thought of any negative thoughts as being entirely destructive. Because of this she could never risk saying 'no' to Judith, however appropriate the 'no' might be. Her partner was very supportive to her, as she worked all this out, and she began to have more confidence in her mothering abilities and to set tentative limits.

One week the family came in, settled themselves down in somewhat of a flurry and produced a bottle of milk for Judith. They said that now she was not having milk at night she needed it during the day. I said they seemed to be telling me in a backwards sort of way that the nights had changed. They told me, beaming, that Judith was waking up only once or twice a night. If she woke up before the parents' bedtime, her mother would go in to her and firmly tell her it was night-time and time to go to sleep. After the parents got to bed themselves they did not go to her, but called to her from their bed. Judith would cry for a few minutes and go back to sleep. Both parents were delighted with this success. What accounted for this change? Of course the parents' new commonsensical, clear and firm manner with Judith was in itself reassuring to her. She was not abandoned by them, she knew they were there and listening, but the limits were set. How did the parents get to the point where this behaviour on their part was possible? If in the first place I had simply mapped out advice on these lines, they would, I am sure, have thought I had not understood the problem at all. What I think was effective was the combination, within this relatively brief, focused work, of both parents telling me something of their childhood, while I also saw them with their child and connected all this through their actual relationship with me.

I must emphasize that the mother had been left very much torn to pieces by her childhood experiences. It took several years of her own very good therapy to help her repair this. But it was essential for me also to know about this, so as to be able to connect it with her feelings about her baby now. The necessary stages were these: first, she told me about her own relationship with her mother and some actual childhood experiences; second, I noticed her anger, both in telling me about her mother and in her reactions to my comments; then we had the episode of my lost voice, when she was able to talk about the destructiveness she felt in herself – the aftermath of a mother who had actually been destructive of her daughter's individuality and real creativity. When she saw that I was hearing all this, with no damage to myself besides a temporarily lost voice, it all seemed less dangerous.

At this point it was appropriate for me to show my appreciation of the real warmth between Judith and her mother. Having really dared to look with her at her worst fears about herself as a damaging mother, it was not now empty reassurance for me to confirm a new belief in herself as a good mother. Her partner's presence was of course essential in underlining this. There was also a chance for them both to look at ways in which anger with each other had made the problem worse.

The next stage was to look at Judith's mother's difficulty in giving up her picture of herself as a deprived baby with nothing good to hang on to. If she were able to give something good to Judith, she might have to acknowledge that somewhere she got something for herself and would therefore have to lose some of the anger and resentment which were so much part of her. I thought that going through all this with me, in our sessions together, led her to trust that it need not invalidate the truth of her early experiences if she did allow things to get better now.

I met this mother several years after this piece of work and found she had developed a real cutting wit, a brilliant kind of black humour. This seemed to be a creative way of expressing the anger still inside her and was much valued by her husband and daughter as well as by her own growing professional circle.

Parents who have felt very undermined by their own parents may easily feel criticized by their babies. Judith's mother felt reproached at times by the look in her complaining daughter's eye. Penny's mother on the other hand felt criticism rather differently. She had started to feed her baby less often and was pleased that she slept for longer. She then panicked, took Penny into bed with her and told me it all sounded too theoretical, that what 'the authorities' said was not always right. I said it sounded as though I was being a 'theoretical authority', not realizing what she and her daughter really needed and simply criticizing her for what she was doing. She agreed and we thought about how devastating criticism appeared to her. I then suggested that perhaps taking her daughter even closer to her in the night than before, having her in bed with her, was a way of stopping the baby's criticisms of her mother's attempts to put more distance between the two of them. Mother took this up enthusiastically and offered me another twist of the generations. She volunteered that perhaps she could not stand being 'criticized' by her daughter, because it would remind her of how vehemently she had criticized *her* mother.

Mothers with sleep problems

I mentioned earlier Giorgis et al. (1987) finding in their study of babies with sleep problems that 26 percent of the babies' mothers had families with sleep troubles, while only 10 percent of fathers did. Of the mothers, 16 percent also had sleep problems themselves. The case of Jesse and his mother shows how a baby's sleep problems can connect with the mother's own sleeplessness as a child. Jesse at nine months was waking often during the night and had to be put to sleep by his mother. It emerged that he was breastfed for four weeks and then his mother stopped, because she felt she was not giving him enough. At four months his mother had *never* left him – when she tried to leave him with her mother while she went out for the evening with her partner, Jesse was beside himself with emotion. Jesse's father described how the veins stood out on his scalp. Jesse's mother volunteered that she herself had been unable to sleep and that her sister had similar problems with her children. When I asked his father, he said there was no such trouble in his family. He added that his mother had been able to get him to sleep and his first wife had been able to get his children from his first marriage to sleep. I commented on his assumption that getting children to sleep was only a mother's job! Jesse's mother confirmed what seemed to be both her own and her baby's belief – that without her presence Jesse could neither get to sleep nor manage during the day.

I asked more about her own sleep problem. She initially said she had had a happy childhood. Then she told me that when she was born her father was in hospital with TB. She was the first child and she and her mother lived in her grandmother's house. An aunt and her children were also there. Everyone seemed to be critical of her mother's handling of her little girl, so that it was an extra strain trying to keep her quiet. It seemed to me that this mother's own mother, separated from her husband and afraid that he would die, might have clung to her baby for comfort. Perhaps the baby had become one of the vigilant babies, feeling responsible for mothering their own mothers and displaying 'reverse attachment' behaviour (see Chapter 12). When she was three, her father came out of hospital; the parents moved into their own home and had another baby. She reported being able to sleep from then on and said she was surprised, because she would have expected a new baby to have had the opposite effect. I suggested that the relief of having her father back safely, and the family together for the first time as a going concern, might have been more influential than jealousy of the baby. The relief was perhaps her own and also a reflection of her mother's. Jesse's mother agreed that here was a key to her own sleeplessness and started to think how it might connect with Jesse's problems. It did seem as though her inability, to an unusual degree, to let herself and her son be out of each other's sight might have its origins in her own childhood overshadowed by her father's illness.

Despite this weighting from the past, it seemed a good time to start work on the present problem. Although he was unable to let his mother out of his sight, Jesse was starting to use words and therefore presumably concepts that could include that of separation. He could say 'Mamma' and 'Dadda' and also 'bye-bye'. In Chapter 7, I suggested that absence is part of the way in which thinking is stimulated. Although Jesse had not yet managed to be absent from his 'Mamma', his use of words to name his parents might indicate a readiness to hold people in mind when they were not there. Following this suggestion, his mother reported some improvement in Jesse's sleep. However, perhaps the most interesting outcome of this piece of work was that at the end of our first meeting, Jesse's mother, intrigued by the connections we had made, planned to talk it over with her own mother. Next week she told me how helpful she and her mother had found it to talk together.

Recalling childhood

Sometimes I find that asking mothers questions about their own childhood makes them realize the gaps in their knowledge. When their mothers are still alive and in touch, then the conversation between mother and daughter can fulfil many functions. It not only provides information or confirmation for the mother about her own early experience, it is also a vehicle for the two mothers to share feelings about what has happened in the past and what is happening now. Fraiberg (1980) describes this vividly, 'In every nursery there are ghosts. They are the visitors from the unremembered past of the parents' (p. 164).

A mother who is being helped therapeutically to consider her childhood may also be able to help her own mother recall and voice regrets about the past. The understanding that can be engendered by this between grandmother and mother has infinitely more value than insights that remain in the consulting-room. However, Pound et al. (1985) warn us that good relationships in the present between the mother and her own mother may come too late to undo the present effect on their parenting of the grandmother's past deficiencies. The mothers' 'earlier evaluation of their mothers was strongly associated with whether their child had a current disorder', (p. 924) even though most women's relationship with their mothers was quite friendly, and they had, as it were, forgiven them for their past shortcomings.

Her own mother's obstetric history can be a crucial factor in the mother's relationship to the child-bearing aspect of her own body. Women whose own mothers had miscarriages and stillbirths may grow up with their mother's confusion, anger and distress about the birth and death their bodies have produced tearing around in their own bodies. One such mother felt guilty about her own survival and not only guilty but apprehensive about the survival of her baby. She felt she had no right to be spared the grief her mother had suffered. She checked so continually on her baby in the night that he was in fact unable to sleep. The agonizing effects of cot deaths can also spread through extended families. Women whose sisters have suffered in this way talk of their guilt and fears and not surprisingly may have sleepless babies. Mothers also may feel guilty about their own child-bearing coinciding with their mother's menopause, as though their ability to have babies has destroyed their mother's ability to do so.

In listening to parents' experiences, it is also useful to notice the way in which they talk about them. Main et al. (1985) have shown that the way parents talk about their relationships with their own parents in a single hour-long interview, the Adult Attachment Interview, can enable a prediction to be made of the baby's response to the parents in a stress situation. They used the Strange Situation Test, described in Chapter 8, to show how babies' behaviour, when briefly separated and then reunited with their mothers, connects with the adults' own upbringing. Strikingly, they found that there are characteristic ways in which parents describe their own childhood experience which connect with the kind of attachment their baby has with them. Parents whose babies had insecure attachments can be classified into three types. Firstly, those who deny and devalue the importance of attachment; these parents have babies who avoid them. Secondly, there are parents who continue to be preoccupied with what has gone on between themselves and their own parents; they have babies who are ambivalently preoccupied with them and may angrily insist on attention. Thirdly, there are traumatized parents who have suffered deaths or separations; they may have babies showing disorganized behaviour.

In contrast to this, parents with securely attached babies are able to talk about their own childhood in a coherent manner. I find Main et al.'s (1985) finding that coherency in the discussion is the best predictor of security extremely interesting. It fits well with my own experience of being told by parents what I describe as a jumble of unassimilated material. In brief work I also make the assumption that the *telling* of the incoherent story within the framework of one or two hour-long sessions, plus the putting together of the story by the listener, are themselves therapeutic. In other words, I think that some of the parents I see become less incoherent by the reviving of their incoherent story – the work does in fact make some sense of the past and connects it to their relationship with their baby in the present.

It is worth ending by referring again to Fraiberg et al.'s (1980) belief that the emotion of childhood experiences must be remembered in association with the facts in order for ill-treatment or neglect not to be inflicted again on the next generation. This is also a comforting thought for workers facing an intergenerational sequence of unhappy childhoods. Things can be changed by remembering and bearing the pain. I also think that the effectiveness of this sometimes lies in the therapist bearing the emotions evoked by the memories, transferred into the therapeutic relationship. In such cases the therapist cannot just pleasantly enjoy being an 'understanding mother' for the first time in the parent's own experience. The therapist must also stand being experienced as though she was the mother who *did not understand*, before she can know what the parent really needs to say.

Chapter 11

Father's role, the parents' relationship, single parents and returning to work

In this chapter, we will examine how both relationships and external circumstances can affect parents' handling of their baby. Firstly, we see how the parents' relationship influences their baby – whether the father is present or not. We see some of the possible implications when the father is absent, temporarily or permanently, and the complex issues for mothers going back to work. We also look at how the external factors of a family's circumstances are, as we might expect, dealt with according to the personalities and relationships within the family.

In my work, either mothers on their own or both parents come to see me; very rarely do fathers come alone. The quality of the relationship does not seem to determine who attends. Fathers who do not come to the baby clinic may be as supportive at home as those who do come. The baby of course is nearly always there as well. Where there are two parents, I always invite both to come. Mothers often say that it is difficult for their partner to take time off work, and they tend to come on their own the first time. After a visit where they see the style of help I am offering, many of them encourage their partners to come the next time. I have not yet worked with any fathers bringing up small children on their own.

Although I do not think the success rate is altered by whether both parents come to the clinic, the content of the work can certainly be very different. When only the mother comes, the theme is very often centred on the mothering she had herself and its influence on her as a mother now, on her physical and emotional experience of pregnancy, childbirth and breastfeeding. The absent father may be represented as supportive and understanding of all this, with mother relating our conversations to him each week, or he may be pictured as not understanding or even hostile to the thoughts mother is developing about herself and the baby. When both parents do come, then each has a chance to look at the present problem in terms of their own childhood experience. They also have a chance to work out with a third party conflicts between them about their philosophies of what to do about their baby. My presence as this other person can be experienced as supportive, provocative or both. The use of me is thus different when one or when two parents come to the clinic. Either can be seen as a helpful way to intervene in a particular family or on the contrary as a way of falling in with the defences and denials of that family's system. It is usual practice now to involve fathers wherever possible in clinics, and in her edited book, *Working with Fathers in Psychoanalytic Parent-Infant Psychotherapy*, Baradon (2019) looks at the issues.

When I do see a mother without the father, it can be truly helpful to work with her, centring on her emotional problems of mothering. She may use me to work through some of her unresolved feelings about her own mother. I often think that, even in the relatively brief time-scale of this kind of therapy, some very deep connections are made. The pitfall of working with only the mother is that a partnership between me and the mother, with the baby in between, can actually seem to have the effect of excluding the father. I make this situation explicit, hoping by doing so to break up the collusive element.

I have also sometimes worked at this emotional level with a mother in the presence of her partner and have found this can be liberating for both partners. It does not usually have the effect of making the father feel excluded; on the contrary, it opens up into the relationship a way of talking about intense emotions. Both parents may be able to start telling each other more about what they feel and what they have undergone. In joint work, when parents are in conflict over what to do about the baby and are upholding different ways of childrearing, they may be amazed to discover where the other's attitude evolves from in their own childhood. Mutual planning of how to deal with the baby's sleep and other problems becomes much easier when the origin of their disagreements has been opened up. Where joint work does not seem useful is when parents are at loggerheads and not in sympathy enough to look at the causes. Some may accept referral for marital or family therapy; in other cases it may be worth doing some limited work with the mother alone, if she feels that the care of the children is in any case left to her.

To give a brief example, Edward's parents came with a conflict between them about how to deal with him. Edward always cried when he was put in his cot. His mother wanted to leave him to get himself to sleep; his father felt he should always be picked up and held until he fell asleep. His father had been left to cry himself, in a way that left him with traumatic memories. In his insistence that Edward should never be left he seemed to be expressing how unbearable his own memories were. He was making his wife stay with the baby, when he had been unable to make his mother stay with him. In a sense he was being as tyrannical with his wife, in making her stay with the baby, as his own mother had been in her neglect of him. His own mother had not read the signs that he needed her and had not known that he was frightened when he was left alone in his room. Equally dogmatically, Edward's father did not read the signs of what his son really needed now; more importantly he did not allow his wife to use *her* judgement of how to carry out her mothering, of when to be with Edward and when to be apart from him. Sharing these memories with his wife allowed him to become more flexible.

Father's role

Let us now turn to the wider question of a father's role in the rearing of babies. I am not assuming that the paternal function is necessarily always carried out by a male, although I use 'father' to represent it. The role is a dual one, involving both a direct relationship with the baby and support for the mother-baby couple. This involvement may depend upon the nature of his relationship with the mother. Kraemer (2017) writes that in modern families, the mother tends to be the gate-keeper for the child's relationships, including that with the father. He continues:

> She introduces the father to his child. Of course a father does not have to wait for the invitation but negotiation of the parental partnership is a necessary and crucial step in any family. The pace of this varies across cultures but it is irreducibly complicated.
>
> (2017, p. 2)

He warns that enmeshment can ensue when mother's partner is excluded, suggesting that 'Children require more than one engaged caregiver' (Kraemer, 2017, p. 9).

Fathers can help with establishing a cut-off point, supporting mothers to say enough is enough. Judith's father (described earlier in Chapter 10) was a case in point. Here it was vital for the mother to know that she had Judith's father's confidence before she had the courage to say 'no' to her at night. It would not have been enough in their case for Judith's father himself simply to say 'no' to her, though this was the vital first move. He both did this and also helped her mother to regain her own authority and limits. We have seen from several examples in Chapter 9 the struggles mothers have between their wish to continue the intimacy of breast-feeding and conversely to hasten their child's independence. At best fathers can remind mothers of how the baby has grown, help her clear her vision and help her find the authority within herself to be more separate from her baby and to share the baby more with the father and the rest of the family. At worst this position of the father's can be felt as an envious intrusion into an intimacy that only mother and baby can share – one of Kraemer's (2017) irreducible complications.

The father may also provide some protection for a baby whose mother is depressed or having other difficulties – interestingly, this works particularly well for boy children (Murray et al., 2010). Guedeney and Kreisler (1987) say the father can help by being 'an effective substitute for a very depressed or withdrawn mother, or by limiting the influence of mother's phobias on the child' (p. 311). The quality of the marital relationship is also a protective factor against depression. Brown and Harris (1978) have shown that a woman without an intimate partner relationship is much more likely to experience a breakdown. If this intimate relationship is protective for the mother, it is also of importance for the baby. When parents have an estranged relationship, the baby's experience will not only be of a mother in difficulties with being emotionally available to him, but he will also sense that his parents are not performing this for each other.

Strong feelings abound in families. We have seen how the problem of separation for the baby at night is rooted in the complexity of his tie to his mother. Another issue which is almost universal is the oedipal situation, where the baby's reason for not sleeping seems to be an anxiety or protest about the parents being together and excluding the child. A baby who cries frequently and requires the attention of one of his parents is very effectively keeping them apart. Often parents are suffering the consequences of this, but have not really thought of it as a cause. They will have become resigned to broken nights, have got used to a small child between them in bed or are often even sleeping separately so that one of them can get an undisturbed night's sleep.

The effect on a marriage can be disastrous, and the stress can affect a whole family. Sometimes this aspect of the problem is obvious at once. For example, Jim's parents were quite explicit about the blight on their sex life. They were ready to take this on at once in our work and to look at the mutual misunderstandings of each other's needs which had led them to the 'musical beds' of the night. Having previously been allowed his pick of the family's beds, Jim was surprised to find himself firmly put into his own bed and told to stay there. He was no longer the centre of interest in the night, as his parents worked out their sexual hesitations and with amusement and pride reported each week's discoveries to me.

In another family, Melanie's parents came to this understanding at a totally different pace. We had worked for some weeks on Melanie's hijacking of the nights. Here there was some painstaking work to be done on her mother's ability to separate herself from Melanie and the need for her father to support this. This work was slow, but very successful. The parents came and told me of a whole week of almost unbroken nights. I remarked on how subdued they both appeared. The success had fallen rather flat. I followed my hunch and asked how they were getting on sexually. Melanie's father told me it was a non-event. Her mother had been too exhausted by the broken nights and had only recently weaned the demanding Melanie. She said, as do many other mothers in this situation, that she felt she wanted her body to herself. It took meetings over several months for us to talk about how she would achieve this and find her own individuality again. Expressing sexuality as *part of* individuality and not as a loss of it again can be quite a problem. It may be that sex too can feel like a demand. A way for a mother not to confront the issue is to be 'too tired' for sex, and a baby can be used to keep some distance.

In both these cases it is also important to spell out that a marital relationship, which in its sexual aspects excludes the child, is in fact just as vital for the child himself as for his parents. A child who by his jealousy manages to keep his parents apart is himself deprived of being able to grow within their flourishing relationship. He will bring less knowledge of emotional involvement to his own marriage in later years. It is worth confronting any immediate jealousy now for this end. In fact parents with a troubled marriage, who have been sleeping separately while their child has had sleep problems, are particularly vulnerable when they come together again. Focusing on the child has given them a respite from dealing with their own problems.

It can often be overlooked that evenings may be just as important for parents as the night as a time together, sometimes as their preferred time for sex, but in any case as a time to relax together after the day's work. It may be as necessary for parents to claim this time for themselves as later in the night. The evening can then be used for parents to become attuned to each other after the separate activities of the day. But this can easily slip away from them under the stress of a baby's demands.

One major source of jealousy of course is that of older children towards younger ones in the family. The father can play a major role in dealing with this. Adam, a three-year-old boy who had always slept badly, became even more difficult after the birth of a new baby who slept in the parents' bedroom. Every night Adam came and got into the parents' bed. In many families this would be an acceptable solution for a while, but Adam, having got into his parents' bed, was unable to settle down. He slept restlessly, kicked his parents and woke them and himself many times during the night. It seemed as though the disturbing feelings which led him to seek their bed were not relieved by being with them; they seemed in fact to be accentuated. Adam's parents decided to try to keep him in his own bed. They explained to him that his father would come to him if he called, but that he was not allowed out of his bed. They offered him a small car as a reward for staying in his bed. On the first two nights he stayed in his bed throughout the night, calling out for his father a couple of times and falling asleep again while his father stayed with him. On the third night he slept throughout the night and came into the parents' bedroom in the morning, saying to his father, 'You've been a very good boy. You stayed in your bed all night. I shall buy you a new pair of cufflinks.' This father indeed deserved a reward for the firmness which relieved his son of the torment of jealousy of both parents and the new baby which he was unable to get away from in the parents' room.

Another small child, David, aged two and a quarter, took a long time to settle in the evenings, continually reappearing downstairs. Eventually the parents realized what was on his mind. They talked to him about the new baby they were expecting and told David he did not need to keep on checking if anything was happening; the new baby would not just suddenly appear. David settled much more easily from then on. A week after his baby sister was born, David again could not settle to sleep. His father talked to him and David said, 'More baby coming.' His father told him not to worry, there weren't any more babies coming. David said, 'Nicholas got two.' Ten months previously his friend Nicholas's mother had had twins. 'I told him that he was right, but we weren't having twins.' 'Where's Gregory?' asked David. His father told me: 'Gregory was in fact the name we had chosen if the baby was a boy. I explained and David settled.'

This little story shows the importance of listening carefully to exactly what is troubling a child. It would have been easy for David's father to assume that it was the birth of the actual baby sister that was now disturbing David and keeping him awake. His father's finding out that his worry was the imagined arrival of yet another new member of the family was an instant relief to David; he could stop being on guard and let himself go to sleep.

This father and son understood each other well. David had a period at about 12 months of waking distraught and being very angry with his father – hitting him if he picked him up and held him or through the bars of his cot. On one such occasion his father said to him, 'David, why are you so angry with Daddy?' David stopped hitting out at his father, gave him a kiss and lay down to sleep. The relief of something being put into words, to a little boy who had as yet very few words of his own, is interesting. With little information we can only speculate as to why David was so angry with his father. Was it something going on between them, or was the anger perhaps a displacement from complicated emotions going on with his mother who had recently weaned him? Whatever the cause, it was the *acknowledgement* of the anger that David needed from his father.

As in many families sleep problems re-emerged at times of stress. After the family moved house David, now nearly three, was again wakeful. His father bought him a clock and pointed out on the clock the time when he could come in to his parents in the morning. After a few genuine mistakes, David got the idea within a week. He then appeared one night, half an hour after going to bed, and said, 'It's pointing to the seven, Daddy', with a twinkle in his eye. The joke between David and his father shows a much more creative internalization by David of the new rule than a solemn acceptance of it might have done.

We see how enjoyably this father interacts with his son and how he helps him through times of stress or change in the family. A crucial element in families is whether the father can be different from the mother, act in a complementary way to her and be able to rescue mother and child from too heightened an emotion.

One topic, full of hidden perils, is whether the father takes turns in getting up for a baby in the night. This is a very complex subject. When a mother is breast-feeding, obviously only she can feed the baby. She may enjoy this exclusivity and wake up quite pleasurably to feed the baby, matching her own sleep rhythms to the baby's. The baby's father may also get up, sometimes to be part of an enjoyable social time or to support the mother. Sometimes more destructive forces are at work – either a father cannot tolerate the exclusive mother-baby feeding or conversely the mother cannot bear her partner to sleep while she is awake.

After weaning or if a feed is not needed, either parent can go to the baby. It has been shown that higher involvement of fathers in their babies' overall care was associated with fewer night wakings (Tikotzky et al., 2011), but once a baby has woken, many mothers complain that fathers cannot wake up properly and perform clumsily, if they do get up to a baby in the night. Is this a reluctance to be helpful or is it that mothers are more able to attune their own sleep/wake rhythms to the baby's and are able to wake as the baby does? It would seem so; McKenna (2014) writes that mothers sleeping near their babies are woken within two seconds of the baby's waking, not necessarily for food; and there may be good physiological reasons for their mutual night-time contact; as the mothers 'touch, hug, inspect or whisper to them we witness on our monitoring screens a suite of physiological changes including increased heart rate and higher oxygen levels . . . remarkable to observe' (2014, p. 43). When fathers have close physical contact with new babies, they also more easily wake to the baby's cries.

If, however, a baby is waking more frequently than the family can manage, where does the father fit in? I have mentioned that he may be needed to help the mother limit the baby's demands, to say when enough is enough. It may be that he can reassure his partner that the baby could go for longer between feeds or that his wakings do not mean he is in need of anything. In this way, mother's partner can reinterpret the baby's signals to her when she is feeling anxious, triangulating them with another perspective, so that she has a chance to understand them in a less urgent way. However, mothers may use fathers to displace on to them annoyance about being woken by the baby. Instead of being firm themselves with the baby about what is going on, they may be angry with their partner either for not providing the firmness or on the contrary for not similarly leaping to attention whenever the baby makes a sound.

Fathers can be supportive by confirming to a mother that it is extraordinarily challenging work she is doing and helping with the problem of trying to understand what to do. One mother rather movingly described how she was able to let her baby's father help, after some months of excluding him. She wrote to me:

> Actually our method for getting Charles to sleep through the night seems to have worked – unless it's just a coincidence. S carried on going into him, instead of me, for a week. He would pick Charles up and give him a cuddle and a drink of water and then put him back into bed and firmly leave the room. To begin with, this had to be repeated several times a night but by about the 5th night he was only waking once, and after a week started to sleep right through! I can't believe it was that simple in the end! Though I think it was a question of timing really – I had reached a point where I was prepared to let S intervene. Before then I always felt I had to be the one to go to him in the night.

This mother had been reading about sleep problems. She said, 'I identified immediately with mothers who feel uncertain that they have given their babies enough good mothering during the day and therefore give in to their demands far more during the night'.

What we see in this fascinating account of family dynamics is how something vital changes in the interactions between all three. The mother says that at first she was not sure about being a 'good-enough' mother and had to keep giving more; she could not allow her baby's father to help her set limits. In such cases saying 'no' is felt to be being a 'bad' parent; the mother is unable to do this herself. She may put into the father this aspect of parenting, but also stop him from effecting it. In fact 'an immediate response may rob the baby from developing a sense of himself, by himself, which could give him great pleasure' (Phillips, 2003). These two parents, in fact very appreciative of each other's qualities, were able to change from this way of operating before it became too fixed. Perhaps as the mother became able to admit to her own wish to say 'no' to the baby, she was able to let the father take over from her. In addition, the baby's father was allowed to be a comforter to him and enjoy the intimacy that comes from this.

The father's role of course changes with the age of the baby. Small breastfed babies need their mothers to some extent exclusively. Fathers come increasingly into their own with weaning and may be especially needed to help mothers and babies separate. With older children, the need for a partnership of parents being firm is obvious. There may be a temptation sometimes for mothers to rely too much on fathers to provide the firmness, letting themselves be the indulgent, 'caring' parent and leaving the father to do the 'heavy' parenting. On the other hand a somewhat surprising pitfall for parents can be when each parent tries to be too much like the other and act in the same way towards the child, as if personal differences can be eliminated and it will not matter which parent a child is with.

One pair of high-powered professional parents each worked part-time and looked after their 20-month-old daughter Amina in turn. She seemed happy during the day, but refused to settle to sleep at night. They told me in detail how consistent they were in their handling of her. It emerged as they talked that in their busy work/baby-minding schedules each of these parents whizzed in and out, not particularly saying 'hello' or 'goodbye' to Amina. They did not feel she was going to miss one parent, because she was always with the other. A moment's thought might let them realize that such an arrangement, as if people were replaceable, would not work for themselves. I suggested to them that Amina might actually be quite angry at this lack of ceremony and at their assumption that one parent was interchangeable with the other at any time. Perhaps to Amina this was not so. I said I thought she was being politely co-operative during the day, but letting them know at night that she felt somewhat pushed around. These parents started to be more careful to signal what was happening to their daughter and also, to their own relief, to behave more spontaneously, so that their style of looking after her corresponded more to their own natural ways. They were able to be different in style from each other and Amina was able to have a slightly different experience with each of them. This was perhaps easier for Amina to understand; at any rate she began sleeping better.

Such issues can be particularly troubling for parents with strongly held views of not wanting to behave in sexist and stereotyped ways with their own children, which they feel marked their own childhoods. This is especially relevant where parents' own mothers have unfairly carried most of the responsibility for bringing up children and the parents do not want to perpetuate the pattern. The constructive wish to share and enjoy time and contact with children and not define rigidly the roles of either a mother or a father can, however, sometimes become confused with not recognizing individual personality or indeed even hormonal biological differences and the creative tension between these differences, which is a major component of a live relationship. The change towards recognizing this was a great relief to Amina and her parents.

The absence of father

A father's importance means that his absence will of course have repercussions. When I saw one-year-old Joanna, mentioned in Chapter 6, she had been sleeping badly since she was six weeks old, when her father had been away for a brief period. It seemed as though the difficulties had started then because of her mother's own panic at this separation and her resentment with her partner for not being there to support her.

Karen's mother also had a strong reaction to her father's business trips. Karen had slept badly for some time, but her mother felt doubly unable to deal with this when Karen's father was away, partly because she herself slept so badly then. She lay awake, worrying about burglars. I suggested that this fear might have its origin in her anger with her partner for being away: perhaps she was rejecting her absent partner, so that in her fantasy if he came back he would be an intruder. This formulation was shocking and also made instant sense to both parents. It also came in the context of the mother thinking of herself as an exile from her own large, warm family. Often in her partner's absences she and Karen went to stay with the grandparents. Neither had trouble sleeping there.

Karen's sleep problems had started when she was five months old, when her mother went back to work. Karen was happy with the babysitter her mother left her with, but she stopped sleeping at night. Her mother continued breastfeeding Karen and the nights were one long agony of Karen refusing to let go of the breast. When she and her mother came to see me, Karen was ten months old. She and her mother were both beautiful, brightly dressed and smiling, but underneath Karen's mother at least was feeling desperate.

We thought about the possible connection between her lack of sense of herself on her own and Karen's problem of separating from her at night. It seemed reasonable that Karen had protested when her mother left her at five months to go back to work. She felt it was an unsuccessful experiment; it had not really suited either of them and she had given up work as soon as it was possible. Why, however, was Karen still playing out this tragic role of the baby who must never be left? It occurred to her mother that in some subtle way she was letting Karen dramatize her own feeling that it was unbearable to be left. She started setting some limits, which Karen accepted. Most importantly, she decided that in her partner's forthcoming absence she was going to stick it out on her own with Karen for the first week of his trip. We agreed that she could telephone me, but we did not arrange a meeting (I always saw these parents together). She did not phone me and managed to keep the improvement going during this week. My interpretation to her that 'burglars' were in part the representation of her own anger left her feeling much less of a helpless victim. Acknowledging this anger gave her added strength and allowed her to start experimenting with a picture of herself as a competent adult woman who could look after her daughter on her own. This new competence came over convincingly to her daughter, who perhaps now felt safe enough to sleep. Karen was maybe also an example of the inverted attachment described in the next chapter, where babies' wakefulness is produced by feeling responsible for looking after their mothers.

Relationship conflict

There is a huge and growing body of knowledge about the impact on small children of conflict in the home. I cannot do this disturbing subject justice here, but it is vital for parents and professionals to know that growing up in a family where your caregiver is frightening or frightened is damaging in a number of important ways (see Kitzmann et al., 2003, for a review and Lieberman et al., 2015, for a guide to intervention). The impact is formative (Balbernie, 2018). On the whole, parents underestimate the levels of conflict that children have been exposed to. Caught up in it themselves, they can often assume children are less aware than they are – in fact they are usually hypervigilant and dysregulated. They are frightened and helpless, and of course it can cause sleep problems. As well as overt rows and shouting, much more subtle signs of relationship discord are also noticeable to babies and young children in a way that parents deny or do not realize. A major part of children's world is the awareness of their parents' emotions, and they tune in from a very young age. The same formative mutuality that we saw earlier establishing psychobiological patterns in a beneficial relationship works against them here.

We have seen, too, how an intimate relationship with the baby's father is one of the protective factors for a mother against depression. If this is difficult and conflicted, she is more vulnerable to depression. The baby then experiences his mother's uneasy state of mind and also his parents' inability to be close to each other. This can make the world feel like an unsafe place in which it is hard to find the comfort of sleep.

Single parents

Single parents are particularly vulnerable when there is no one easily available to support them. Many parents in this situation are also aware that they are unsure whether they really want their small child to go off to bed and leave them alone. The parent may be torn between needing a respite from a child's demands and dreading loneliness. It may be that difficulties in a child going off to bed may be an unconscious protest by both child and parent about the missing parent who is not there to help and that perhaps what both are doing is keeping a place open for this absent parent.

One family illustrated, albeit dramatically, some of the problems of single-parent families. Just before the summer holiday a five-year-old girl, Dawn, and her eight-months-pregnant mother were referred to me. Dawn was not sleeping and was refusing to go to school. Dawn's father had left her mother some years before, and the expected baby's father had just left after beating up the mother violently.

In the first session I got Dawn's mother to tell me some of this story in front of her. I listened and commented that Dawn was also listening, while she played with toys. I then asked about Dawn's sleeping difficulties and her mother told me of her reluctance to go to sleep and of her nightmares. I talked about what I thought was Dawn's worry about her mother after all the dreadful experiences. Dawn listened carefully. I then asked Dawn herself to tell me of her recurrent nightmare. She crossed the room, stood in front of me and told it to me at great length. I had not become attuned to her speech and could not understand anything she said.

However, it was obvious that her mother could; she was listening as avidly as Dawn had earlier listened to her. I solemnly said that the dream was very frightening and that Dawn should tell her mother every morning what her dreams had been about.

Next week they reported to me that there had been no nightmares. Dawn had gone to bed easily each night and slept well. That week Dawn told me in vivid detail of the time the mother's boyfriend had smashed up the flat. Mother told me that she had not been able to get Dawn to talk about it at all before. I said it seemed to need an outside person to help them both talk about such things. Possibly, Dawn and her mother may have used me not just as an outside listener but as a missing father. We talked about Dawn staying home from school to look after her mother and about how bossy she had needed to become. When I once said to her that she was a little girl and that she didn't decide what happened, that Mummy decided, she said to me, 'No, you decide'. How frightening to be experienced as in control when you are five, and how relieved Dawn seemed to be that I was someone who could take charge.

Mothers returning to work

Mothers may also have difficulties in setting boundaries when they go back to work. They and their babies may actually need more time together to become reunited after the day's separation, but this can merge into a guilty reluctance to face the baby's feelings about being put down. One professional mother found that her one-year-old boy, Henry, was having great difficulty in sleeping, when she started back at work. She then realized that one problem was how she separated from him in the daytime. She had been taking him to the childminder, waiting until he was happily settled and playing and then slipping out of the room without saying goodbye to him. This mother had gone back to work reluctantly and found the separation from her little boy very painful. She realized she was saving herself the pain of saying goodbye to him during the day but had to have the confrontation with him at night instead. When she managed to let him know in the mornings that she was going away, he was able to make his protest to her at the appropriate time and not displace it to the evenings. He also perhaps felt more generally secure, by always knowing when his mother was leaving him and when she was not. With this settled between them his mother was able to look at her feelings about leaving him and found them to be more complex than she had imagined. She had previously not owned that *she* was leaving her son; she had thought the *job* was taking her away from him. Once she had worked out that her son perceived her as leaving him, she became more able to feel this herself. She took the responsibility for the separation and became more able to enjoy her job, while still regretting the time away from her son.

Another mother returning to work found herself with a different version of this problem. Coming back home after a day's separation from her baby and toddler, she found herself puzzling about how hard it seemed to be to cuddle them and talk to them. It was easy to do things for them – cook their supper, get the bath ready, even sit down and look at a book with them – but it always seemed as though there had to be something else to relate to the children through. She could not just physically touch and play with them. She then realized that this extended to the perfunctory way she put them to bed. Thinking all this over, she decided that feeling and showing the children that she knew she mattered to them most seemed to make the separation of the day more painful. If books and toys came first, then the babyminder could provide these just as well as her. When she began to acknowledge that it really was painful to be away from her children through the day, she could have a reunion that was more satisfying for them all. Bedtime became more of a time for cuddles and games and both children started to sleep better.

Perhaps the greatest stress for working mothers is not having the freedom to attune exclusively to the baby's sleep rhythms but having also to be subject to the alarm clock. Mother and baby have the problem of working out a sleep/wake rhythm with limited time available to them to do it. Several mothers have told me that the prospect of going back to work has broken in to their experience of the early weeks, even when they were actually able to be full-time with their babies. They were not able to be totally in the present because of the future separation looming. Brazelton (1988) has found similarly that in a prenatal interview when parents anticipate the pressures of having to return to work 'too early', they guard against talking about the future baby as a person or about themselves as parents. They talk instead about the concrete problems of timetables and finding substitute care for the baby. He suggests that they are already defending themselves against too intense an attachment because of the pain of separating prematurely from the new baby. Brazelton implies that the impending return to work robs parents and baby of some intimacy ahead of the actual separation. He cites three months as being 'too early', but I have seen parents suffer with later dates for the return to work.

This gives us an interesting glimpse into the way time is experienced by mothers and babies together. Freud has said that the unconscious is timeless. It seems as though the experience of the early weeks of babyhood needs to be timeless and thus infinite to be fully enjoyed by both mother and baby. Just as, in memory, the summers of our childhood seem to be endless, so mother and baby need to share a 'timeless time' together. If they are able to have this, then the mother can also, as Stern and Winnicott show, look at her baby and imagine him growing into future stages of development.

When a separation that seems premature is imminent, mothers often seem unable to comprehend the phases and cycles of needing to be close and the ability to move apart that they and the baby might otherwise naturally have. Most important, they may attribute separation from the baby as only due to the job that takes them away. Put outside their relationship, there is no way to absorb it and deal with it as part of self and baby starting to move away from each other.

Gerhardt (2004) describes the difficult and complex nature of this whole area and does not shy away from the huge responsibilities of parenting, especially given the mutual regulation we have looked at between mother and baby of many important physiological and emotional systems, laying a secure foundation for the future. She acknowledges too the struggle for women to establish themselves outside the home in a variety of workplaces and resists the notion of blame. There is also the question of a wider social and economic context that means women are often not in a position to choose to stay at home, even if they would prefer to.

There is some debate about whether working leads to a lower incidence of depression in mothers. Brown and Harris (1978) have suggested that it does. However, Moss and Plewis (1977) dispute the beneficial effects for mothers of going out to work:

> In our study no such positive relationship [of an increase in self-esteem] was observed. This may be because the experience of employment, and therefore the protection it affords through supporting a sense of self-esteem, varies among women. Data from our study, for instance, suggests that women employed full-time in manual jobs are less likely to be satisfied with their employment experience than those employed part-time, especially in non-manual jobs.
>
> (p. 649)

This job satisfaction of women with part-time work bears out evidence (Newell, 1992) that mothers want both to be able to attend to their babies and to have some work outside the home. Although there was no significant relationship between employment and distress, there was a connection between distress and the desire to start work expressed by women at home full-time at the time of the survey. Ginsberg (1976) showed that women with conflicting feelings about being full-time mothers were four times as likely to have been prescribed sedatives, tranquillizers and other similar medication in the previous year as those who experienced no such conflict. It should also be taken into account that depressed women are less likely to be able to organize themselves into getting a job – the ones at work are therefore more likely not to have been depressed *before* seeking work.

Lozoff et al. (1985) have given unaccustomed maternal separation as a cause of sleep problems – that is, the mother's return to work may cause distress to babies rather than the family routine of her being at work over a period of time. Likewise, the mother's unaccustomed absence in hospital having a new baby also causes sleep disturbance. Zuckerman et al. (1987) did not find a significant difference in sleep problems where mother was regularly at work or away during the day (or night). On the other hand, Giorgis et al. (1987) found that 60 percent of babies with sleep problems had working mothers, compared with 41 percent of babies without such problems who had working mothers.

The conflicts for working mothers are often and variously described in terms of the opposing pull between work and home and the pain of being separated from a baby weighed in the balance with economic necessity or professional ambition.

But something more serious and far-reaching has been missed in such an account of the debate.

Stern (1985) describes the process by which mother and baby become attuned to each other. He describes the minute steps of mutual recognition and adjustment which build up to this state between them. He also describes the various stages of development of the baby's own self (see Chapter 7). Klein, Anna Freud and Winnicott do something similar in their own various psychoanalytic languages. My suggestion is that going through these stages is as crucial psychologically for the mother as for the baby. She is not simply enabling something to happen for the baby; she is also going through an integrating process in her own right, for herself, finishing a cycle that starts with conception. If she has to be absent from the baby for more than a few hours a day, or has an inflexible timetable outside the home that takes no account of herself with the baby, then this process is interfered with. This is nothing to do with the rights or wrongs of working or not, it is simply a description of what the mother will miss, to the degree that she is absent during the first year.

What the mother may feel cheated of is a triple process:

1   working out with the baby his regulation of his own physiological states;
2   witnessing the baby's own process of integration;
3   physically and emotionally absorbing and working through her own experience of labour, birth, lactation and the restarting of the menstrual cycle *in the presence of the baby*.

To give a small example: the postnatal six weeks check-up is no doubt arranged for administrative economy, but I suggest that, as it is often performed for both mother and baby by the same doctor at the same time, it is also of emotional significance to both mother and baby. It acts as a confirmation of the interconnection between mothers' and babies' states of being.

Housing conditions

Turning to external conditions, I see many families who are badly housed and at times have to remind myself that there is some evidence that bad housing does not necessarily in itself create emotional problems in children. It is certainly one aspect of childhood adversity that cumulatively has a seriously negative impact on a child's life (Felitti et al., 1998). This impact is buffered or not through the child's relationships – under pressure from the effect of these difficulties upon the parents' state of mind and capacity to cope. What I see is that anger and stress in parents brought about by their bad living conditions make it difficult for them to bring up their children in these conditions. This anger is often constructive, the only effective weapon that might change something for them, but the fury in the family and the impotent waiting for outside bureaucracy to find a solution can be extraordinarily stressful and make it very difficult for emotional issues to be dealt with effectively within the family unit. These include the setting of limits for sleeping.

One such family lived in a one-bedroomed flat, with parents and the two boys sleeping in this one bedroom. The mother came to see me about the sleep problems of the two-year-old. This family had been promised the house next door, but squatters had got in and the council seemed to be delaying evicting them. This mother was so brimming over with the need to tell me each time we met of this injustice and of the outrageous behaviour of the squatters that she was unable to think about how, in the meantime, to calm down her two-year-old. It is really a moot point as to what is the most effective survival behaviour in such circumstances. Is it making life more tolerable in the short term to change what it is in one's own power to do within the family or is it essential to keep looking outwards at what must be changed externally, even at the cost of keeping the status quo of the problem within the family?

In this vein I was sceptical about the referral of another family by their doctor. The referral letter mentioned their harassment by a neighbour who had just moved out. I said to the doctor that I doubted whether this was a family who would have the capacity to work on their problems. I was therefore pleasantly surprised when I met two-year-old Alex and his parents. They poured out a horrifying story of a mad neighbour in the house next door who abused them verbally and physically, threatening Alex and his mother and implying that she would set her ferocious-looking Alsatian dog on them. After the relief of having me listen to all this seriously, they then said that they thought Alex's sleeping problem was also their own problem; it had started before this neighbour moved in. With this acknowledgement there was a chance to work on the idea of how much of the trouble was caused by the horrendous external problems and how much from within the family and their intergenerational history.

The neighbour had now moved away so we looked in detail at the present family situation. Alex's father's job in a hospital obliged him to work late on many evenings; Alex clamoured to stay up until his father came home and then wanted to stay up playing with him. Alex's mother said she was exhausted, with no chance to rest in the evening. As we talked, it emerged that in fact she was in two minds whether she wanted Alex in bed or whether she needed his company in the evenings. We talked about whether, although Alex's mother backed her partner's choice of profession, she was angry about him being out till late so often. Perhaps Alex's protest was partly on her behalf.

Talking about all this cleared the air and the parents decided that Alex's mother would put him firmly to bed in the evening, telling him he would see his father in the morning. They decided to give Alex a special decorated night-light, in case he was frightened on his own in his room. After only a fortnight of this they told me the nights were greatly improved. Alex settled to sleep in the evening and was awake only once in the night.

The problem now was that Alex's eating habits were worrying them. He ate very little and they worried about his low weight gain. From his mother's description of what food she gave Alex, it sounded as though she herself was a 'faddy' eater and I commented on how thin she was and asked *her* weight. She confirmed that she did have an eating problem herself. I asked when it had started and she recalled that it was soon after the accidental death of her elder sister, when she herself was ten. I pondered on the thought that she might have felt she did not have the right to live, that is, eat to keep herself alive, when her sister was dead. She then revealed that her sister had been schizophrenic and ill for some years before her death.

I felt we had come full circle to the content of the original referral. Here perhaps was a key to how to put externally based and internal precipitating factors together. I said that although her fear of the mad neighbour was based on external reality, the degree to which she was shaken by it, to the extent of being unable to leave the house without her partner escorting her, was produced by the fear of madness within herself and within her family. This acknowledged fear of madness within made her powerless to deal with the actual madness existing outside in this neighbour.

Another example, albeit much less extreme, of displacing feelings from inside the family on to neighbours is when parents tell me they have been unable to experiment with letting their baby cry for a little while, because of 'what the neighbours will say'. Sometimes, unfortunately, it is only too true that intolerant neighbours complain about the most innocuous noises coming from young families, and the inhibitions resulting from this may be one of the causes of trouble in sleep. However, it is often worth questioning whether the disapproval from next door, real as it may be, is not also a displacement of the parents' own inability to bear some crying; or again the neighbour may also represent a fierce critical aspect of the parents themselves that feels they are getting their child care wrong. This can be similar to parents' use of professionals' opinions or of 'advice' in books on bringing up children, referred to in Chapter 2, as a way of displacing their own opinions on to others.

We have looked at how parents can support and enhance each other's relationship with their baby, and also at how external stress can put pressure on family relationships and exacerbate any difficulties. One thread that has gone through this chapter is that of disowning an aspect of the self, a part of one's character, and attributing it either to another person or to external circumstances. The result is an impoverishment of the self and a restriction of possible action.

Chapter 12

Disturbed sleep as a psychosomatic problem

It is clear from the neuroscience and development research of the last three decades just how interconnected are states of mind and body (Schore, 1994; Perry et al., 1995; Pally, 1998). Psychosomatic disturbances are the body's expression of emotional conflict. We have seen how when things go well, a regulating connection arises between the baby's mind and body and the subtly attuned responses of the parent; a 'protoconversation', like a duet (Trevarthen, 2005), which helps the baby to establish her own regulated sleep and other rhythms in her physiological and emotional development. In particular, we have seen how the relationship between mother and baby, including satisfying physical needs like feeding and sleeping, is the ground on which emotional resilience is built. Intimacy is established, and from this grows a feeling of security and the baby's ability to be an individual, feeling herself to be separate in relation to someone who goes on knowing about her and protecting her. When something goes wrong in this process, perhaps particularly in the rhythms of mother and baby being together and apart, then something often also goes badly wrong with the baby's experience of her own body and her feelings about it. Psychosomatic – mind/body – symptoms are one aspect of this. Sleep disturbances are basically a psychosomatic problem.

Psychosomatic disturbances

Fain and Kreisler (1970) studied babies suffering from serious psychosomatic disturbances in the first months of life, and found one group of infants only able to sleep if rocked continually in their mothers' arms, otherwise suffering from almost total insomnia. The suggestion is that these mothers have partially failed in their function as a protective shield against exciting stimuli, paradoxically because they have overexercised the protective function. Instead of developing a primitive form of psychic activity akin to dreaming, which permits most babies to sleep peacefully after feeding, these babies require the mother herself to be the guardian of sleep. There is here a breakdown of the capacity to recreate a good internal state of being in symbolic form. The researcher's observations led them to conclude that these babies do not have a *mère satisfaisante* ('satisfying mother'), but a *mère calmante* ('tranquillizing mother'). The mother, because of her own problems, cannot permit her baby to find a way of getting to sleep without continual contact with her. Winnicott's transitional space is missing, and with it the capacity to imagine, and to play, or dramatize feelings.

McDougall (1986) examines psychosomatic conditions and their origins and shows how psychosomatic conditions can arise through being out of touch with feelings. She uses the term *alexithymia* from the Greek *a-lexis-thumos*, meaning *without-word-heart*. It refers to the state of patients who have difficulty both in describing their affective state and in distinguishing one affect from another. They were often babies whose mothers did not put into words their feelings. She writes that emotions are connecting links, being both psyche (mind) and soma (body). One of their functions is appraisal. They alert the mind – or in the case of the baby, the parent's mind – to situations requiring readiness and mental action. These ideas are in tune with Panksepp, whose work integrates neuroscience and physiology. He alerts us to the signalling function of emotions:

> Emotional feelings (affects) are intrinsic values that inform animals how they are faring in the quest to survive. The various positive affects indicate that animals are returning to 'comfort zones' that support survival, and negative affects reflect 'discomfort zones' that indicate that animals are in situations that may impair survival. They are ancestral tools for living.
>
> (2010, p. 533)

If these signals do not achieve mental representation in the mind, originally the parent's, then the emotional arousal runs the risk of only alerting the body, which is likely to respond with psychosomatic dysfunctioning, since the soma, following its own specific biological law, will frequently react as though defending itself against *physical* rather than psychological dangers. We may all at times 'fail to contain and reflect upon the experiences that besiege us' (McDougall, 1986, p. 100) and may then be likely to fall ill. Infants tend to show conflict in psychosomatic terms, and the fundamental functions of breathing, digestion, evacuation or sleeping can be affected by conflicts that arise from personal and emotional relationships.

Failure to regulate psychic pain causes not only psychosomatic illness but can also lead to a personality organized around addiction. Individuals plunge into *action* to dispel emotional pain, because the capacity to contain and process it mentally has not been relationally developed at the optimal time. Drugs, alcohol and addictive use of sexuality are all examples of action symptoms. The temporary relief offered by addictive behaviour allows the basic psychic conflict to be dissociated. Without relational mediation of emotional signals, the dysregulation stays in the body and presents as psychosomatic illness.

The addictive personality arises partly from an early failure of containment (Bion, 1962). This is the process by which a baby's emotional states are taken in by the mother, mentally digested, reflected upon and returned in a more manageable form, named, and with added understanding, which in itself moderates distress. There is a clear link here with development research on emotional regulation (Gianino & Tronick, 1988). There is also a link with Winnicott's ideas about transitional phenomena. Winnicott (1971) has shown how the ability to use transitional phenomena follows from internalization of this quality in the early mother-baby relationship. The use of a transitional object then itself allows the process of internalization to gather speed, as the mother sanctions the use of a symbol in place of her actual body, something the mothers of the insomniac babies (Fain & Kreizler, 1970) seemed unable to do.

As an infant's earliest external reality is the mother's physical presence, the baby is profoundly affected by the mother's emotional state, including feelings the mother herself is not consciously aware of. The way in which she relates to her child's body will influence his somatic functioning, vitality and affectivity. Many of McDougall's (1986) psychosomatic patients talk of their bodies or their bodily functions as though they did not really possess them. It seems as though they still unconsciously belong to the mother, who could not accept distance or separation. Children of such mothers may also conceive of their emotions as not being truly their own possessions but their mother's.

By putting these ideas about psychosomatic disturbance, emotional regulation, containment and transitional phenomena together, we can see how they fit in with sleep problems in infants. Firstly, some parents are unable to divest themselves of being the only means of getting their baby to sleep. They feel they can only be the 'guardians of sleep' for their baby when they are physically present; the baby has no chance to internalize them in their absence. McDougall (1986) shows how the parents she describes are able to deal with physical actions, while ignoring emotions and experiences. They are *mères calmantes*, or mothers who foster a concretely addictive, rather than an imaginatively processing, state of mind. Next, we see how a failure to contain, regulate and process a baby's emotional states leaves him unable to self-regulate as he grows. Thirdly, it seems that the child's ability to deal with physical sensations and pain is equally impoverished by the failure to help the child differentiate his experiences from those of his mother. The joke 'A sweater is a garment a child puts on when his mother feels cold' comes to mind. Here, there is no exchange about whether the child himself feels cold. The implication of this for sleep problems is that we may have a baby who cannot trust his own bodily signals to know whether he wants to go to sleep and has to check back continually with his mother. It is worth surmising also that, if such a baby is sleepless in the night, his mother is unable to communicate a wish of her own to sleep and hence provide an atmosphere of sleep.

People who work shifts and have to sleep during the day often report the difficulty of changing their sleep rhythms, of having to sleep at the wrong time, when everyone else is awake. For most of us, the background to being asleep is being part of a sleeping world. One of the special pleasures of adolescence is overturning such general perceptions, going to bed and getting up at quite different times from parents and other boring, ordinary people. A baby wakeful during the night is unable to join in with the shared perception of the ordinary way of things – or has not been offered it. Of vital importance, too, in connection with night-time patterns, is the way the mother relates to the child's father. This influences what she expects of her child and, particularly at night, whether she gives priority to her relationship with the father or with the child.

Disturbed attachment

Moore (1989) explains the origin of some psychosomatic symptoms in terms of disturbed attachment. When attachment develops normally, a child feels protected by his attachment figure and can sleep within the security of this relationship. When the attachment system is not switched off because of continuing threat, the child is left feeling anxious, and this in turn has a damaging effect on the ability to sleep. This anxiety-related sleep dysfunction includes a reduction in the deepest restorative sleep stages and in REM sleep, with its integrating dream function. A failure in the protective role of an attachment figure thus plays a key role: the deeply unconscious state which occurs during Stage 4 sleep renders the individual vulnerable to external threat. Children perceiving themselves to be in danger cannot risk falling deeply asleep.

McDonald et al. (1976) have shown how unusual

electrodermal storming during slow-wave (Stage 4) sleep is *positively* correlated with anxiety and stress and *negatively* correlated with *amount* of Stage 3–4 sleep . . . if one function of storming is to reduce the amount of Stage 3–4 sleep this might have survival value in the presence of environmental threat.

(p. 128, author's italics)

We can thus see how secure attachment plays a part in allowing sleep with its restorative functions, and how disturbances in attachment connect with disturbed sleep. Threats can be surmounted if there is sufficient protection for a child or an adult. In contrast to this, a child subject to stressful or traumatic events without such protection will feel chronic anxiety and often a pervasive sense of helplessness and depression.

Following Bowlby's (1973) insights about attachment, Moore (1989) argues that where parents are themselves anxious about the availability of their own attachment figures, they may unconsciously invert the normal parent-child relationship and require that the child be the parent figure to the mother. We saw earlier how this was the case for Dawn. In cases of inverted attachment roles, it is the child's responsibility to remain available to the mother; it is the mother or attachment figure who might wander off or be hurt, abandoning the child. Thus a child in this situation has the primary responsibility for remaining aware of the environment, including the whereabouts of the mother. Deep sleep precludes any awareness of the environment and might be experienced as threatening to the attachment bond.

In normal attachment, mothers of young children do not go 'off duty' during the night. They sleep lightly (McKenna, 1986) and are conscious of not wanting to fall into deep sleep. This wish is so strong that even depressed mothers given anti-depressant medication do not usually take it, because they cannot risk being unable to hear their child in the night (Pound et al., 1985). This being so, the normal readiness of mothers to wake up when their child needs them is echoed in the young child who, in the reverse process, cannot sleep deeply when he feels he is responsible for his mother.

The inverted attachment need not always seem to be morbid, however. A.A. Milne in the poem 'Disobedience' (1924) describes for posterity the three-year-old in charge of his mother.

> James James Morrison Morrison Weatherby George Dupree
> Took great care of his Mother
> Though he was only three.
> James James said to his Mother,
> 'Mother', he said, said he,
> 'You must never go down to the end of the town if you don't go down with me.'

His mother disobeyed these instructions and 'hasn't been heard of since'. We can see how the child learning to move away from his attachment figure (James is pictured on his tricycle) needs to be sure that she will not move away from him. The reasonable desire for security can change imperceptibly to a tyrannical demand that she remain available and interested only in him.

One of the characteristics of more disturbing forms of this inversion may be a discrepancy between the affect of the mother and her external behaviour. The mother who comes into the child's bedroom ostensibly to soothe him may in fact herself be angry and disturbed, so that she has to be calmed by the child. The child feels anxious both on his own account and on behalf of his mother. His anxieties are not dealt with and a vicious circle may be set up. The unmet needs of the child make it hard for him to sleep. He has disturbed Stage 4 sleep that may lead to increased somatization, which may mean more night waking. The cycle can be endless.

Shining another light on these links between sleep difficulties and disturbances in attachment, a study (McNamara et al., 2003) found that infants with insecure-resistant attachments – those who are preoccupied with seeking out contact with the caregiver – are more likely to have clinically significant sleep problems than those with insecure-avoidant attachments, who are adapted to a distance-maintaining stance. Researchers looked at the interesting role of REM sleep in terms of the emotional link with the mother. It activates hormonal circuits that support parent-child bonding systems, which in turn facilitate proximity-seeking behaviours. Thus the babies need to fall asleep to get to REM; however, their relatively high REM activation levels eventually awaken them. This makes for the paradoxical sleep pattern of insecure-resistant infants, who have no difficulty falling asleep but then a high frequency of long night-waking episodes. The study concludes that indicators of REM activation levels such as night wakings vary with attachment status.

Disturbed attachment relationships may thus have bodily repercussions, depending on a child's attachment status and the kind of sleep that is compromised or prioritized. There may be a link here with asthma and allergies. Kales et al. (1970) found that compared to normal children of the same ages, asthmatic children had a significant reduction in Stage 4 sleep. In the sample studied, no asthma attacks occurred during the first third of the night (i.e. during Stage 4 sleep). It appears, however, that these children were unable to relax into *enough* deep Stage 4 sleep, which might itself have provided a protective factor against the asthma. This leads us to the fascinating question of the function of Stage 4 sleep, which is perhaps best answered by default. What are the results of this loss?

One finding is that it is during the deepest sleep, in the initial period of Stage 4, that a significant percentage of daily growth hormone is normally produced. Thus children who have failed to thrive in abusive homes, that is, situations where they have not been safe, have started to grow when removed to foster homes, where their sleep pattern changes. This does not of course mean that all low-growth children are in unsafe home situations, but it may be that many low-growth children have needed to be 'vigilant' and have not had enough Stage 4 sleep.

Recent research findings reveal that important restorative immune system functions occur during slow-wave sleep and not during REM or lighter stages of sleep. A major repercussion of insufficient Stage 4 sleep is an impaired immune system. Indeed, Guedeney and Kreisler (1987) found that half the children referred to them for severe sleep problems had associated diseases, such as infantile colic, allergy and otitis. Crucially, Guedeney and Kreisler did not feel that colic and so on *caused* the sleep problem but that they were *associated* with it. We might therefore conclude that the disturbed sleep itself had interfered with immunity in such a way that these children were vulnerable to a number of other disorders. This is a good example of how, as we have seen in this chapter, mind and body influence each other to produce psychosomatic conditions.

We have touched in this chapter on disturbed attachment, and I would like to note here that there is not scope in this book to fully take up the issue of child abuse and the long-term damaging impact on children of all its forms (see Glaser, 2000, 2005). We are dealing here on the whole with more everyday sleep and relational disturbance, for the parents who consult me about their babies' sleep problems seem to have had less dire instances of family dysfunction on their minds. However, I do think that some families coming to see me only once, and failing to turn up again without further explanation, may have been worried that I would 'discover' something they were either not ready to talk about or felt that I was not the person to tell. When families have broken off prematurely, I have sometimes had an intuition and shared with their doctor, nurse or health visitor my concerns about possible sexual abuse. These serious concerns are best tackled jointly among professionals. It is important to be aware that some of the more bizarre sleeping arrangements in families, reported as an aspect of a child's sleep problem, may be in fact symptoms of more troubling forms of family dysfunction.

Chapter 13

Mothers' mental health and wellbeing

How do mothers' own physical and mental health conditions relate to their children's wellbeing and sleep? Research clearly shows the vital importance for the baby's future development of parent-infant mutual regulation (Gianino & Tronick, 1988) and responsive synchrony (Feldman, 2007) in the earliest months of life. The lack of this lively mutuality seems to be key in understanding early psychopathology and particularly sleep disorders. We will look here at how maternal states of mind and health can have this negative impact, and in the next chapter we will turn to aspects of the baby's physiology and particular needs that can present challenges to this communicative musicality (Malloch & Trevarthen, 2009).

Perinatal anxiety and sleeplessness

It has become very clear that a mother's state of mind and wellbeing or otherwise during pregnancy affect both mother and baby after the birth. Of eighteen cases of severe infant sleep disorders dating from the early weeks, seven mothers had had serious health issues (four of which were a threat to the pregnancy) and nine others a noticeable depression during pregnancy (Guedeney & Kreisler, 1987). Interestingly, they suggest that mothers themselves attribute the cause of their baby's sleep disorder to their own state before her birth. They also show that anxiety during pregnancy is related to a high level of activity in the baby after birth and to the onset of sleep disorders. There is a great deal of research showing that babies are susceptible to the impact of stress-induced raised cortisol levels in the womb, which in turn affects a number of other developing biochemical systems, potentially having a long-term impact on the establishing of regulating rhythms (Gerhardt, 2004, p. 56). These mutual rhythms are vital for a baby's wellbeing and overall development.

In this context, there is a clear connection between the vulnerability of mothers to distressing or disruptive symptoms and their babies' tendency to very early sleep problems. As we have seen in Chapters 4 and 5, the weeks after birth show that the attainment of sleep patterns is a sensitive balance of regulation of the baby's neurophysiological states with the emotional interaction between mother and baby. If a mother has a somatic disorder during pregnancy, her physical condition may affect her emotional response to her baby or, reversing this, she may be converting her emotional ambivalence about the baby into a somatic form. The chain of bodily expressions of conflict is then passed on to the baby, who, like any baby, adapts to his own particular social and relational context. He responds to his mother's ambivalence and to her way of expressing it and learns from her that emotions are expressed in bodily form.

Some mothers feel 'used up' by the foetus and exploited by its residence in their bodies. Such a mother might come to terms with her baby after its birth and feel that she has enough reserves for it after all, or she might continue with her feeling of being drained by her baby's needs. In any case we could guess that, just as the babies of mothers who had disorders threatening their pregnancy have early sleep problems, so the babies of mothers who feel drained by the pregnancy might also be among those with sleep difficulties.

We saw in Chapter 7 how the events of the birth itself can cause difficulties in the relationship between mother and baby and to sleep problems. Adverse events during the birth, or a very long labour, can lead to increased night waking.

The mother's own ability to sleep is also significant, and insomnia in the mother can be one of the earliest signs of postnatal depression (Karacan & Williams, 1970). They note that insomnia starts before the onset of the psychosis and that clinical symptoms first appear during this period of sleep disturbance, or 'miserable sleeplessness', to use a classic colourful term (Savage, 1896).

This sleeplessness is not only an early symptom of postnatal depression but also itself increases the mother's vulnerability to such a depression. The loss of sleep and its restorative function, particularly of Stage 4 and REM dreaming sleep, means that the restructuring necessary to take in the physiological and emotional upheaval of giving birth is affected. Sleep helps an integrating process; loss of sleep means the mother is more vulnerable to a feeling of disintegration. The lack of sleep also makes it more difficult for her to relate to the baby and impairs the process by which mothers can usually feel themselves recovering from the birth through the emotional interchange with their baby. Insomnia is thus both the result and a cause of serious postpartum depression. I will turn now to look at the impact of parental mental illness upon the developing child, and then focus particularly on postnatal depression.

Parents' mental illness

Parental psychiatric symptoms negatively affect a whole range of adverse infant outcomes:

> First, there may be a direct pernicious impact on the child of exposure to the parental disorder. Second, there may be an indirect impact via the effect of the parental disorder on interpersonal behaviour in general and parenting in particular. Finally, the impact may be via third factor variables, such as the social adversity commonly associated with psychiatric disorder, or genetic

or constitutional factors. Depression arising in the postnatal period could have an impact on infant development via each of these causal pathways. The infant's extreme dependency on their caretaker, their sensitivity to interpersonal contacts, and the fact that, in the great majority of cases, the mother constitutes the infant's primary environment in the first postnatal months, make the question of the impact of depression occurring at this time one of particular importance.

(Murray & Cooper, 1997, p. 99)

Stern (1985) gives the example of a 'paranoid schizophrenic' mother who overprotects her ten-month-old daughter inappropriately. He describes a visit by the mother and baby when the baby was asleep as they arrived.

> The mother gently took her sleeping baby and began to lay her on the bed so she would stay asleep. The mother did this with enormous concentration that left us closed out. After she had ever-so-slowly eased the baby's head onto the bed, she took one of the baby's arms, which was awkwardly positioned, and with her two hands carefully guided it to a feather-like landing on the bed, as though the arm were made of eggshells and the bed made of marble.
>
> (p. 205)

Stern shows how this mother, by being over-careful, was reacting against harmful impulses in herself. Although in the instance witnessed this over-careful handling did allow the baby to remain asleep, we can see how puzzling this sort of behaviour might be to a baby building up its picture of the world from its mother's cues.

Similarly, in looking at dreams and nightmares in Chapter 6, we saw how a schizophrenic father's violent and unpredictable behaviour led his infant son Jerry to suffer from night terrors. These appeared to be a direct result of traumatic attacks that frightened the child and could not be made sense of by the child or his mother. The trauma of the father's violent and chaotic behaviour inevitably impacted on the child's sleep, which, as we have seen throughout the book, is a function of the flow of mutual physiological and psychological regulation between parents and child.

Postnatal depression

In a prevalent example of the disruption of this flow, there is an established and mutually reinforcing link between infant sleep problems and postnatal depression (Hiscock & Wake, 2001). Postnatal depression is so widespread that at one time it was thought of as a 'natural' reaction to birth, perhaps due to hormonal changes. At least one in ten mothers experience depression after giving birth to a baby (Cox et al., 1982). It seems now as though its severity can be partly a reactive response either to trauma or to adverse social situations, that mothers without support are vulnerable to it and that providing support greatly helps recovery from it. Henshaw

(2003) reviews connections and distinctions between the 'baby blues' experienced by many women in the first few days after giving birth and more severe cases of postnatal depression. Although these two categories overlap, there are also important differentiations to be made. Henshaw has shown how women are differently vulnerable to longer-term depressive symptoms; 'blues and dysphoria during pregnancy, a past history of depression, neuroticism and premenstrual depression' (2003, p. 33) are all risk factors. Whether or not there will be subsequent serious postnatal depression, she suggests, is apparent by eight days after birth. Postnatal depression can be seen partly as a reaction to the event of giving birth and to having a vulnerable new baby to care for and partly to pre-existing vulnerability in the mother. She sees sleep deprivation as an important factor. It can also include the reaction to the situation of being a mother, possibly isolated, at home. Depression in mothers of pre-school children may include those mothers who have not yet recovered from traumatic reactions to giving birth and can also include new sufferers who represent a response over time to adverse conditions.

Difficult births may provoke postnatal depression, by leaving a mother feeling shocked, upset and inadequate at not having given birth 'properly'. I have previously suggested that difficult births often lead to sleep problems in the baby. One of the routes by which this happens is that depression ensuing from the birth experience makes it harder for the mother to tune into and be in touch with the baby's sleep rhythms.

Brown and Harris (1978) have argued that depression is a social phenomenon. They found that at least a quarter of working-class women with children living in London suffered from a depressive disorder. By contrast, crofters in the Outer Hebrides were apparently practically free of depression, and London middle-class women had a much smaller incidence of depression than had working-class women. They suggest, however, that bad housing and other difficult conditions, which working-class women are more likely to be subject to, are *provoking* agents and not the only cause of depression. Oddly, it seems that more recently, middle-class women with high-status jobs are reporting more depression and might be suffering from the radical change in their life style, both in time away from work and the effect of having moved far from their family.

There is in fact a second set of factors. If a woman does not have an intimate relationship with a partner, one in which she feels she can confide and trust, she is much more likely to break down in the presence of a major life-event or difficulty. Similarly, she is also at greater risk if she has three or more children under 15 at home, is unemployed and lost her mother (but not her father) before the age of 11. We call these *vulnerability factors*, although they can be seen as the presence or absence of protective factors. None are capable of producing depression on their own, but they greatly increase chances of breakdown in the presence of a provoking agent (Brown & Harris, 1978, p. 229).

Some of these vulnerability factors to depression apply particularly to postnatal depression. We have seen earlier (Chapter 10) that the lack of a confiding relationship and the loss of the mother's own mother have an effect on mothering ability.

Other important factors are the impact of being responsible for the life of a vulnerable new baby, the social isolation of many mothers, the low esteem accorded to childrearing and the loss of identity for mothers who have given up their jobs or lost touch with friends at work or friends without babies.

Even though it is clear from Brown and Harris's findings that there are sociological factors determining which mothers may be depressed, it is vital for us to think of each depression as having individual meaning. The content of each mother's depressive thoughts are hers and hers alone. Brown and Harris have cited vulnerability factors, such as the death of a mother, and although this has statistical significance, it is essential to know about the personal route by which such a loss leads to a depression now.

It is also significant that the birth of a baby may itself reawaken feelings about the loss of the mother. The mother's own infantile feelings are stirred up by the experience of her new baby's needs. Mourning needs to be done in various stages through life, and bereavement reactions are provoked at each new life-event, including childbirth. Also relevant are the universal feelings of loss of the unborn baby that are experienced in giving birth to a baby. Sometimes the real baby outside cannot make up for the loss of the 'ideal' baby that belonged only to the mother inside herself. The change from being an individual to being a parent should also not be underestimated as another focus for the feeling of loss.

Time spent by professionals with a vulnerable mother before and after the birth dramatically reduces depression. Current advice around supporting mothers and babies, based on the neuroscience of development, encourages the mother's imagining of her unborn baby. The richness of antenatal maternal representations is significantly linked with the security of the infant's attachment to the parents at one year of age (Benoit et al., 1997). The Family Nurse Partnership model (Olds, 2006), keeping in mind the importance of the antenatal start to the bonding process, works with mothers in adverse circumstances from pregnancy until the child is two years old. Much of this may help to provide what is missing in the mother's own social network. A crucial facet of any help seems to be the opportunity to talk through the details of the baby's birth; the mother often needs to relate this to one of the workers involved in some stage of the pregnancy or the baby's birth, either in antenatal care, labour or postnatal care. The person who listens may equally be the doctor, nurse, midwife or health visitor, but part of the process for the mother of absorbing the experience of labour is facilitated by this narrative.

All mothers may need this chance to talk, but a few are in particular need of it. By noting that a motherless mother-to-be is vulnerable, professionals may be alerted to the fact that it is important to spend time in listening to the mother's experiences. Although this cannot replace the interest of an actual grandmother, there can still be a real possibility for the mother to have a confirmation of herself as a mother from these exchanges with the worker. Talking about the mother that she has lost and her memories of having been mothered herself is particularly valuable. Doing this reminds her of what she has inside herself from her mother to pass on to her baby, as well as allowing her to think about her loss in the context of being a mother herself. This process may also help the mother move on and find a substitute 'mother' in her family, neighbours or friends who will take a continuous interest in her and her baby.

This brings us to the critical effect a mother's postnatal depression may have on her baby. Lozoff et al. (1985), among others, suggest that sleep problems may ensue when the mother is emotionally unresponsive to the baby. I will then turn to look at the nature of a depressed mother's relationship with her baby and try to reconstruct the way in which this influences the baby's sleep.

The effect of postnatal depression on infant development

Murray (1988) explores the effect of postnatal depression on infant development in the context of normal parent-infant interactions during the baby's earliest weeks. At a time when the infant is not yet able to make much use of physical objects, she is captivated by a carer's attentive gaze. Mother and baby spend long periods looking at each other, and each partner's experience of being in relation to the other appears to exist as an end in itself. In pioneering work on early communication between mothers and babies, Trevarthen (1974) recorded and described the reciprocal 'conversations' between mothers and two-month-old babies. A depressed mother's ability to focus, engage in a lively way and hold up her side of the conversation is impaired.

In order to gain some idea of the effects such a difficulty in engaging might have, studies on the effects of contrived disruptions of normal infant-mother couples were carried out, setting up 'perturbations' in ordinary communications between mothers and babies. In one perturbation the mother became still and expressionless for a period of 45 seconds, while continuing to look at her baby; in the second perturbation the timing, not the form, of the mother's acts in relation to the infant's were interfered with, playing them back after an interval of some 30 seconds, so that the infant sees and hears the same maternal behaviour that occurred during the live sequence, but sees it as unrelated to its own act (Murray, 1988, p. 17). Not surprisingly, the babies quickly became disturbed. Thirty seconds of mistiming between a mother and baby is a serious matter. The baby's reaction to being shown a blank-faced (normally responsive) mother was of protest followed by withdrawal, with his gaze averted from the mother's face; the reaction to the replay sequence was puzzlement or confusion.

> The results of perturbation studies show how sensitive two- and three-month-old infants are to the quality of their mother's communication. Infants can not only discriminate subtle variations in maternal behaviour, but their distress when the mother behaves inappropriately and their apparent protests or efforts to solicit communication are also evidence for a strong motivation for the particular forms of interpersonal engagement that mothers spontaneously provide in normal face to face encounters.
>
> (Murray, 1988, p. 179)

Over time, as a result of being with a postnatally depressed mother – who may indeed either have a blank face or mistime her signals to her baby – the baby will devise some kind of behaviour to deal with the mother's inattention. One reaction may be to give up trying to get her attention and instead withdraw, and he may then go on being withdrawn after the mother has recovered from her depression. Mother and baby will therefore continue to be out of touch with each other. We can see how this may then stop them being in touch about sleep rhythms.

It is important to consider depression in the mother not only as a state of mind that impairs her ability to focus on the child. It may be useful sometimes to start the other way round with the hypothesis that some psychologically vulnerable mothers are thrown into a state of depression by their very attempts to focus on their child. To such mothers, the life-and-death communications from a newborn baby, both as direct bodily needs and as emotional signals, are terrifying and unbearable, and some mothers may switch off into a state of not noticing the intensity of the baby's communications. As we have seen, Main et al. (1985) have observed that some mothers cannot notice their babies' signals because they remind them of their own unmet needs as babies. Depression and withdrawal in the mother may sometimes be an extreme version of this inability to notice, because noticing is so painful. We will turn now to experimentally engineered disruptions in contingent connection.

Experimentally induced mother-infant detachment

Papousek and Papousek (1975) have looked at infants' reactions to their mothers' 'incomprehensible' actions. In their study we can see, by default, how important the understandability of each other's behaviour is for mother and baby. The Papouseks looked at sequences of behaviour in which the mother-child interaction became erratic and thus 'incomprehensible' for the child. They analyzed the capacity of four-month-old infants for 'comprehending' their mothers' behaviour and asked the specific question: how do infants react to the deliberate omission from a behaviour chain of an important segment containing key information?

Initially the mother was asked to leave her child six times for 15 seconds each time and to act in the same way she would act at home. All mothers tended to employ similar routines on leaving (making eye contact, verbal repetitions) and on returning they experienced no difficulties in renewing happy contact with their children. In the next part, with a different group of infants, the mother was required to leave her child without any preparations when overhead lights were turned off for 3 seconds, and then to return under the same conditions after 15 seconds.

> This 'incomprehensible' disappearance and reappearance of the mother produced rather conspicuous changes in the child's behavior . . . At first the infant reacted cheerfully to his mother on her return. Although still rather quiet during her absence, after her later reappearance the child gradually rejected the renewal of contact with his mother more and more strongly. Thereafter the

mother's efforts to renew contact only intensified the baby's turning away; in some of these infants such renewals even led to listless or whining rejection of the mother. Control experiments in yet another study showed that the short periods of darkness as such did not produce changes of this type. These experiences surprised the mothers as well as the observer, and we noted with some relief that the children's relationship with their mothers recovered quickly after the experiments ended!

(p. 257)

The Papouseks' study has particular relevance for our study of sleep disturbances in its examination of the result of a mother's unheralded departure in the dark. What it shows is the importance for babies of clear messages about the mother's intentions. The ordinary visual and verbal means mothers ordinarily used communicated an intention to the baby, which appeared to make the absence manageable for him. We could add that it seems as though this prepared absence also contained the idea of the mother's return. Incomprehensible disappearances and reappearances, such as might happen during parental mental illness, destroyed both the infant's cognitive attempts to learn about intention and of course the mother's trustworthiness.

This rather odd little test shows the possible effect on an infant in her own home if her parents are unable to signal their comings and goings to her at night. The problem for the baby may not be so much in being left but in *not knowing* when the parents are going to leave and when, or why, they will return. This reminds us that one very ordinary situation that can lead to sleep problems is when a baby wakes up and finds herself, unprepared, with a babysitter instead of with her parents. After such an experience many babies will wake on subsequent evenings to check who is there and who is not, or they may wake later in the night to see whether their parents have returned.

The effects of maternal depression on a baby's sleep

In their study assessing the effects of a mother's depression on the child, Guedeney and Kreisler (1987) ask, what is more puzzling for the child, the mother's slow responses or her mood disorder and emotional flatness? They suggest that this emotional flatness is an important and painful element in depression, hampering attunement of feelings between mother and child and subsequently damaging the mother's ability to match the infant's own interactional rhythm and thus to understand her sleep rhythm. Tronick et al. (1978) have shown how even a temporary disruption to a mother's sensitive responsiveness, a 'still face', is disturbing to her baby.

Guedeney (1989) contrasts the capacity to understand and respond to the baby with a depressed mother who is preoccupied with fantasies about the baby which get in the way of her being able to perceive the real baby and its needs. Such a mother does not understand her baby's sleep.

Zuckerman et al. (1987) have also identified an association between mothers' depressed feelings and children with sleeping problems, particularly whether children's sleeping difficulties cause mothers to feel depressed or whether mothers' depressed feelings affect their handling of their children, resulting in sleep problems.

> The longitudinal nature of this study allowed us to demonstrate that mothers' depressed feelings do not appear to be a *consequence* of children's sleep problems between eight months and three years of age. This conclusion is reached because of the similarities of newly identified maternal depression at three years whether or not the child had a sleep problem at eight months.
>
> (Zuckerman et al., 1987, p. 669)

Anecdotally I know of instances of mothers who do claim to have become ill and depressed because of their babies' sleeplessness. It is, however, possible that some of these were actually suffering from undiagnosed postnatal depression early on and did not really notice at the time whether their general feeling of *malaise* started before or after their baby kept them awake at night.

Zuckerman et al. (1987) suggest that depressed mothers may be awake more often themselves and are thus more aware of their children's night waking, whether the child cries or not. They also surmise that some mothers may have been depressed but had recovered by the time of their study of babies at eight months. Thus unrecorded depressions might have influenced some other of the sleep problems seen at eight months. Looking at cause and effect, they suggest that stressful life-events do not necessarily affect children directly but rather through the impact on their mother's emotional world and consequent changes in the way she is able to take care of them.

In relation to this, it is worth noting that Pound et al. (1985) have studied depressed mothers and their children and came across a group of depressed mothers whose sensitivity to their children's needs did *not* seem to be affected by their depression. In spite of their problems, these mothers were able to enjoy their relationship with their babies, play with them and contain their emotions, and for many of them the baby was the best thing in their lives. Some of the depressed mothers also reported changes in their child's behaviour when they themselves were particularly low. 'Most became less active and more clinging and often attempted to comfort the mother in a very touching way, for example, by bringing her their teddy bear to make her feel better' (p. 243). It may be that these children developed the parentified reversed attachment style we looked at in the last chapter. However, the authors argue that whether a mother's depression leads to the child developing behaviour disorders which include sleep problems 'seems to depend mainly on whether he and his mother maintain an intimate and satisfying relationship in which he is not exposed to (nor provokes) high levels of hostility' (Pound et al., 1985, p. 249).

Maternal criticism and hostility

Some mothers do pass on their own feelings of misery or low self-esteem to their child. One form this can take is maternal criticism, which can have a devastating effect on children. Richman et al. (1982) cite this as the single most predictive factor for child disturbance, closely followed by lack of warmth. They saw these factors as more important than maternal depression, parental conflict or environmental stress.

Maternal criticism can be thought of as a distorted perception of the child. Such distortions by a mother in how she sees her baby have been shown to be associated with sleep problems. In a study of normal mothers and infants (Nover et al., 1984), it was found that the majority of mothers perceived their babies' temperaments very similarly to the way the researchers viewed them. However, a minority saw their babies differently, usually as being more difficult than the researchers did; these babies had a greater tendency to sleep problems. The suggestion is that the mothers' misperceptions were associated with more anxiety; they were less responsive to their children and interfered more with their play. The implication is that the mother's negative response to the child affects his ability to sleep. They also suggest that a sleep problem could tire and anger a caregiver, so that the negative perceptions might also be the result of a sleep problem. As ever, it is in the relationship between the two that ruptures and disharmonies arise. A key factor in maternal criticism and hostility is the mother's blaming of the child for his own problems and perhaps for her own also. She has cut herself off from seeing problems as something going on between the two of them. Where sleep is concerned, this will therefore intensify a reaction that a baby who is not sleeping is to blame.

Externalizing

An interesting fact related to depression is that many mothers consulting me about their baby's sleep problem eventually tell me how untidy their homes are. At times I have measured therapeutic success by the number of filled plastic bags taken to Oxfam or put in the bin. As a general problem, extreme untidiness may have many psychological meanings. When mentioned in the context of parent-baby relationships, a few are particularly relevant. In the first place, of course, it is a well-known sign of depression. Secondly, it may simply reflect the feeling of a new mother that there is too much to do, that she does not know what to attend to first. It may illustrate anger at being saddled with child care and household tasks. On the other hand it can also have a positive value as a lack of rigidity, a lessening of obsessional ways of coping. If extreme untidiness continues, however, the chaos of the house may reflect the disintegration experienced by the mother trying to come to terms with her own and her baby's feelings about the 'primal separation' from each other (McDougall, 1974). The fragmentation that is described to me in consultations, where parents do not know which aspect of their babies' needs to attend to first, is physically demonstrated in the objects strewn inappropriately round the house.

Another facet of extreme untidiness can be the parents' attitude to their own toilet-training and the way their own parents carried it out, stirred up by the need to toilet-train their young child. Molly's mother was a good example of this.

Two-year-old Molly was having sleeping difficulties and also being toilet-trained. Molly's mother told me at length how untidy her house was and how much her own mother, who was coming to stay, would disapprove. She developed this theme to tell me how she also expected her mother to criticize Molly's lack of progress in toilet-training. I asked her if she knew about her own toilet-training and indeed she did. Her mother made sure that she knew that she and her sisters had been definitively trained at about one year. I pointed out that her descriptions to me of her untidy house were not only despairing, they were also conveying that a messy baby part of herself that she felt had been cleaned up too quickly still needed to communicate with her own mother. Getting in touch with the idea of this, through the medium of our words, seemed to be sufficient to mobilize more adult motivations, and she went home, intending to tidy up her kitchen before her mother's visit. Molly's toilet-training ceased to be a fraught issue and was resolved within the next few weeks.

The result of acute untidiness can also be similar to a psychosomatic condition. We will look shortly at how a psychogenic factor can cause or exacerbate the body's fall into a physiological condition which has its own repercussions (that is, the individual then suffers from an illness which follows its own course, however it originated). In the same way, extreme untidiness can have its own effect and appears to the sufferer to be the *cause* of their depression and feeling of ill-being. Babies brought up in such a setting have an additional difficulty in making sense of their physical surroundings – like the incoherence of mothers who are unable to respond to their babies' signals appropriately. This is also a useful word to describe the ambience of extreme untidiness.

Mother's eczema

There are many ways, some obvious, some more subtle, by which a mother's state of health affects her baby. We can speculate about this from a clinical example of a mother and baby who both had eczema. Was it an inherited condition, either as a physiological allergic reaction or as a family tendency to somatize? Or was it transmitted by psychological communication? And what effect did the eczema have on their relationship?

Simon and his mother, whom we saw in Chapter 9, both suffered from eczema. Simon's mother said her eczema was related to a milk allergy and to stress. Simon seemed to share the milk allergy and, when mother had any milk product in her diet, it affected her breastmilk and the baby. This mother attributed the origin of her eczema mainly to stress. She told me of her own difficult family life and said that on a recent visit to her parents her eczema, dormant for several months, had reappeared.

When Simon was born, his mother was isolated, and this was a time when she particularly mourned and resented not having the backing and understanding of her mother. Her eczema flared up. Crucial in the relationship between Simon and his mother was how the eczema then affected them both; his mother found it very difficult to hold him, when her own skin was so vulnerable. When Simon himself was affected by eczema, he likewise did not want to be held. Simon cried much of the time, day and night. Out of the mutually unsatisfied needs of this mother and baby couple a situation arose where, once their eczema had subsided, holding seemed the only solution. For this baby, who had little continuous sleep, we can also imagine that he was deprived of much-needed Stage 4 sleep and that his vulnerability to the eczema was increased by this.

This mother and her baby suffered at times from similar uncomfortable states of mind and body. There is often a clear connection between how both mother and baby feel and, of course, how a mother behaves towards her child affects him directly. A mother who is over-stimulating, for example, will naturally tend to have an active, excited child who also may not sleep.

As we saw in Chapter 1, Lozoff et al. (1985), in looking at the causes of sleep problems, cite five different kinds of precipitating factors that range from external events to maternal mood. They describe how stress in the family (accident or illness, unaccustomed absence of the mother during the day, maternal depressed mood, co-sleeping with parents and maternal ambivalence towards the child) are experiences significantly differentiating children with sleep problems from those without, especially when some of these factors are linked. They claim that 'specifically, disturbance of sleep seems to occur in children where mother's psychological attention had been withdrawn from them' (p. 481).

What we have seen in this chapter is the profound connection between mothers and babies. Through this communicative connection the baby makes sense of the world. When the responses of the mother are impaired because of her own state of wellbeing in her relational, social and economic context, then the baby's ability to deal with the world outside and with the regulation of her own body, including sleep rhythms, is affected.

Chapter 14

Children with particular needs and abilities

This chapter includes a whole range of very disparate parent-child relationships. They involve problems with different origins and degrees of severity. We will look at sleep for premature babies, for parents and babies after the tragedy of a sibling's stillbirth or sudden infant death syndrome, and for those who are ill. I will include a case study of a child with a particular disability that affected her sleep, and will finally turn to sleep difficulties that can be encountered by those with a particular ability, sometimes called 'gifted' children. All involve a very particular and sometimes very demanding level of response from the parents. The baby's state and the parents' attempts to respond to it colour the parents' and babies' relationships. Many babies in all these categories have sleep problems. The disturbed sleep may be a direct result of the baby's condition. It may also result from both the parents' feelings about the baby's condition and the relationship that develops in this context.

In all these situations, especially when they are distressing or traumatic, parents' confidence in themselves as parents can be affected. The normal ebb and flow of anxieties that parents have about their babies may be replaced by a continuous experience of anxiety that does not go away. A feeling of being responsible and having to go on being responsible for the baby is unremittingly there for some parents; for others, the hospital seems to have taken over all initiative, leaving nothing for them to do.

One mother of a baby who had been in intensive care was typical of many. She told me that she herself had been sleepless in the baby's first few months. She felt she had to stay awake to keep the baby alive. We can see here an intensification of the normal process by which a mother's thinking about her baby is one part of her care for him. This mother could not stop thinking about her baby, even to go to sleep for very long herself. When a baby is in a special-care unit, looked after by professionals, there may be little chance for a mother to care physically for the baby herself. In such cases, *keeping him in mind* is what she can offer her baby, Winnicott's primary maternal preoccupation, in line with Lozoff's (1985) assertion mentioned earlier, of the vital importance of the mother's psychological attention.

Premature babies

A large number of premature babies, of course, have sleep problems. Born into the sensory onslaught of the neonatal intensive care unit (NICU), 'premature babies have been traumatised already by unbearable intrusive events which are nevertheless part of their survival' (Urwin, 1998).

The premature baby's experience after the birth is of a setting which is noisy and unpredictable and seldom able to be influenced by what she feels about it. The noise level within an incubator is very high from the high-tech machinery to which the baby is wired up and is added to by the clatter of metal instruments (Bender & Swan-Parente, 1983). The premature baby's brain suffers from developing at a critical time not in the quiet darkness of the womb but in this relative bombardment, before her system is ready for it. Normal babies soon develop an idea of predictability from the routine of their care and also are likely to have a preponderance of good experiences. Premature babies have to suffer many painful and invasive procedures and have few good experiences to hold on to. Many of the necessary treatments are shocking to the baby's system, which in any case is immature and physiologically incomplete.

The premature baby's need for survival overrides her rights to agency. She is impotent, unable to influence her world. She is attended to because of the needs of her immature system, not because she himself has expressed a feeling of wanting something. Even her feeding is a passive experience; fed through a tube, her hunger goes away without her doing anything. She does not have the experience of actively seeking breast or bottle and actively sucking to acquire the milk. She also misses out on the feeling in her mouth of sucking a soft and responsive nipple or teat and instead has hard objects, tubes, pushed into her nose or mouth. Objects are pushed or injected into her; she cannot use her hand to push away the hand that 'assaults' her.

The parents' experience, when their baby is in such a situation, comes partly from identifying with the baby, and partly from the direct effect it has on their own parenting, and perhaps partly from the experience of pregnancy and birth. This may have been difficult and even dangerous if the mother, for example, had high blood pressure. If there has been a caesarean, particularly an unexpected one, this can in itself affect the future relationship of mother and baby (Trowell, 1982), given the potential shock and sense of failure caused to the mother. The fact of the caesarean, too, may imply a complication in the pregnancy. Furthermore, a mother who has had any unexpected and traumatic experience during the birth can be looking for a representative of the badness and may feel as though the 'bad' delivery is the baby's responsibility and be angry with her. Such a feeling is very difficult to acknowledge, let alone express, but it can underlie the mother's dealings with the baby, the father and hospital staff.

Parents are likely to feel helpless as a reflection of what their baby feels, but also impotent and peripheral, because in all the sophisticated technology surrounding their baby there is little for them to do. The baby in an incubator is denied contact with her parents, she lacks the bodily contact with them and she lacks the building up of a picture of the world through anticipating and then experiencing interchanges with them. Parents are denied their reciprocal part in this. With no opportunity to care routinely for their babies, they have few ways to *be* parents except as an abstract idea. For parents who are already knocked sideways by the unexpected circumstances of the birth and their baby's ensuing difficulties, there are no easy means by which they can take reparative action and be part of what makes the baby 'better'.

> The mother cannot pick her baby up, hold him or feed him . . . she feels she is not really the mother, or that this is her baby . . . that he belongs to the nurses . . . the mother's function as the giver of meaning is interfered with. She will probably find it hard to function as the interpreter of her baby's feelings, wishes, even thoughts as for large amounts of time she will not be present and she is not able to interpret the world to the baby because it is a world over which she has little control, a world that she herself may find hard to understand.
>
> (Cohen, 2003)

This is all the more painful because of the baby's dramatically increased need for the regulating functions of the 'ordinary devoted mother' (Winnicott, 1949). In Als's study of the premature baby's brain development, she points out that the frontal lobe, involved in emotional processing, containment and regulation is badly affected by this overload at a critical time:

> In the good enough full term situation, (the frontal lobe) appears to be nurtured in the social-emotional communicative matrix of good enough parenting in good enough social groups. In violated situations, it requires special attention and ameliorative care.
>
> (1995, p. 462)

Realizing this, many baby units are now changing their methods. It was in fact a major reform when beds were provided, so that parents were allowed to stay in baby units. Now more and more attempts are being made to allow and encourage parents to have physical contact and to be part of the baby's caring. Wolke (1987), however, warns that although holding by parents during the early sensitive period after birth enhances the parent-infant relationship for robust, healthy pre-term infants who can cope with handling, it is not appropriate for the fragile and ill baby, who may become distressed in his breathing and even collapse and need to be resuscitated because he just cannot cope with the handling. He says this experience may then become traumatic for the parents. Wolke points out that, left to use their own initiative, parents will in fact discriminate and handle the very sick baby less and that, if assisted by empathic nursing staff, they will take over more of the care when their baby recovers.

The mutual need for parents and babies to have as much contact as possible seems to be overriding. Babies in incubators recognize their parents' touch from early on; often the parent has a special place on the baby's body where they touch. Minde et al. (1978) observed that these babies open their eyes more often for their parents than for others. It is poignant to think of the way in which a baby is able to know his parents from among a multiplicity of caretakers handling him.

Bender (1981) has also pointed out the value of dummies for premature babies to suck, particularly while undergoing invasive procedures. These babies have 'bad' mouth experiences, when something is rammed into it; a dummy can counteract this and provide a 'good' sucking experience. This can be both an ongoing satisfying experience and also a way for the baby of focusing and having a feeling of something to hold on to through the mouth when having to deal with interventions. Paediatricians have also discovered that premature babies who have dummies to suck on may gain weight faster.

Sleep may be a particular problem in an intensive care unit, if it is organized in such a way that there is no quiet time and the sleep states of the baby are not respected. In premature babies under 32 weeks gestation, the baby does not attain deep sleep states; with older babies their rhythms are often not sufficiently taken into account. A trail of people with a need to carry out procedures on behalf of the baby have their own timetable. This rarely fits in with the baby's sleep rhythms, so that the baby's sleep is frequently and unpredictably disrupted. In addition to this the baby may not go to sleep and wake up in the near presence of the parent, as most ordinary babies do. A different person may be there when the baby falls asleep and when he wakes up. We saw earlier how the negotiating of the baby's sleep rhythms was one of the main tasks between mother and baby in the early weeks; we see here how deprived both are of this crucial means of contact.

Furthermore, Wolke (1987) has shown that in NICUs there may be a lack of clear diurnal rhythms. Light levels, non-speech sounds and handling of babies may be similar over the 24-hour period. The lack of diurnal rhythms in the unit affects the baby's ability to develop his own rhythmicity. A trial by Mann et al. (1986) showed that pre-term infants who were cared for in a nursery where the intensity of light and noise was reduced between 7pm and 7am spent a significantly longer time sleeping, less time feeding and gained more weight after being discharged home than those housed in perpetual light and noise.

Premature babies suffer the double effect of being less able to regulate their behavioural states than full-term babies are, while having more disturbance inflicted upon them. Wolke (1987) stresses the importance for pre-term infants of obtaining sufficient deep non-REM sleep. At under 32 weeks gestation, they spend only 10 to 20 percent of their sleep time in quiet non-REM sleep. To achieve physiological stability, deep non-REM sleep is essential. Wolke shows that by implementing day-night rhythms, dimming the light and reducing noise and handling at night, the infant's sleep need not be interfered with. The infant thus can attain sleep rhythms which allow him to have longer periods in deep sleep. This means that the baby gets accustomed to sleep for long periods during the night, with the dual gains of the immediate benefit to his development of physiological stability and the later benefits of this for establishing patterns at home with the parents.

The return home

Parents and babies returning home from a NICU are often in a vulnerable situation. The parent, who may already feel inadequate because of the circumstances of the birth, goes on feeling this way, simply because the baby has needed intensive care – that is, more than the parent is able to give. From having felt impotent themselves when their baby needed a dozen people to keep him alive, suddenly they are on their own. Many parents feel panic-stricken at this stage. For the first time they are fully responsible and also at liberty to follow or influence their baby's needs and rhythms for sleep or other functions. With no practice, this freedom may be daunting.

Parents who have not been able to share actively in their baby's care may have focused their love and optimism for their baby by looking at him and thinking about him. This thinking may be a way of 'holding' a fragile baby and keeping him alive. The thinking may include anticipatory grief about a baby who may not survive. Whatever the elements, it is difficult for parents who have taken their baby home, even though he may have become stronger, to switch gear and be able to stop this hyper-intense thinking and looking. Many parents report not expecting their babies to settle to sleep and not being able to leave them to do so. Richards (1983) remarks on parents in this position feeling that they do not know their baby when they bring him home.

I saw one family who experienced many of these problems. They had had twins, a boy and a girl, born at 26 weeks and each weighing under two pounds. The girl died at five days, the boy, Felix, survived but was in intensive care for the first four months of his life. In the first weeks he collapsed and had to be resuscitated several times.

Felix's parents came to see me when he was four years old, distraught about his uncontrollable outbursts and his sleeplessness. For me to know what they had been through I needed to ask them to describe in detail the experiences of Felix and his twin sister's birth, of the baby girl's death and of the events of the four months in hospital. I needed to know all this as background to how Felix was behaving now. Even more, the parents needed someone to tell their story to. I have mentioned that all parents need to tell the story of their baby's birth. When something has gone wrong at the birth, there is even more need to do so. However, when the baby itself is in extreme need of care, the baby's survival becomes the only focus. Attention is of necessity on keeping the baby alive and the mother has no one, no place for telling the story of the birth. There may be a heartbreaking story that goes untold. As I got to know Felix's parents, it emerged how much else had been left unsaid. These parents had had twins. As so often happens when one dies and one survives, the emotions, the grief for one baby and the hopes for the other, become confused. Hospital staff attempt to cheer the parents after the death by talking of the live baby. Parents themselves may fear thinking about the dead baby in case it magically affects the one they are trying to keep alive with their thoughts. Mourning for the dead baby gets set on one side and may never happen.

This mother told me of spending most of her days during these four months sitting by Felix's incubator, thinking about him. She fetched her older child after school. He was not allowed inside the unit, but stood by the door. Father joined them after work. It seemed in retrospect that although Felix's mother had spent most of her time in the unit and had felt the staff there to be caring and helpful, there had never been the right moment to pour out her feelings about having a baby in such a vulnerable state. Perhaps she *had* done so and later forgotten she had. I suspect, however, that, glued as she was to the side of the incubator, being with her baby and willing him to live, no one perceived her as being distanced enough to talk about her feelings, in contrast to just having them. It was not until this belated opportunity to talk to me came that this mother and father were able to put their feelings in perspective.

They told me of the distress and exhaustion of the first four months, when they absorbed the situation of having a baby who might not survive. Also in their minds was the worry about how normally he would develop. When they brought him home, they felt overwhelmed by his vulnerability. They continually expected him to collapse and did not feel they could safely take their eyes off him. Felix slept in fits and starts, mostly in the parents' bed. Even there he was restless, kicking and bumping into his parents. During the day he had constant explosions and tantrums; the parents could rarely take him out without incident. He could not tolerate any new experience and often bit and ripped up his own clothes, toys and bedding. All this had continued day and night for the four years until they came to the clinic. Felix had now started school and to his parents' surprise and relief settled down well. His behaviour at school was quite different from at home. He was able to respond to the school's matter-of-fact firmness and control his outbursts. In other ways he was tentative and fearful but able to use staff to help him last through the day.

This confirmation that Felix could survive in the outside world made an enormous impact on his parents. They started to think seriously about his problems being in relation to themselves and the early experience they had all shared. Their thoughts went in two directions: firstly, that Felix's behaviour must have been at least in part a reflection or communication of his early experiences in intensive care and secondly, that their handling of him reflected their own confused reactions to all this.

They started to connect Felix's rejection of anything new with the repeated unpredictable interventions in intensive care; his present explosions and anger might represent a feeling of not being able to tolerate what was happening to him, of having no focus for explaining it and holding it together for himself. For their own part, they thought about how, with their fragile picture of him, they had not been able to look after him in a firm, consistent way. They had always worried that he would collapse. They had responded to him in an immediate panicky way; no firm routine had been built up for him to fit in with. They then confessed, perhaps for the first time, the anger they themselves felt and the unfairness of having a baby like Felix. At the back of their minds continued the fear that he was even now not really 'normal'. Their doctor then arranged more tests that showed he was not brain-damaged. They now worked out that Felix's outbursts had seemed so extreme that they felt he must be damaged and ordinary parenting could not reach him. They were then able to agree to my suggestion that at times they might have wished Felix had not been born.

These acknowledgements seemed to lift an enormous weight from them. They were firstly able to remind themselves that they were successful parents with their older son. Then they started to talk with Felix about the experiences in the hospital and about the sister who had died. They were able to speculate on what it might feel like to Felix to be the survivor when his twin sister had died. They did not discuss this directly with him, but thinking about the confusions or guilt he might have experienced about being the one who held on to life helped them feel they understood him better. They showed him the marks on his body from transfusions, blood tests and drips. They had broached this before and wondered if it was necessary to do it again. This time he appeared to understand and take in what they were saying much more clearly. It occurred to them that talking from time to time about the overwhelming central circumstances of Felix's existence would help them all to take it in. They noticed at once that he was calmer and more able to take part in conversations about everyday matters.

Felix's father decided to be firmer with him and found that during his outbursts he could hold him until his rage subsided, preventing the orgy of destruction that he had previously felt was unstoppable. Possibly acknowledging their own anger at the situation allowed both parents to separate anger from firmness and hold him without doing harm. Felix not only got over these outbursts quicker, he also had fewer of them.

It seemed time to look at the sleep problems. Felix would only go to bed with the parents in their bed. The parents decided that even though Felix would end up in their bed later, he must start off in his own bed. His father lay beside him for hours till he got to sleep. Later in the night Felix would wake and call until his father fetched him to the parents' bed. This was a small first step, but it seemed to alter some perception in Felix. He had always woken up again 'swearing'. Now, though he still woke and called for his father, he was not so angry and explosive in his words. As we thought about the next changes to make, Felix's mother poignantly described his position as he slept. His leg had to poke out from under the duvet and he lay with his arms spread outwards above his head on the pillow. She said he looked as he had done in hospital in the incubator.

We talked about the feeling the parents had had then of their helplessness in not being able to pick up their baby, cuddle him and wrap him up. His exposed sleeping position now seemed a continuation of this unreachability. I suggested that Felix need not still be a child beyond their reach; that what they as parents did could now make a difference. Perhaps setting limits for Felix could be a way of wrapping him around with their care. Furthermore he was now a little boy who could understand words. At bedtime, his father could perhaps stay with him for a while, tell him he was going out and would come back again. The parents had tried to make up for the unreachable time by going on being physically there for Felix. I suggested that being *reliably* there was more important now than being *always* there. Expected and understood separations might be what was necessary now. If Felix had slept well when he was with his parents, these thoughts would not have been relevant. In such a case he might have been communicating that he needed still more of his parents' presence before being separate from them. But Felix's anger and disturbance, even when he was in their bed, might have been a sign that he needed to find a bearable way to be able to leave them, not to go on being with them. At the time of writing this issue is still not resolved between Felix and his parents.

Babies born after stillbirths

One of the griefs that Felix's parents had to bear was the death of Felix's twin sister five days after her birth. They had to cope with their anxiety about Felix's survival and try to deal with their mourning for the dead twin all at the same time. Felix also grew up with his own confused feelings about the death that took place so close to his own birth. I have mentioned that one problem for families in such a situation can be that because they do not want to confuse their feelings about the live baby with their grief about the dead one, mourning gets put on one side and may never properly be done. Because there has not been the time and space really to feel the grief about the death, this grief may in fact stay around, unrecognized, for years.

Babies born after stillbirths may be in a similar position. Bourne and Lewis (1984) have shown how 'After a perinatal death everyone hopes the next pregnancy will set things right' (p. 31). However, the mourning of stillbirth and genuine recovery are difficult processes that require time and, if the next pregnancy starts before the mourning process has had enough time to take place, then the new pregnancy can cut short the mourning for the last baby, predisposing the mother to mental disturbance. Bourne and Lewis show how difficult it is in fact to mourn a stillbirth and how difficult it is also for professionals to help with this task.

Beyond ordinary pain and disappointment, stillbirth is complicated by extraordinary sensations of confusion and unreality as birth and death have been fused. After months of expectation and growing fullness, there is sudden emptiness with nothing to show. (Even after a live birth women may have a sense of emptiness and sadness mingled with their joy.) Women complain that, after a stillbirth, people expect them to go on as if nothing had happened. The mother feels the stigmata of disease although she usually has no illness. She feels ashamed, inferior and guilty without reason. If the baby's body is whisked away to an unknown grave, the reality may be yet harder to grasp.

It is important for the parents to have memories on which to base their mourning. They need a chance to see and to hold the dead baby, to have photographs taken, to have a proper funeral and also to name the baby. The more that the dead baby has a real identity the easier it is to mourn him or her. If the mourning has been helped along in this way, then there is less risk of the next pregnancy producing a confusion between the dead baby and the expected one. Although parents will still be more likely to be anxious and depressed than the average expectant parents, the new pregnancy offers consolation and fulfilment.

After the birth parents may be puzzled by their reactions to the new live baby. They may be overwhelmed by sadness in the middle of their joy; painful memories of the dead baby will be reawakened and at times they may confuse the live baby with memories of the dead baby. Telling parents in advance that they may feel like this gives them 'permission' to be confused and afraid.

There is thus a chain of circumstances which can lead from the experience of stillbirth to subsequent difficulties in the care of later, live babies. Parents who have lost confidence in their child-bearing capacities, who are anxious and confused, will have difficulty in understanding and responding to their baby's signals. We can see how sleep problems sometimes develop out of this confusion of past and present.

Sudden infant death syndrome

As with parents who have had stillbirths, parents who have lost a baby through sudden infant death syndrome have the traumatic event of the death itself to deal with, as well as the loss of their baby. If these parents have a later baby, almost universally they are unable to leave the baby to himself during the night. Quite understandably their need to keep checking whether the baby is still alive is uppermost in their minds and may in fact continually disturb the baby. This in itself may be a relief; an awake baby is an alive baby.

We looked earlier in Chapter 8 at parents' ordinarily ambivalent feelings about their babies and saw that the hostile part of this ambivalence can be expressed as death fears. Most parents have the good fortune that their babies survive. For parents whose babies do not survive, it can feel as though it was indeed the ambivalence that caused the death. Irrational it might be, but it can be part of the conscious and unconscious feelings that make up the parents' grief.

One such mother, with a sleepless nine-month-old, had earlier had twins who had died from sudden infant death syndrome a few weeks after their birth. She told me, dry-eyed and factually, the story of their deaths. She said that if she started to cry, she would never be able to stop. The acute unbearableness of the two babies' deaths, a grief beyond the relief of tears, was there every night as she put her live baby to bed. It did seem as though sleep and death were still entangled in her mind.

Ill babies

Parents of ill babies also have the problem of finding a balance between giving their baby the care he needs and divining the moment to allow him to work out his own bodily processes. Infant mental health workers have the same problem. Campbell Paul suggests,

> We should begin by acknowledging the mind, the self of the baby, and working with that concept in our own mind. This helps the baby with severe illness, prematurity, or malformation to develop a stronger sense of self, of confidence in his own 'damaged' body without needing to have recourse to excessive defensive withdrawal.
>
> (2014a, p. 19)

One mother whose baby had recently recovered from a severe illness told me how impossible it was to look after a baby *and* do the washing. I puzzled over what she meant. It emerged as we talked that when her baby was seriously ill, she had thought about him all the time, willing him to stay alive. This had succeeded, in the sense that he had survived and was now well and flourishing. But what his mother had been unable to do was to switch off from this total preoccupation with him and belief that he could not survive if she stopped thinking about him. This carried over to other areas of responsibility, even the washing-machine. She could not, so to speak, bundle the clothes in and let it get on with 'doing the washing'. She went on thinking about the washing-machine and this conflicted with thinking about her son; she could not manage both.

Parents of ill children have to deal with anxieties about their children's illness. They also may have to deal with separations, when their children have to be in hospital and, also, if the parents are unable to be with him, with the repercussions from the separation when the child is back home.

Robertson's (1953) touching films show the effects of separation on young children during limited stays in residential nurseries and hospitals. Bowlby (1961) found that a child of 15 to 30 months who has not been previously parted from his mother will show a predictable sequence of behaviour. The phases of this can be described as protest, despair and detachment.

> At first with tears and anger he demands his mother back and seems hopeful he will succeed in getting her. This is the phase of protest and may last several days. Later he becomes quieter, but to the discerning eye it is clear that as much as ever he remains preoccupied with his absent mother and still yearns for her return, but his hopes have faded and he is in the phase of despair. Often these two phases alternate: hope turns to despair and despair to renewed hope. Eventually, however, a greater change occurs. He seems to forget his mother so that when she comes for him he remains curiously uninterested in her, and may seem even not to recognize her. This is the third phase – that of detachment. In each of these phases the child is prone to tantrums and episodes of destructive behaviour, often of a disquietingly violent kind.
>
> (Bowlby, 1961, p. 48)

This work reveals the seriousness of the effects on a young child of being away from his parents in hospital, both being away from family and home and having to deal with frightening situations and possible painful treatment without the emotional protection of his parents. Before these careful observations, the phases of behaviour described by Bowlby, ending with the phase of 'detachment', were usually misread as indicating that the child had 'settled in' to the hospital.

On the child's return home after such an experience, it was then observed that the longer the stay in hospital, and particularly if parents did not visit, the longer it took the child to re-establish relationships at home. The child would at first be unresponsive and undemanding. When this broke, the intense ambivalence of his feelings for his mother was shown in intense clinging and anxiety. These findings brought about a change of policy in hospitals, so that now most children's wards allow and encourage parents to stay with their young children where possible.

When there has been such a separation, however, one of the consequences on coming home may be sleep disturbances. The child may need to reassure himself of his parents' presence and they themselves may be anxious to spend as much time as possible with him. The ambivalence of the reunion between parent and child may be played out through a sleep disturbance. The child may 'blame' the parents for allowing both the separation and any painful experience in hospital; parents may feel reciprocally guilty.

In some instances, children who sleep badly at home may actually sleep better in hospital. Occasionally children are taken into hospital for observation for acute sleep disturbances. If the child does sleep better there, then we may guess at some family disturbance and that this is one of the 'vigilant' children, described by Moore (1989), who do not feel protected by their parents. Similarly some children, sleeping in a laboratory for research purposes, may sleep better with the 'protection' of the researchers.

At 14 months, Claudia, who had severe sleep problems, was admitted to hospital because of low weight gain. Her mother went into hospital and slept with her, and while in hospital Claudia slept very well. It seemed as though both Claudia and her mother felt protected by the hospital and that this feeling of protection was able to override the uncertainties the two of them felt together at home. Claudia had also slept well when staying with her mother in her grandparents' home. The hospital seems to have had the same parenting quality as the grandparents for this mother-baby couple.

Hospital procedures need not lead to sleep problems. In one family two little girls needed operations and splints for a congenital dislocation of the hips at the end of their first year. Their mother or father stayed in hospital much of the time with each baby. Both babies ate little and had unsettled sleep while in hospital and for the first few nights at home again, but they both settled back quickly into their sleep patterns, even though they were in plaster casts for a couple of months. It seems as though a basic feeling of security in these babies was not destroyed, even by the experience of the operations and the ensuing immobilization. Their parent's almost continual presence will have helped keep this feeling of security going.

Other children, however, will feel unbearably helpless and may have frightening dreams of being attacked, which disturb their sleep in such a situation.

A case study

Babies with particular disabilities may suffer severe sleep problems. It has been shown that a range of problems, including sleep disturbance, cause stress in mothers caring for such children (Quine & Pahl, 1985) and is one of the reasons for requests for long-term care.

Clements et al. (1986) show that sleeping difficulties occur with considerable frequency amongst children of all ages with neurodevelopmental disorders. There is a specific link between self-injury and night waking, and there have been speculations about a bio-rhythmic component to self-injurious behaviour. Here again we can see that there may be both a failure in the functioning of the central nervous system to attain the normal development of sleep stages and a disturbance in the relationship between parents and infants because of the way in which these difficulties influence the normal negotiating of sleep rhythms. We can see how the need for parents to adapt their parenting to the different circumstances of a particular child's development can in itself impair the ordinary parenting approaches that the child still needs. Providing for special needs may mean that ordinary ones go unmet. Furthermore, a compromised or a missing response from a disabled child to ordinary spontaneous parenting has a very dispiriting effect on parents and can hinder their capacity to go on offering it.

Tracy, aged five, was a little girl who had had a difficult birth. She suffered physiological and neurodevelopmental consequences and had had a great deal of treatment for the many facets of her condition. The diagnosis of Tracy's condition was uncertain, and it was difficult for Tracy's parents, in recounting the story of her first year, to know which elements in the course of her illness and its treatment were the provokers of the various aspects of her state and her behaviour. However, it seemed clear that her birth had been normal until the last 15 minutes of labour, when the cord became wrapped round her neck and she became blue. Her father felt that her illness started at that point. It gradually emerged that Tracy's development was slow and she had epileptic fits. She had cried a great deal as a tiny baby, but at seven and a half months she had a hernia operation and her crying increased even more after that. She started having some shaking movements which were like sleep jerks. At this point she had a wiped-out, vacant look. She was put on steroids at 11 months and after a month of taking these she suddenly stopped shaking. Her mother said it was like an iron curtain lifting. She would smile and look at people. Although her fits resumed, she was never so detached again. However, because she was full of adrenalin she was always active and hungry, never still.

How all this fitted in with Tracy's sleep pattern is complex. Her mother said that even on the day of her birth Tracy was wakeful. She was born, with the traumatic last stages described earlier, at midday. That night a nurse took her away from her mother's side, because she would not go to sleep. She spent the entire night on her tummy being rocked. Throughout the first few months she was difficult to settle and had to be wheeled in her pram round and round the garden to send her to sleep. The movement would send her to sleep, but she might wake as the pram was bumped up the stairs back into the house.

After her hernia operation she cried and cried in hospital and her shaking started shortly afterwards. When she went on the steroids, which cured the shaking, the effect seemed to be acutely stimulating. She hardly slept at all and her mother's memory was of her and Tracy's father being with her all the time. Tracy remained on the steroids for six months, and after she came off them some sleep patterns started to develop. Even so she was awake between one o'clock and three o'clock every night. Her mother would go and get into bed with her and would lie with her as Tracy breast-fed. At 18 months, in order to achieve some separation, they bought her a cot. Tracy did not like the cot and would cry angrily while lying in it. One night her mother became so angry in response to this crying that she shut the door and left her to cry. After that Tracy would never go in the cot again, and they reverted to using the bed. However, Tracy's mother's next attempt to separate from her was more successful. At two years and four months, she weaned her by asking Tracy's grandmother, who was staying, to lie with Tracy for the two wakeful hours in the night.

Looking back at this time, Tracy's mother observed that most babies with a dis-ability do not go through all this. She felt that the explanation lay in the assaults on Tracy's body. She had had painful injections daily from a home care team who visited at home. Her mother held her during these injections and fed her after-wards to help her recover.

It seemed to me that the origin of Tracy's sleep disturbance and failure to estab-lish sleep rhythms lay in the initial onslaughts on her central nervous system and the stimulation from medication. Following from that, what psychological ele-ments can we see in her sleeplessness? The element of reaction to painful proce-dures, such as the injections, perhaps bridges two kinds of responses and includes a psychological as well as a physiological response.

Even for a little girl as physically assailed as Tracy was, we can see strong con-nections with emotional processes in Tracy's responses to her parents' attempts to manage her and mitigate her condition. Tracy's mother felt that her baby survived because of the breastfeeding, which they kept going throughout the traumatic events of the first couple of years. During the time of Tracy's operation, her injec-tions and the worst of her fits, they maintained a relationship through the breast-feeding. Without this, her mother felt that Tracy would have turned in on herself, as so many children with a severe disability do. By keeping the breastfeeding going, Tracy's mother kept this closeness with her; the adverse effect of this from her mother's point of view was that Tracy needed her continuously. To fall asleep she needed a person lying touching her, preferably (though not essentially) her mother and her breast. Her mother felt trapped. It was also presumably not really satisfactory to Tracy, judging by the way in which, when sleeping in the parents' bed, she slept fitfully and pushed aggressively against them.

However, things changed. As Tracy grew and developed speech, a sleep routine became established. Tracy became able to take part in a bedtime routine, which meant that her mother had to stay *near* her room while Tracy went to sleep but no longer had to lie with her. When she woke in the night, she still went into the parents' bed. At this point her sister asked her, 'Why do you get into Mummy and Daddy's bed?', and she replied, 'Because I feel lonely'. Here we see how much Tracy had developed. This self-awareness is a totally different state of being from the inconsolable baby who had to be held or pushed in her pram without stopping. We can also see how the parents' sensitivity to Tracy's needs and their wish to be there for her constantly, if that was what she wanted, then produced its own problems. Her mother's capacity to remain available to her day and night was probably a major factor in bringing Tracy out of her apparently unreachable state. However, being so available also meant that her mother at times felt unbearably trapped. What also needs to be recognized is that at some point her mother changed from a policy of being always available to Tracy to one of firmly setting up a bedtime routine and gradually expecting Tracy to take more responsibility for getting to sleep herself, her mother moving step by step away from her side.

It seems that both these stages (of being always available and gradually moving away) are essential ones. What is particularly difficult for the parents of children with disabilities, who may need their parents more than do normal children, is to work out when the child needs and is ready to be more separate. Many parents miss the cues, which are much less apparent than in other children. Tracy's mother in fact said that Tracy never initiated anything new, and all changes had to be lengthily negotiated with her.

How did a little girl like Tracy get from the stage where she seemed, paradoxically, to be both unreachable and also to need her mother's constant holding, to become the child who could be separate enough and able to conceptualize enough actually to say that she was lonely? It seems quite plain that her mother's availability was crucial. Perhaps also the moments of rejection, as when her mother shut the door and left Tracy in her cot, were necessary in order to signal to Tracy that her mother had needs of her own. With hindsight, this mother might perhaps have been less devoted and insisted earlier to Tracy that she existed outside of their mother-baby relationship. If she had done so, she might not have had to dramatize her feelings so intensely, as when she had to get away to leave Tracy to cry in her cot. She also described how Tracy's very skilled and sensitive speech therapist played a vital part in helping her find the words to express her emotions.

In thinking about the meaning of Tracy's difficulty in getting to sleep, her father guessed that she might be fearful of the hypnagogic stage (the transitional stage of losing consciousness while falling asleep) – that this might be for her like the losing of consciousness of her fits. In thinking of her as making these comparisons and fighting sleep as a response to her fear, we are seeing her as no longer just swept along by neurological processes, but as having a sense of her own ability to protect herself. Tracy had come a long way.

There was also, if Tracy's parents were correct in their connection, an unassimilable shock for Tracy from the hernia operation. Her parents attributed the onset of her shaking to the operation. Also important is that before the operation she had attained a preverbal 'babble'. She lost this after the operation and reverted to an insistent early-baby cry. Not till her grandmother went away when she was 17 months did she say her first words, 'Bye-bye'.

Children with particular abilities

I have included issues about gifted children in this chapter about children with special needs because, although the circumstances of particular need may be different, there is in common a situation where parents are 'responding to a difference' in their child from the normal run of children. As we have seen, this affects the parents' handling of their child and their ability to respond to the universal and ordinary aspects of their children's needs.

Gifted children are often thought to need less sleep. However, Freeman (1979) has interestingly demonstrated in her research study, 'The Gulbenkian Project on Gifted Children', that 'sleep was not a function of giftedness but of social expectation' (p. 122). In this study children who had not been measured as gifted, but were seen by their parents as being gifted, were compared with two control groups, the first of similar intelligence to the 'designated' gifted group and the second group chosen at random as far as their intellectual ability was concerned. The target group was found to be hyperactive and to sleep poorly compared with both control groups, that is, children of parents who had joined the National Association for Gifted Children appeared to be the ones with sleep problems. This may link with my earlier thoughts about parental perceptions. Research (Rosenthal & Jacobson, 1968) shows how children live up or down to teachers' ideas of their potential; presumably parental expectations have a similar if not a greater force.

In looking at the early development of such children, alertness at birth is an important aspect. Freeman (1979) says:

> It was only the target children who were described as more alert at birth in comparison with the control groups . . . However, no differences in early alertness were reported between the high IQ children and the moderate IQ children, nor between the adjustment groups. It cannot be said therefore, on the evidence from this study, that children who are intellectually gifted are objectively more alert at birth. It is possible that a high proportion of the target parents were anticipating a very bright child, even before the baby's birth and readily accepted their own and the nurses' description of their babies as 'bright' or 'clever' in support of this.
>
> (p. 221)

What Freeman's findings suggest is that parents who associate 'alertness' in their babies with desired giftedness may encourage and stimulate alertness in their babies to the detriment of more peaceful ways of being. I would surmise that such babies may be encouraged both to interact with parents and be spurred on to activity of all kinds in a way that does not allow enough of the kind of relaxation that develops into the drowsiness necessary before a baby can fall asleep. In this vein, the parent may continue to encourage 'ambitious' play, which consists of accurate building, puzzles, etc., and not give the child adequate opportunity for play involving less motor co-ordination, particularly reflective play. Playing with sand or water or apparent aimless sorting through of small toys can allow the dreaming play which helps the small child to sift through in his mind the conflicts and experiences of the day. In particular a small child who is occupied with learning new skills for much of the day needs time to absorb the changes in himself that this new learning represents. Such reflective time enables him to start to process the anxieties that taking on new experiences brings. By beginning this process during the day, there is less backlog of anxiety to be dealt with at night. The small child's REM time can then effectively deal with the consolidating of new learning, and he is less likely to be disturbed in the night by arousals of anxiety.

From this it would follow that 'bright' children in fact need as much or even more sleep than the average child, in order to assimilate new knowledge and achievements and metabolize them into the personality without them being a cause of anxiety. The clever children who are always anxious about possible future failure may be those who have not had enough sleep to metabolize the changes of past learning and to keep their confidence going. The remedy would seem to be more time spent in non-learning activity, so as to allow relaxation that leads to sleep.

We have seen in this chapter how illnesses and adversities concerning their children affect the confidence and self-esteem of parents and can seriously influence their handling of their children in a way that impairs the establishment of sleep rhythms. Anything that means the child is perceived as unusual by the parents, including a perception of 'giftedness', may start off a chain of responses which leads to sleep difficulties.

Conclusion

This book has been about reflecting about putting difficulties into the context of both past and present experiences and relationships. It is about the need for several kinds of theoretical knowledge on which to base our thoughts about the nature of infants' sleep problems, even though it can be difficult to put these different approaches together. It is also about the way in which dreams put us in touch both with what is going on in our minds now and with our memories of the past, and how they help us organize our experiences.

I more or less started with a dream of my own, to illustrate my principal theme of the connections in thought between parents and their children; I also end with one.

The night before starting to write on the sleep problems of infants, I dreamt that I had a baby who was waking and feeding repeatedly in the night. I was confused and despairing about how to sort it out. This baby obviously represents in part the sleepless inner-city London babies that I have thought about. What is also illustrated is the integrative process that a dream carries out (together with the hidden wish-fulfilment!) that allowed me to some extent to translate my jumbled thoughts and experiences into the structure of a book. As one appreciative parent said, 'It worked like a dream'.

Bibliography

All books are published in London unless otherwise indicated:

Ainsworth, M.D.S. and Wittig, B.A. (1969) 'Attachment and exploration: behaviour of one-year-olds in a strange situation', in B.H. Foss, ed. *Determinants of Infant Behaviour*, vol. 4. Methuen, pp. 111–36.

Als, H. (1995) 'The preterm infant: a model for the study of fetal brain expectation', in J.P. Lecanuet et al., eds. *Fetal Development: A Psychobiological Perspective*. Hillsdale, NJ: Erlbaum, pp. 439–71.

Als, H., Tronick, E., Lester, B.M. and Brazelton, T.B. (1977) 'The Brazelton neonatal behavioural assessment and scale (BNBAS)', *Journal of Abnormal Child Psychology* 5(3):215–31.

Alvarez, A. (2012) *The Thinking Heart: Three Levels of Psychoanalytic Psychotherapy with Disturbed Children*. Routledge.

———. (2018) 'Paranoid/schizoid position or paranoid and schizoid positions?' in K. Long and P. Garvey, eds. *The Klein Tradition: Lines of Development – Evolution of Theory and Practice Over the Decades*. Routledge, pp. 392–408.

Anders, J.F., Keener, M., Bowe, T.R. and Shoaff, B.A. (1983) 'A longitudinal study of night-time sleep-wake patterns in infants from birth to one year', in J.D. Call, E.G. Galenson and R.L. Tyson, eds. *Frontiers of Infant Psychiatry*. New York: Basic, pp. 150–70.

Armitage, R., Flynn, H., Hoffmann, R., Vazquez, D., Lopez, J. and Marcus, S. (2009) 'Early developmental changes in sleep in infants: the impact of maternal depression', *Sleep* 32(5):693–96.

Balbernie, R. (2018) 'Circuits and circumstances: importance of earliest relationships and their context', in P. Leach, ed. *Transforming Infant Wellbeing*. Routledge.

Baradon, T., ed. (2019) *Working with Fathers in Psychoanalytic Parent-Infant Psychotherapy*. Routledge.

Barlow, J. and Svanberg, P.O., eds. (2009) *Keeping the Baby in Mind*. Routledge.

Beebe, B. and Lachmann, F.M. (2002) *Infant Research and Adult Treatment: Co-Constructing Interaction*. Hillsdale, NJ: Analytic.

Beebe, B., Lachmann, F.M., Markese, S., Buck, K., Bahrick, L., Chen, H., Cohen, P., Andrews, H., Feldstein, S. and Jaffe, J. (2012) 'On the origins of disorganized attachment and internal working models: paper II an empirical microanalysis of 4-month mother-infant interaction', *Psychoanalytic Dialogues: International Journal of Relational Perspectives* 22(3):352–74.

Bell, S.M. and Ainsworth, M.D.S. (1972) 'Infant crying and maternal responsiveness', *Child Development* 43:1171–90.

Bender, H. (1981) 'Experiences in running a nursing staff group in a hospital intensive care unit', *Journal of Child Psychotherapy* 7:152–9.

Bender, H. and Swan-Parente, A. (1983) 'Psychological and psychotherapeutic support of staff and parents in an intensive care baby unit', in J.A. Davis, M.P.H. Richards and N.R.C. Robertson, eds. *Parent – Baby Attachment in Premature Infants*. Beckenham: Croom Helm, pp. 165–76.

Benoit, D., Parker, K. and Zeanah, C. (1997) 'Mother's representations of their infants assessed pre-natally: stability and association with infants' attachment classifications', *Journal of Child Psychology, Psychiatry & Allied Disciplines* 38:307–13.

Ben Simon, E., Oren, N., Sharon, H., Kirschner, A., Goldway, N., Okon-Singer, H., Tauman, R., Deweese, M.M., Keil, A. and Hendler, T. (2015) 'Losing neutrality: the neural basis of impaired emotional control without sleep', *Journal of Neuroscience* 35(38):13194–205.

Bick, E. (1964) 'Notes on infant observation in psychoanalytic training', *International Journal of Psycho-Analysis* 45:558–66.

Bion, W.R. (1962) *Learning from Experience*. Heinemann.

Blurton-Jones, N., Rosetti Ferreira, C., Farquar Brown, M. and MacDonald, L. (1978) 'The association between perinatal factors and later night waking', *Developmental Medicine and Child Neurology* 20:427–34.

Bourne, S. and Lewis, E. (1984) 'Pregnancy after still birth or neonatal death: psychological risks and management', *Lancet* 31–3.

Bowlby, J. (1961) 'Childhood mourning and its implications for psychiatry', *American Journal of Psychiatry* 118:481–98; reprinted in Bowlby (1979), pp. 44–66.

———. (1969) *Attachment and Loss*, vol. 1, *Attachment*. Hogarth.

———. (1973) *Attachment and Loss*, vol. 2, *Separation*. Hogarth.

———. (1979) *The Making and Breaking of Affectional Bonds*. Tavistock.

Braten, S., ed. (2007) *On Being Moved: From Mirror Neurons to Empathy*. Amsterdam: John Benjamins.

Brazelton, T.B. (1973) 'Neonatal Behavioural Assessment Scale', *Clinics in Developmental Medicine, no. 88. Spastics International Medical Publications* 1984, pp. 1–125.

———. (1988) 'Stress for families today', *Infant Mental Health Journal* 9:65–71.

Breen, D. (1975) *The Birth of a First Child*. Tavistock.

Broughton, R. (1968) 'Sleep disorders: disorders of arousal?' *Science* 159:1070–8.

Brown, G. and Harris, T. (1978) *Social Origins of Depression*. Tavistock.

Chisholm, J. and Richards, M. (1978) 'Swaddling, cradleboards and the development of children', *Early Human Development* 2/3:255–75.

Clements, J., Wing, L. and Dunn, G. (1986) 'Sleep problems in handicapped children', *Journal of Child Psychology and Psychiatry* 27:399–407.

Cohen, M. (2003) *Sent Before My Time: A Child Psychotherapist's View of Life on a Neonatal Intensive Care Unit*. Karnac.

Cox, J.L., Connor, Y.M. and Kendall, R.E. (1982) 'Prospective study of the psychiatric disorders of childbirth', *British Journal of Psychiatry* 140:111–17.

Cunningham, N., Anisfield, E., Casper, V. and Nozyce, M. (1987) 'Infant-carrying, breast-feeding and mother-infant relations', *Lancet* 14:379.

Davis, M. and Wallbridge, D. (1981) *Boundary and Space: Introduction to the Work of D.W. Winnicott*. Karnac.

Daws, D. (1989) *Through the Night: Helping Parents with Sleepless Infants*. Free Association.

———. (2008) 'Sleeping and feeding problems: attunement and daring to be different', in L. Emanuel and E. Bradley, eds. *What Can The Matter Be? Therapeutic Interventions with Parents, Infants and Young Children*. Karnac, pp. 237–53.

Daws, D. and de Rementeria, A. (2015) *Finding Your Way with Your Baby: The Emotional Life of Parents and Babies*. Routledge.

Department for Education (2015) *Working Together to Safeguard Children: A Guide to Inter-Agency Working to Safeguard and Promote the Welfare of Children*. Retrieved from: https://assets.publishing.service.gov.uk/government/uploads/system/uploads/attachment_data/file/592101/Working_Together_to_Safeguard_Children_20170213.pdf#page=93

Douglas, J. and Richman, N. (1984) *My Child Won't Sleep*. Harmondsworth: Penguin.

Dunn, J. (1977) *Distress and Comfort*. Fontana.

Emde, R. (1988) 'Introduction: reflections on mothering and on reexperiencing the early relationship experience', *Infant Mental Health Journal* 9: 4–9.

Emde, R. and Robinson, J. (1979) 'The first two months: recent research in developmental psychobiology and the changing view of the new-born', in J. Noshpitz, ed. *Basic Handbook of Child Psychiatry*, vol. 1. New York: Basic, pp. 72–105.

Fain, N. and Kreisler, L. (1970) 'Discussions sur la genèse des fonctions representatives', *Revue Française de Psychanalyse* 34: 285–306.

Feldman, R. (2007) 'Parent-infant synchrony and the construction of shared timing; physiological precursors, developmental outcomes, and risk conditions', *Journal of Child Psychology and Psychiatry* 48(3/4):329–54.

Felitti, V.J., Anda, R.F., Nordenberg, D., Williamson, D.F., Spitz, A.M., Edwards, V., Koss, M.P. and Marks, J.S. (1998) 'Relationship of childhood abuse and household dysfunction to many of the leading causes of death in adults. The Adverse Childhood Experiences (ACE) Study', *American Journal of Preventive Medicine* 14:245–58.

Ferber, R. (1987) 'The sleepless child', in C. Guilleminault, ed. *Sleep and Its Disorders in Children*. New York: Raven, pp. 141–63.

———. (2013) *Solve Your Child's Sleep Problems*. Vermilion.

Fraiberg, S. (1950) 'On sleep disturbance of early childhood', *Psychoanalytic Study of the Child* 5:285–307.

———. (1959) *The Magic Years*. Methuen, 1968.

Fraiberg, S., Adelson, E. and Shapiro, V. (1980) 'Ghosts in the nursery', in S. Fraiberg, ed. *Clinical Studies in Infant Mental Health*. New York: Basic Books, pp. 387–421.

Fraiberg, S. (1980) *Clinical Studies in Infant Mental Health: the first year of life*. New York: Basic Books.

Freeman, J. (1979) *Gifted Children*. Lancaster: MTP.

Freud, A. (1953) 'Some remarks on infant observation', in *The Writings of Anna Freud*, vol. 4. New York: International Universities Press, pp. 569–88.

Freud, S. (1900) 'The interpretation of dreams', in J. Strachey, ed. *The Standard Edition of the Complete Psychological Works of Sigmund Freud*, 24 vols. Hogarth, 1953, vol. 4, pp. 509–622.

———. (1916–17) Introductory lectures on psycho-analysis. *S.E.* 15, pp. 84–7.

———. (1920) *Beyond the Pleasure Principle*. *S.E.* 18, pp. 3–64.

Gerhardt, S. (2004) *Why Love Matters: How Affection Shapes a Baby's Brain*. Routledge.

Gianino, A. and Tronick, E.Z. (1988) 'The mutual regulation model: the infant's self and interactive regulation and coping and defensive capacities', in T.M. Field, P.M. McCabe and N. Schneiderman, eds. *Stress and Coping Across Development*. Hillsdale, NJ: Lawrence Erlbaum, pp. 47–68.

Ginsberg, S. (1976) 'Women, work and conflict', in N. Fonda and P. Moss, eds. *Mothers in Employment*. Uxbridge: Brunel University, pp. 75–88.

Giorgis, F.G., Camuffo, M. and Cascioli, P. (1987) 'Influenza dei disturbi precoci del sonno sullo sviluppo cognitivo', in *Atti dell' Vili Convegno di Neurologia Infantile*. Università la Sapienza, Roma: Istituto di Neuropsichiatria Infantile, pp. 1–10.

Glaser, D. (2000) 'Child abuse and neglect and the brain – A review', *Journal of Child Psychology and Psychiatry* 41(1):97–116.

———. (2005) 'Child maltreatment', *Psychiatry* 4(7):53–7.

Glasser, R. (1986) *Growing up in the Gorbals*. Chatto & Windus.

Glover, V., Onozawa, K. and Hodgkinson, A. (2002) 'Benefits of infant massage for mothers with postnatal depression', *Seminars in Neonatology* 7(6):495–500.

Goldsmith, J. and Cowen, H. (2011) 'The inheritance of loss', *Journal of Child Psychotherapy* 37(2):179–93.

Goldstein-Ferber, S., Laudon, M., Kuint, J., Weller, A. and Zisapel, N. (2002) 'Massage therapy by mothers enhances the adjustment of circadian rhythms to the nocturnal period in full-term infants', *Developmental and Behavioural Pediatric* 23(6):410–15.

Guedeney, A. (1989) 'Les Troubles de l'endormissement et du sommeil au cours des trois premiers semestres de la vie', in B. Cramer, ed. *Proceedings of World Infant Psychiatry Congress, Stockholm, 1986*. Paris: Eshail.

Guedeney, A. and Kreisler, L. (1987) 'Sleep disorders in the first eighteen months of life: hypothesis on the role of mother-child emotional exchanges', *Infant Mental Health Journal* 8:307–18.

Harlow, H.F. (1961) 'The development of affectional patterns in infant monkeys', in B.M. Foss, ed. *Determinants of Infant Behaviour*, vol. 1. New York: Wiley, pp. 75–97.

Harlow, H.F. and Zimmermann, R.R. (1959) 'Affectional responses in the infant monkey', *Science*, pp 130–421.

Hartmann, E. (1973) *The Functions of Sleep*. New Haven, CT: Yale University Press.

———. (1984) *The Nightmare*. New York: Basic.

Henshaw, C. (2003) 'Mood disturbance in the early puerperium: a review', *Archives of Women's Mental Health* 6(Supplement 2), S33–S42.

Hiscock, H. and Davey, M.J. (2018) 'Sleep disorders in infants and children', *Journal of Paediatric Child Health* 54(9):941–4.

Hiscock, H. and Wake, M. (2001) 'Infant sleep problems and postnatal depression: a community-based study', *Pediatrics* 107(6):–22.

Hopkins, J. (1986) 'Solving the mystery of monsters: steps towards the recovery from trauma', in A. Horne and M. Lanyado, eds. *An Independent Mind: Collected Papers of Juliet Hopkins*. Routledge, 2015.

———. (1996) 'The dangers and deprivations of too-good mothering', in A. Horne and M. Lanyado, eds. *An Independent Mind: Collected Papers of Juliet Hopkins*. Routledge, 2015.

Hunziker, V.A. and Barr, R.G. (1986) 'Increased carrying reduces infant crying: a randomized controlled trial', *Pediatrics* 77:641–8.

Insana, S.P., Foley, K.P., Montgomery-Downs, H.E., Kolko, D.J. and McNeil, C.B. (2014) 'Children exposed to intimate partner violence demonstrate disturbed sleep and impaired functional outcomes', *Psychological Trauma: Theory, Research, Practice, and Policy* 6(3):290–8.

Jones, A. (2006) 'How video can bring to view pathological defensive processes and facilitate the creation of triangular space in perinatal parent-infant psychotherapy', *Infant Observation: International Journal of Infant Observation & Its Application* 9(2):109–23.

Kahn, J.H. and Wright, S.E. (1980) *Human Growth and the Development of Personality.* Oxford: Pergamon.

Kales, A., Kales, J., Sly, R., Scharf, M., Tjiauw-Ling, T. and Preston, T. (1970) 'Sleep patterns of asthmatic children: all-night electroencephalographic studies', *Journal of Allergy* 46:300–8.

Karacan, I. and Williams, R.L. (1970) 'Current advances in theory and practice relating to postpartum syndromes', *Psychiatry in Medicine* 1(4):307–328.

Kirkland, J. (1985) *Crying and Babies: Helping Families Cope.* Beckenham: Croom Helm.

Kitzmann, K., Gaylord, N.K., Holt, A.R. and Kenny, E.D. (2003) 'Child witnesses to domestic violence: a meta-analytic review', *Journal of Consulting Clinical Psychology* 71:339–52.

Klaus, M.H. and Kennell, J.H. (1976) *Maternal-Infant Bonding: The Impact of Early Separation or Loss on Family Development, Parent-Infant Bonding.* 2nd edn. St. Louis, MO: Mosby, 1982.

Klein, M. (1932) 'The psychological foundations of child analysis', in *The Psycho-Analysis of Children.* Hogarth, pp. 3–15.

———. (1959) 'Our adult world and its roots in infancy', in *Envy and Gratitude and Other Works.* Hogarth, 1980, pp. 247–63.

Kraemer, S. (2017) 'Narratives of fathers and sons: there is no such thing as a father', in A. Vetere and E. Dowling, eds. *Narrative Therapies with Children and Their Families: A Practitioners Guide to Concepts and Approaches.* 2nd edn. Routledge.

Kreisler, L. (1974) 'Insomnie de premier semestre', in L. Kreisler, M. Fain and M. Soule, eds. *L'Enfant et Son Corps.* Paris: Presses Universitaires de France, pp. 70–99.

Leach, P. (2010) *Your Baby and Child.* Dorling Kindersley.

———. (2015) 'Controlled crying: what parents need to know', *International Journal of Birth and Parent Education* 2(4):13–17.

———, ed. (2018) *Transforming Infant Wellbeing.* Routledge.

Lebovici, S. (1980) 'L'experience du psychoanalyste chez l'enfant et chez l'adulte devant le modèle de la nervose infantile et de la nervose de transfert', *Revue Française de Psychanalyse* 44:733–857.

Lee, G.Y. and Kisilevsky, B.S. (2014) 'Fetuses respond to father's voice but prefer mother's voice after birth', *Developmental Psychobiology* 56(1):1–11.

Lieberman, A.F., Ghosh Ippen, C. and Van Horn, P. (2015) *Don't Hit My Mommy: A Manual for Child-Parent Psychotherapy with Young Children Exposed to Violence and Other Trauma.* 2nd edn. Washington, DC: Zero to Three.

Lipton, E., Steinschneider, A. and Richmond, J. (1965) 'Swaddling: a child care practice: historical, cultural and experimental observations', *Journal of Pediatrics* 35:519–67.

Lowy, F.H. (1970) 'Recent sleep and dream research: clinical implications', *Canadian Medical Association Journal* 102(10):1069–77.

Lozoff, B., Wolf, A.W. and Davis, N.S. (1984) 'Co-sleeping in urban families with young children in the United States', *Journal of Pediatrics* 74:171–82.

———. (1985) 'Sleep problems seen in pediatric practice', *Journal of Pediatrics* 75:477–83.

Lyons-Ruth, K., Bruschweiler-Stern, N., Morgan, A.C., Stern, D.N., Sander, L.W., Nahum, J.P., Harrison, A.M. and Tronick, E.Z., Process of Change Study Group, Boston,

Massachusetts (1998) 'Implicit relational knowing: its role in development and psycho-analytic treatment', *Infant Mental Health Journal* 19(3):282–9.

Magagna, J. (1986) 'Night terrors in latency children'. Paper given at the 11th International Congress of the International Association for Child and Adolescent Psychiatry. Paris, July 1986. Obtainable from Hospital for Sick Children, Great Ormond Street, London WC1N 3JH.

Mahler, M. (1975) *The Psychological Birth of the Human Infant: Symbiosis and Individuation*. Maresfield Library, 1985.

Main, M. (1989) 'Parental aversion to physical contact with the infant: stability, consequences and reasons', in T.B. Brazelton, ed. *Touch: The Foundation of Experience*. New York: International Universities Press.

Main, M., Kaplan, N. and Cassidy, J. (1985) 'Security in infancy, childhood and adulthood: a move to the level of representation', in I. Bretherton and E. Waters, eds. *Growing Points of Attachment Theory and Research*, Monographs of the Society for Research in Child Development, vol. 50, (1–2, serial no. 209), pp. 66–104.

Main, M. and Solomon, J. (1986) 'Discovery of an insecure-disorganized/disoriented attachment pattern', in T.B. Brazelton and M.W. Yogman, eds. *Affective Development in Infancy*. Norwood, NJ: Ablex, pp. 95–124.

Malloch, S. and Trevarthen, C., eds (2009) *Communicative Musicality: Exploring the Basis of Human Companionship*. Oxford: Oxford University.

Mann, N.P., Haddow, R., Stokes, L., Goodley, S. and Rutter, N. (1986) 'Effects of night and day on pre-term infants in a newborn nursery: randomized trial', *British Medical Journal* 293:1265–7.

McDonald, D., Shallenberger, H., Koresko, R. and Kinzy, B. (1976) 'Studies of spontaneous electrodermal responses in sleep', *Psychophysiology* 13:128–34.

McDougall, J. (1974) 'The psychosoma and the psychoanalytic process', *International Review of Psycho-Analysis* 1:437–59.

———. (1986) *Theatres of the Mind*. Free Association.

McKenna, J.J. (1986) 'An anthropological perspective on the sudden infant death syndrome (SIDS): the role of parental breathing cues and speech breathing adaptations', *Medical Anthropology* 10:9–92.

———. (2014) 'Night waking among breastfeeding mothers and infants: conflict, congruence or both?' *Evolution, Medicine & Public Health* 1:40–7. Retrieved from: www.ncbi.nlm.nih.gov/pmc/articles/PMC3982898/

McKenna, J.J., Ball, H. and Gettler, L. (2007) 'Mother-infant cosleeping, breastfeeding & SIDS: what biological anthropologists have learned about normal infant sleep and pediatric sleep medicine', *Yearbook of Physical Anthropology* 50:133–61.

McKenna, J.J., Mosko, S., Dungy, C. and McAninch, J. (1990) 'Sleep and arousal patterns of co-sleeping human mother/infant pairs: a preliminary physiological study with implications for the study of sudden infant death syndrome (SIDS)', *American Journal of Physical Anthropology* 83(3):331–47.

McNamara, P., Belsky, J. and Fearon, P. (2003) 'Infant sleep disorders and attachment: sleep problems in infants with insecure-resistant versus insecure-avoidant attachments to mother', *Sleep and Hypnosis* 5(1):7–16.

Meltzer, D. (1983) *Dream-Life: A Re-Examination of the Psychoanalytic Theory and Technique*. Perth: Clunie.

Metcalf, D.R. (1979) 'Organizers of the psyche and the EEG development: birth through adolescence', in J. Noshpitz, ed. *Basic Handbook of Child Psychiatry*, vol. I. New York: Basic, pp. 63–71.

Miller, L., Rustin, M., Rustin, M. and Shuttleworth, J., eds (2002) *Closely Observed Infants*. Duckworth.

Milne, A.A. (1924) 'Disobedience', in *When We Were Very Young*. Methuen.

Minde, K., Trehub, S., Corter, C., Boukydis, C., Celhoffer, L. and Marton, P. (1978) 'Mother-child relationships in the premature nursery: an observational study', *Pediatrics* 6:373.

Moore, M.-S. (1989) 'Disturbed attachment in children: A factor in sleep disturbance, altered dream production and immune dysfunction: I. Not safe to sleep: chronic sleep disturbance in anxious attachment', *Journal of Child Psychotherapy* 15(1):99–111.

Moore, T. and Ucko, L.E. (1957) 'Night waking in early infancy', *Archives of Disease in Early Childhood* 32:333–42.

Morrell, J. and Steele, H. (2003) 'The role of attachment security, temperament, maternal perception & care-giving behaviour in persistent infant sleeping problems', *International Mental Health Journal* 24(5):447–68.

Moss, P. and Plewis, I. (1977) 'Mental distress in mothers of preschool children in Inner London', *Psychological Medicine* 7:641–52.

Murray, L. (1988) 'Effects of postnatal depression on infant development, direct studies of early mother-infant interaction', in K. Kumar and I. Brockington, eds. *Motherhood and Mental Illness*, vol. 2. Wright, pp. 159–90.

Murray, L., Arteche, A., Fearon, P., Halligan, S., Croudace, T. and Cooper, P. (2010) 'The effects of maternal postnatal depression and child sex on academic performance at age 16 years: a developmental approach', *Journal of Child Psychology & Psychiatry* 51(10):1150–9.

Murray, L. and Cooper, P.J. (1997) 'Effects of postnatal depression on infant development', *Archives of Disease in Childhood* 77:99–101.

Music, G. (2010) *Nurturing Natures: Attachment and Children's Emotional, Sociocultural and Brain Development*. New York: Psychology.

———. (2019) *Nurturing Children: From Trauma to Growth Using Attachment Theory, Psychoanalysis and Neurobiology*. Routledge.

Newell, S. (1992) 'The myth and destructiveness of equal opportunities: the continued dominance of the mothering role', *Personnel Review* 21(4):37–47.

Nover, A., Shore, H.F., Timberlake, E.M. and Greenspan, S.I. (1984) 'The relationship of maternal perception and maternal behaviour: a study of normal mothers and their infants', *American Journal of Orthopsychiatry* 54:210–23.

Olds, D.S. (2006) 'The nurse-family partnership: an evidence-based preventive intervention', *Infant Mental Health Journal* 27(1):5–25.

O'Shaughnessy, E. (1964) 'The absent object', *Journal of Child Psychotherapy* 1:34–43.

Pally, R. (1998) 'Emotional processing: the mind-body connection', *International Journal of Psychoanalysis* 79:349–62.

Palombo, S. (1978) *Dreaming and Memory*. New York: Basic.

Panksepp, J. (2010) 'Affective neuroscience of the emotional BrainMind: evolutionary perspectives and implications for understanding depression', *Dialogues in Clinical Neuroscience* 12(4):533–45.

Papousek, H. and Papousek, M. (1975) 'Cognitive aspects of preverbal social interaction between human infants and adults', in *Parent-Infant Interaction*, Ciba Foundation Symposium 33. New York: Elsevier.

Paret, I. (1983) 'Night waking and its relation to mother-infant interaction in nine-month-old infants', in J.D. Call, E.G. Galenson and R.L. Tyson, eds. *Frontiers of Infant Psychiatry*. New York: Basic, pp. 171–7.

Parker, R. (2005) *Torn in Two: Maternal Ambivalence*. London: Virago.

Paul, C. (2014a) 'Feeding, the self, and working through the infant's pathological defences: the seriousness of playfulness', in C. Paul and F. Thomson-Salo, eds. *The Baby as Subject*. Karnac.

———. (2014b) 'The sick baby in hospital', in C. Paul and F. Thomson-Salo, eds. *The Baby as Subject*. Karnac.

Perry, B.D., Pollard, R., Blakely, R., Baher, W. and Vigilante, D. (1995) 'Childhood trauma, the neurobiology of adaptation, and user-dependent development of the brain: how "states" become "traits"', *Infant Mental Health Journal* 16:271–91.

Phillips, A. (2003) *Saying No: Why it's Important for You and Your Child*. Faber & Faber.

Pine, F. (1986) 'The "symbiotic phase" in light of current infancy research', *Bulletin of the Menninger Clinic* 50:564–9.

Pines, D. (1982) 'The relevance of early psychic development to pregnancy and abortion', *International Journal of Psycho-Analysis* 63:311–19.

Pound, A. (1982) 'Attachment and maternal depression', in C.M. Parkes and J. Stevenson Hinde, eds. *The Place of Attachment in Human Behaviour*. Tavistock, pp. 118–30.

Pound, A., Cox, A., Puckering, C. and Mills, M. (1985) 'The impact of maternal depression on young children', in *Journal of Child Psychology and Psychiatry* 28(6):917–28.

Quine, L. and Pahl, J. (1985) 'Examining the causes of stress in families with severely mentally handicapped children', *British Journal of Social Work* 15:501–17.

Radesky, J., Miller, A.L., Rosenblum, K.L., Appugliese, D., Kaciroti, N. and Lumeng, J.C. (2015) 'Maternal mobile device use during a structured parent-child interaction task', *Academy of Pediatrics* 15(2):238–44.

Raphael-Leff, J. (1982) 'Psychotherapeutic needs of mothers to be', *Journal of Child Psychotherapy* 8:3–13.

———. (1983) 'Facilitators and regulators: two approaches to mothering', *British Journal of Medical Psychology* 56:379–90.

———. (1986) 'Facilitators and regulators: conscious and unconscious processes in pregnancy and early motherhood', *British Journal of Medical Psychology* 59:43–55.

Rayner, E. (2019) 'Matching, attunement and the psychoanalytic dialogue', in J. Edwards, ed. *Psychoanalysis & Other Matters: Where Are We Now?* Routledge.

Reid, S., ed. (1997) *Developments in Infant Observation: The Tavistock Model*. Routledge.

Richards, M. (1983) 'Parent-child relationships: some general considerations', in J.A. Davis, M.P.H. Richards and N.R.C. Robertson, eds. *Parent – Baby Attachment in Premature Infants*. Beckenham: Croom Helm, pp. 3–21.

Richman, N. (1981a) 'A community survey of characteristics of one- to two-year-olds with sleep disruptions', *Journal of American Academy of Child Psychiatry* 20:281–91.

———. (1981b) 'Sleep problems in young children', *Archives of Disease in Childhood* 56:491–3.

Richman, N., Stevenson, J. and Graham, P. (1982) *Preschool to School – A Behavioural Study*. Academic.

Robertson, J. (1953) Film: *A Two-year-old Goes to Hospital*. 16mm, 40-minute and 30-minute versions, in English and French. Concord Video and Film Council.

———. (1958) *Young Children in Hospital*. Tavistock.

Robertson, J. and Robertson, J. (1967–75) Film series: *Young Children in Brief Separation*. Tavistock Institute of Human Relations. Obtainable from Concord Films Council, Ipswich, Suffolk and New York Universities Film Institute.

———. (1971) 'Young children in brief separation: a fresh look', *Psychoanalytic Study of the Child* 26:264–315.

Rosenthal, R. and Jacobson, L. (1968) 'Teacher expectations for the disadvantaged', *Scientific American* 218(4):19–23.

Sander, L.W., Stechler, G., Julia, H. and Burns, P. (1976) 'Primary prevention and some aspects of temporal organization in early infant-caretaker interaction', in E. Rexford, L.W. Sander and T. Shapiro, eds. *Infant Psychiatry*. Yale University Press, pp. 187–204.

Savage, G.H. (1896) 'Prevention and treatment of insanity of pregnancy and the puerperal period', *Lancet* 1:164.

Schore, A.N. (1994) *Affect Regulation and the Origin of the Self: The Neurobiology of Emotional Development*. Hillsdale: NJ: Erlbaum.

———. (2000) 'Attachment and the regulation of the right brain', *Attachment & Human Development* 2(1):23–47.

Scott, W. and Clifford, M. (1975) 'Remembering sleep and dreams', *International Review of Psycho-Analysis* 2:253–354.

Sendak, M. (1963) *Where the Wild Things Are*. Harmondsworth: Puffin and Penguin, 1970.

Smith, C.R. and Steinschneider, A. (1975) 'Differential effects of prenatal rhythmic stimulation on neonatal arousal states', *Child Development* 46:578–99.

Spock, B. (1946) *Baby and Child Care*. New York: Pocket, 1957.

Stern, D. (1985) *The Interpersonal World of the Infant*. New York: Basic.

Sternberg, J. (2005) *Infant Observation at the Heart of Training*. Karnac.

Stevenson, A. (1983) 'Poem to my daughter', in The Raving Beauties, eds. *In the Pink: The 'Raving Beauties'*. Women's Press, p. 38; and in A. Stevenson, *Minute by Glass Minute*. Oxford University Press, 1982.

St James-Roberts, I. (2012) *The Origins, Prevention and Treatment of Infant Crying and Sleeping Problems*. Routledge.

Sutton, S. (2014) *Being Taken In: The Framing Relationship*. Karnac.

———. (2019) *Psychoanalysis, Neuroscience and the Stories of Our Lives: The Relational Roots of Mental Health*. Routledge.

Terr, L. (1987) 'Nightmares in children', in C. Guilleminault, ed. *Sleep and Its Disorders in Children*. New York: Raven, pp. 231–42.

Tham, E.K., Schneider, N. and Broekman, B.F. (2017) 'Infant sleep and its relation with cognition and growth: a narrative review', *Nature and Science of Sleep* 9:135–149.

Thomson-Salo, F. (2018) *Engaging Infants: Embodied Communication in Short-Term Infant-Parent Therapy*. Routledge.

Tikotzky, L., Sadeh, A. and Glickman-Gavrieli, T. (2011) 'Infant sleep and paternal involvement in infant caregiving during the first 6 months of life', *Journal of Pediatric Psychology* 36(1):36–46.

Tomson, M. (1989) 'Mothers to wives, history of a sleep group'. Unpublished.

Trevarthen, C. (1974) 'Conversations with a two-month-old', *New Scientist*, 2 May, pp. 230–5.

———. (2005) 'First things first: infants make good use of the sympathetic rhythm of imitation, without reason or language', *Journal of Child Psychotherapy* 31(1):91–113.

Tronick, E., Als, H., Adamson, L., Wise, S. and Brazelton, T.B. (1978) 'The infant's response to entrapment between contradictory messages in face-to-face interaction', *Journal of American Academy of Child Psychiatry* 17(1):1–13.

Trowell, J. (1982) 'Effects of obstetric management on the mother-child relationship', in C.M. Parks and J. Stevenson Hinde, eds. *The Place of Attachment in Human Behaviour*. Tavistock, pp. 79–94.

————. (1983) 'Emergency caesarean sections: a research study of the mother-child relationship of a group of women admitted expecting a normal vaginal delivery', *Child Abuse and Neglect* 7:387–94.

Tustin, F. (1972) *Autism and Childhood Psychosis*. Hogarth.

Underdown, A. (2009) 'Exploring infant massage', in J. Barlow and P.O. Svanberg, eds. *Keeping the Baby in Mind: Infant Mental Health in Practice*. Routledge.

Urwin, C. (1998) 'Psychic links and traumatic events: some implications of premature birth', *Journal of Child Psychotherapy* 24(1):61–84.

Walker, M. (2017) *Why We Sleep*. Penguin.

Weissbluth, M. (1987a) 'Sleep and the colicky infant', in C. Guilleminault, ed. *Sleep and Its Disorders in Children*. New York: Raven, pp. 129–40.

————. (1987b) *Sleep Well*. Unwin Paperbacks.

Winnicott, D.W. (1947) 'Further thoughts on babies as persons', Chapter 13 in *The Child, the Family and the Outside World*. Harmondsworth: Penguin, 1964, pp. 85–92.

————. (1949) 'The ordinary devoted mother and her baby', in *The Child and the Family*. Tavistock, 1957.

————. (1958) 'The capacity to be alone', in *The Maturational Processes and the Facilitating Environment*. Hogarth, 1965, pp. 29–36.

————. (1964) *The Child, the Family and the Outside World*. Harmondsworth: Penguin.

————. (1971) *Playing and Reality*. Harmondsworth: Penguin and Tavistock, 1974.

Wolff, P.H. (1974) 'The classifications of states: state and neonatal activity', in L.J. Stone, H.T. Smith and L.B. Murphy, eds. *The Competent Infant*. Tavistock, pp. 257–82.

Wolke, D. (1987) 'Environmental and developmental neonatology', *Journal of Reproductive and Infant Psychology* 5:17–42.

Wolke, D. and St. James Roberts, I. (1987) 'Multi-method measurement of the early parent-infant system with easy and difficult new-borns', in H. Rauh and H. Steinhausen, eds. *Psychobiology and Early Development*. Holland: Elsevier Science, pp. 49–70.

Zelenko, M., Kraemer, H., Huffman, L., Gschwendt, M., Pageler, N. and Steiner, H. (2005) 'Heart rate correlates of attachment status in young mothers and their infants', *Journal of the American Academy of Child and Adolescent Psychiatry* 44(5):470–6.

Zuckerman, B., Stevenson, J. and Bailey, V. (1987) 'Sleep problems in early childhood: continuities, predictive factors and behavioural correlates', *Journal of Pediatrics* 80:664–71.

Index

Printed in Great Britain
by Amazon

36054826R00119